THE MAKING OF
D U N E™

by Ed Naha

BERKLEY BOOKS, NEW YORK

THE MAKING OF DUNE

A Berkley Book/published by arrangement with
Merchandising Corporation of America, Inc.

PRINTING HISTORY
Berkley trade paperback edition/December 1984

ISBN: 0-425-07376-9

ACKNOWLEDGMENTS

In astoundingly random order, I'd like to thank the following people who, through various behavioral quirks, helped me perpetrate this book: Susan Allison, Nancy Cushing-Jones, Raffaella De Laurentiis and Dino De Laurentiis, Michael Levett, David Lynch, Anne Strick, Robin Snelson, Janelle Balnicke, Kyle MacLachlan, Francesca Annis, Richard Jordan, Sting, Paul Smith, Everett McGill, Molly Wryn, Frank Herbert, Sean Young, Lee Guthrie, Linda Hunt, Golda Offenheim, Cristina Espinosa, Ian Woolf, Freddie Francis, James Devis, Ed George, Gordon Hayman, Tony Masters, Giles Masters, Bob Ringwood, Carlo Rambaldi, Barry Nolan, Chuck Finance, Brian Smithies, Emilio Ruiz Del Rio, the late Aldo Puccini, Kit West, Tony Gibbs, Penny Shaw, Kiyoshi Yamazaki, Roy Larner, Ken McMillan, Frances Doel, Diane Williams, Rachelle Blaine, John Allison, George Whittear, Allison Klarfeld, Blair Brown, Jim Mones, Ginny Nugent, Patricia Ostraff, a tolerant mob of friends and family and all those kind people on and about the *Dune* set who never once fired a handgun in my direction.

For the ticket buyers

CONTENTS

THE MAKING OF
D U N E ™

INTRODUCTION

In recent years, whenever a big movie has been made—a movie that cost a lot of money—someone has written a book about it. It has usually been a nice book, telling the world how much everyone who made the movie liked every moment, how the relatively few little problems that arose were quickly solved. Too often, such books are only fairy tales.

Making a movie, an inexpensive movie or one on the scale of *Dune*, is always an exercise in the impossible. There are *no* small problems: personal difficulties, technical foul-ups, financial over-runs, the weather, the food—all become major concerns. Fortunately, on *Dune*, the large, international cast and crew got along, but on many days—from the time in 1976 when I first decided to make *Dune* into a movie, through pre-production and principal photography, into the post-production and special effects phases—film-making was an adventure into the unknown. In film, there is a fine line between disaster and triumph.

This book tells of many of these adventures and captures the ebb and flow of making a movie. Though *Dune* is a fantasy, a film of an imaginary world, this book is not a fairy tale. It is the true story of an epic, often difficult, often hilarious, ultimately gratifying struggle.

As I look at the nearly final version of the film, I see on the movieola what I saw in my mind when I first envisioned *Dune* as a movie eight years ago. We have the movie we want. Now, as always, it is up to the audience to say how "big" the movie will be.

There is a much-abused expression in the movie business: "You can see the budget on the screen." Much of the time, this is far from true. I am proud to say that, trite or not, the vast portion of our $40 million–plus budget *is* on the screen. The sets, the actors, the lo-cations and the special effects are what made this film so expensive—but money is no guarantee of quality. I like to think that what was spent is visible.

I am a father, but I am also a filmmaker, and it is as a filmmaker that I must share with you my pride in the work of my daughter, Raffaella, who produced *Dune*. I stayed in the background, which

1

was never easy for me, to be there just to support her. Yet she knows so much about all the various aspects of making a movie; her mind and her heart helped to shape this movie into what I believe is an unmatched production of a brilliant novel.

Please enjoy this book and, most important, enjoy the movie. I have no doubt that there will be more.

Dino De Laurentiis
New York City
May 1984

PREFACE

You have to be a little crazy to want to make a movie. Honest. There is nothing glamorous about it. Sets are hot. Hours are long. Costumes are uncomfortable. During the long and tedious production process, illusion and reality somehow never mesh quite right.

A torrid love scene, for instance, might take place two feet away from a fat technician wearing a sweat-stained shirt who's just dying for the scene to be over so he can start chewing his gum again.

A massive battle that on the screen will look as if it's being fought on some exotic locale may be shot in a patch of public park five minutes away from downtown Hollywood.

Half of the fun of making movies lies in the fact that it's such a reality-distorting process.

If making movies, in general, is a strange process, then making a movie in a foreign country is even *stranger*. It's like going to war except you have lunch breaks. Everyone is homesick. No one can get used to the food...or the weather...or the different customs...or the different language...or...well, you get the idea.

The "glamorous" reality of filming on the planet Dune...
the Samalayuca Desert outside of Juarez.

Which, in a roundabout way, brings us to *Dune*. As of this writing, *Dune* is one of the biggest motion pictures ever made. Its budget is over the $40 million mark. It boasts an international cast and crew, its members representing over a half dozen different countries. It needed an entire studio complex to house its seventy-five sets. It was filmed in Mexico by a European producer, an American director and a British cinematographer. The cast includes a British rock idol, a European screen legend and a few dozen giant mechanical worms. Its star has never made a movie before.

In short, it's one major example of the *ultimate* in moviemaking experiences; a manic whirlwind of activity laced with genius, laughter, frustration, heartache and exhilaration.

The book you hold in your hand is, I hope, an accurate reflection of the dedication and dizziness that went into the making of *Dune*. It's not a scholarly tome tracing the film's progress in a precise and orderly manner. Rather, it's a roller-coaster ride through the moviemaking process, almost as crazy as the actual moviemaking itself.

You'll learn about the uniqueness of *Dune* from the people who actually stomped across its celluloid turf: the cast, the crew, the director, the producer, the effects wizards. The dedicated people who invested over two years of their lives in the creation of a motion picture.

It's their story.

I.
PRE-PRODUCTION

We spent six years developing DUNE. I didn't want to rush this one and make a silly film.
Dino De Laurentiis

1.
<u>DUNE</u>

Why make a movie out of DUNE?
The reasons are all in the book.
Raffaella De Laurentiis, producer

A lot of people have tried to film DUNE. They all failed.
I tried writing a screenplay of it, once. It was rotten.
Frank Herbert, author of DUNE

Nobody is as crazy as I am.
You have to be crazy to make a movie like DUNE.
Dino De Laurentiis

Arrakis, the third planet of Canopus. A barren, desert world, it has become one of the most famous fictitious planetary bodies in literary history. Known as Dune to both its denizens and its fans, it first materialized in 1965, the centerpiece of a book of the same name written by Frank Herbert.

Although the book has sold over ten million copies and spawned four sequels, its magical realm has eluded the grasp of filmmakers for nearly two decades... until now.

Dune, the planet, has finally been physically assembled for the screen on a vast studio complex in Mexico. *Dune,* the book, with its layers of adventure, mysticism, philosophy and politics has, at last, been translated into startling visual terms for eager moviegoers by writer/director David Lynch. This metamorphic process, however, has been long and hard. The behind-the-scenes adventures in making the film are almost as epic as those found in the novel.

Nineteen years ago, author Frank Herbert's futuristic hero Paul Atreides was given a description of the planet Dune by the wise, old Reverend Mother.

"You'll learn about the funeral plains," she'd said, "about the wilderness that is empty, the wasteland where nothing lives

7

except the spice and the sandworms. You'll stain your eyepits to reduce the sun glare. Shelter will mean a hollow out of the wind and hidden from view. You'll ride upon your own two feet without 'thopter or groundcar or mount."

On this hot and smoggy day at Churubusco Studios outside Mexico City, Herbert's harsh description of Dune sounds almost idyllic compared to the real world of filmmaking. A small slice of the immense backlot has been converted into a section of the barren planet. During a one-week period 150 tons of sand have been imported from the nearby Samalayuca desert circling Juarez, Mexico and spread over a set covering nearly a city block. Large, man-made rocks and cliffs rise, ominously, towards an all-too-real, relentless summer sun.

A young actor, Kyle MacLachlan, making his screen debut as Paul, is crawling slowly backward in the sand. He is wearing a form-fitting rubber stillsuit. His face is covered with a layer of red grit. Nose plugs, extensions of the suit design, are firmly stuffed into his nostrils. His hair is caked with sand.

Surrounding MacLachlan is a small army of crew members. Director David Lynch, who won critical raves with *The Elephant Man*, must direct both his actor and the elements.

Gigantic fans blow countless pounds of tinted dirt across the background in an effort to simulate the treacherous sandstorms of the fictional world. Closer to the actor, a technician pours sacks of earth in front of a blower, sending out a steady stream of grit in Kyle's direction.

Nearly everyone on the location is wearing goggles and surgical masks. It is almost impossible to breathe. The air is a solid wall of sand.

"Could we have more sand in the background?" Lynch asks, apparently to no one in particular.

Orders are barked into walkie talkies and, presto, the sandstorm increases in intensity.

Lynch now concentrates on the clouds of sand billowing closest to the camera. "A little more...a little more," he coaxes as the technician shakes the bag carefully. "Perfect," Lynch nods. "Peachy keen."

The tall, seemingly imperturbable filmmaker takes his place next to cinematographer Freddie Francis at the camera. Actor MacLachlan is called upon to do his backwards crawl a few times as the red dust roars around him and the crew members. He cannot react to the sheets of grit, only to the object of his character's attention...a

Actor Kyle MacLachlan as Paul confronts the effects of a man-made sandstorm.

Paul and the Lady Jessica (Francesca Annis)
seek shelter from the harsh surface of Arrakis.

monstrous sandworm that will not be matted into the scene until months later when the special effects will be completed for the movie. MacLachlan valiantly struggles through the dirt. The sandstorm never flags.

Finally, after what has to be the longest half hour in history, director Lynch has what he wants. "Great, Kyle, great," he says cheerfully. Lynch sits back in his director's chair. He removes his goggles. His face has been reddened but the goggles have framed his eyes in large, white circles. He looks like a lanky raccoon. Crew members work on the next setup, coughing and wheezing.

Surveying the dust-stained scene, Lynch offers a sheepish grin. "Around here," he laughs, "'Dune' is a four-letter word."

2.
FROM PAGE TO PROJECTOR

I think the movie is a big fairy tale,
a fairy tale about reality.
Jurgen Prochnow, actor (Duke Leto)

You can't get a movie like this done worrying about it as a
whole. You have to take it scene by scene ... or go crazy.
David Lynch, director

I call it my mastodon.
Raffaella De Laurentiis, producer

Since its first publication, Frank Herbert's novel *Dune* has always had a larger than life quality to it. Within the confines of a fairly linear science-fiction storyline, its readers were able to find ample areas devoted to religion, philosophy, politics and human behavior.

Appearing during the turbulent 1960s, it became a cult novel, appealing to an optimistic youth culture. Basically, *Dune* espoused a life-affirming metaphor (human potential, developed to its loftiest power, can triumph over all evils—political, technological, cultural), while hinting that its happy ending would have a darker side in tales to come.

The story begins on the lush planet Caladan, home of the royal family of Atreides. Duke Leto is the archetypal benevolent leader, wise and just, yet militarily adept. His consort, the Lady Jessica, is an independent, powerful woman, trained in the ancient mental arts by the mysterious Bene Gesserit order.

Their son, Paul, seems a perfect heir to the throne. He has been schooled by the realm's experts: weaponry masters, seers and scholars with computer-keen minds. Most important, he has been coached by his mother to develop his mental skills to the highest of PSI potential—that is, to master the use of telepathy, clairvoyance and

11

psychokinesis—despite the fact that these ways of the Bene Gesserit are usually passed on only to females. Paul's prowess at parapsychology leads some to wonder if he is the legendary Kwisatz Haderach: the "one who will bridge space and time" and overcome the evil forces dominating the universe.

The family Atreides is inadvertently thrust into a history-making situation when the conniving and powerful Emperor Shaddam IV and one of the Spacing Guild's third-stage navigators hatch a plot to weaken and ultimately destroy the popular and powerful House of Atreides.

The Duke and his followers will be sent, under order of the Emperor, from lush, water-rich Caladan to the desert planet Arrakis, Dune, to oversee the mining of spice melange. Melange is "the spice of spices." Found only on Dune, the spice is required to travel long distances through space. The spice holds mystical properties as well. It can alter the mental state of a user and, physically, can also lead to a longer life.

The House of Atreides is ordered to replace its bitter enemy, the Harkonnen, as rulers of Arrakis. The order, however, is a trap. After the Duke and his family have arrived on the planet, the evil Baron Harkonnen will carry out the Emperor's orders to launch a massive surprise attack from his planet, Giedi Prime.

With the aid of the traitorous Dr. Yueh, one of the Duke's closest advisors, the attack is launched. The Duke is killed. Paul and Jessica escape, taking flight into the desert. There, they are befriended by the natives of Dune, the sietch-dwelling Fremen. While with the Fremen, Paul begins a strange metamorphosis that is destined to shape both his own future and that of the entire universe.

"I didn't set out to write a classic or a best seller," laughs *Dune's* creator, Frank Herbert. "In fact, once it was published, I wasn't really aware of what was going on with the book, to be quite candid. I have this newspaperman's attitude about yesterday's news, you know? I've done that one, now let me do something else."

Frank Herbert does not look or behave like the stereotypical literary seer. He is bearded and jovial, open and friendly. He will just as soon crack a joke as utter a philosophical profundity. Yet, the Washington-born journalist-turned-novelist has managed to impress millions of readers with a book that most fans consider a philosophical milestone.

Herbert is genuinely modest about it all. "It was just a combination of things I was interested in," he says, recalling the novel's origins. "During the early 1960s, I went down to Florence, Oregon,

The royal ruling family of Caladan:
Paul, Duke Leto Atreides (Jurgen Prochnow), and Lady Jessica.

to do a piece, illustrated with aerial shots, detailing the Department of Agriculture's projects concerning sand dunes. They had assembled experts from all over the world—Israel, Tehran, mainland China—to share what they had found out about controlling these dunes.

"You see, when these sand dunes decide to move, they have a tendency not to worry about politeness. They overrun things like highways, plantations, houses, whatever. Intrigued by this idea of controlling sand movement, I did some additional research.

"Coincidentally, I had also done a lot of research for a book I was planning on the messianic impulse; why we have a tendency to follow charismatic leaders without question. One thing led to another and, about a year later, it occurred to me that both trains of thought would make a great beginning for a novel. I guess I researched for about six years. It took me about a year and a half to write the book.

"But during that period, the ideas just started to flow. I actually wrote most of *Dune Messiah* and *Children of Dune* during the same time period. I wrote the last chapter of *Dune* before the novel was completed. Things just happened. I thought of all this in the round."

While Herbert saw the *Dune* saga as a sprawling space history that was different from most other science fiction novels, he didn't encounter too much initial encouragement from any of his professional peers.

"The publishers didn't really think it would be big," he smiles. "They didn't know what they had. When the book hit, it hit, largely, via word of mouth. The publishers couldn't keep up with the demand."

With the novel a cult classic, it was just a matter of time before the movie world took note of its popularity. The sheer magnitude of the plot, however, made many film producers a bit nervous about taking the plunge.

"Nobody exactly broke down my door with movie offers," Herbert shrugs. "The first offer came from Arthur P. Jacobs, the fellow who produced the *Planet of the Apes* films. That was in 1972. He took a nine-year option out on the book. Nothing really came of that deal. Jacobs died (in 1973) and the project was tied up in his estate for quite a while. Then, a French consortium purchased the rights from the estate."

Director David Lynch (far left) and producer Raffaella De Laurentiis (to the right of Lynch) concentrate on a battle scene being filmed.

And the entire pre-production process began all over again, with one filmmaker after another trying to tackle the book. In 1975, it finally looked as if *Dune* the movie would be made. "Alejandro Jodorowsky *(El Topo)* spent a couple of million dollars in pre-production on his version," Herbert says wistfully. "He even hired Salvador Dali as his production designer. Nothing ever happened. I'm not quite sure why it fizzled. Without exaggeration, his script would have made an eleven-or-twelve-hour movie. It was the size of a phonebook. It was pretty anti-Catholic, too. I used to kid Alejandro about that. I told him that his biggest disappointment in writing the script was probably not finding a way to horsewhip the Pope in it.

"Oh, I don't know how many scripts floated around during this time period. I tried one. It didn't work. It would have been *shorter* than Jodorowsky's, though.

"At one point, there was going to be an incest version made. I won't mention the filmmaker's name but someone actually wanted to have a romance between Paul and his mother. That would have outraged every *Dune* fan in the world! I was rather bemused by it all. I'm a calm man. I found it all grist for the mill. After a while, though, I honestly didn't think that a movie would ever be made. The nine years were almost up."

Unbeknownst to Herbert, however, he had two very loyal fans who were determined to see the book successfully translated into cinematic terms. Raffaella De Laurentiis and her father, Dino.

For the elder De Laurentiis, *Dune* seemed a naturally audacious project. The outspoken Italian filmmaker had fashioned a career out of defying the motion picture establishment, jumping headfirst into projects that were termed unfeasible for one reason or another. He was known as a risk-taker. Sometimes his cinematic high-rolling failed but, much more often than not, he managed to tickle the public's fancy with his eclectic film fare. De Laurentiis, responsible for countless films spanning four decades and including everything from *La Strada* and *The Bible* to *Serpico* and *Ragtime,* had been aware of *Dune*'s critical reputation since its publication.

"I had a special feeling about *Dune,*" the seasoned filmmaker admits. "I knew about the book since before I moved my head-quarters to America from Italy; since the late 1960s. Once I established myself here in America, many producers approached me about working with them on this project. But I was scared. Frankly, *Dune* was the kind of movie that I wanted to have a strong hand in. If I was going to make it, I had to be able to call the shots. Here

David Lynch and Dune author Frank Herbert on the first day of shooting, at Churubusco Studios in Mexico City, March 30, 1983.

were these offers with another producer already attached. That would limit my input. So, I stayed away."

While Dino was biding his time, his daughter Raffaella was becoming a *Dune* fanatic. "I read the book ten years ago," Raffaella states. "In those pages was a movie that had to be made. The book just had so much potential. At that time, I was working in movies during summer vacations from school. Working in wardrobe or the art department. But when I read that book I said that I had to produce it... no matter what. I went on to other jobs, other films. But that thought never left my mind."

Happily, for all concerned, the lack of progress on the *Dune* film front allowed Dino De Laurentiis to enter the picture formally. In 1976, he bought the rights to the picture from the French consortium. He was not particularly fazed by his predecessors' lack of success.

"I don't know why other people hadn't succeeded with *Dune* before," he says. "There's no logical reason why they failed. Maybe they were scared about the script. Maybe they were scared about the money. Maybe they were scared about so many major roles.

"I'm too long in this business now to get frightened by things that should frighten me. If you feel panicked by life, you shouldn't do anything but sit home and hide. In life you must take chances...especially in moving pictures. You take a chance every time you make a movie. I knew I would be taking a big chance with *Dune*. It would be very risky. It would be very expensive. But I never worry about money when I make a movie. If you have the right idea, the money will come. You just have to be patient.

"We spent six years developing it," he says proudly. "You have to have special faith in special projects. I didn't want to rush this one and make a silly film."

Dino's relaxed attitude worked to everyone's advantage. Recounts Raffaella: "I remember writing a letter to my father years ago. I was going to Tahiti for two and a half years to work on two pictures (*Hurricane* and *Beyond the Reef*) and build a hotel. Before I left, I put a note on his desk that said 'No matter what happens during the time I'm away, you're not allowed to start *Dune* without me!'"

Herbert was delighted about the new development. When Dino hadn't produced a movie at the end of the nine-year option, the filmmaker asked to renegotiate, buying the rights not only to *Dune* but also to the sequel books (both written and unwritten). Says Herbert: "We put together a contract and I don't know what Dino did after that. I do know that he brought Universal into the picture and raised a lot of money. The next thing I knew we were in Mexico."

By the time *Dune* was ready to enter the pre-production stage, Raffaella had served her apprenticeship in her father's filmmaking domain, earning producing credits on both *Beyond the Reef* and *Conan, the Barbarian*. In June of 1981, she eagerly grabbed the producer's reins on *Dune* and the movie was ready to go...almost.

There was some consternation concerning who would write and direct the movie. While Raffaella had been working on *Conan*, her father's organization had contacted director Ridley Scott, whose credentials as an excellent science-fiction filmmaker were established by the success of *Alien*. Scott toiled unsuccessfully on launching the movie. H.R. Giger, the artist who worked with Scott on designing *Alien* was commissioned as production designer. Rudy Wurlitzer was hired to translate the book into cinematic terms. The book's plotline proved too unwieldy for a conventional script, however, and Scott departed the project. Work had to begin, again, from scratch. The pressure was now on Raffaella.

At that point, fate intervened. Raffaella saw a movie. It was called *The Elephant Man*. Recalls the producer: "There's so much *heart* in that movie. I don't cry in movies. I'm tough. I haven't cried in a movie in years. But I had tears in my eyes several times during *The Elephant Man*. After I saw it, I had to talk to the director."

Enter David Lynch... and a fresh approach to the making of *Dune*.

3.
TRIUMVIRATE

David had no idea why I was calling him.
He didn't know DUNE. He said, 'What? JUNE?' He thought
we were making a summer movie.
Raffaella De Laurentiis, producer

My first reaction was ... it's not going to work.
David Lynch, director

I think David Lynch is a genius.
There aren't too many of them left.
Dino De Laurentiis

It is a hot, summer day in Mexico. On the Churubusco lot, things seem more frenzied than usual. A group of two hundred extras, all wearing Fremen stillsuits, are huddled under a large tent erected next to one of the lot's lackluster brick office buildings. They try their best to avoid the sun's rays. Sweating construction workers amble by. Sets are being torn down so that others may be erected in their place. *Dune* is at the three-quarter mark in its live-action filming and work is slowly beginning for its second phase, the five months of miniature and model work necessary for the production's impressive special effects.

Hammers and saws can be heard reverberating from all of the large sound stages on the lot. In the midst of the construction and destruction, a $40 million movie is lurching to life. The calm in the center of this hurricane consists of three of the most unlikely comrades imaginable: director David Lynch, producer Raffaella De Laurentiis and her father, Dino.

Today, Dino is visiting the set on a brief trip. Dino is a compact, silver-haired, energetic man. He doesn't walk as much as he marches across the lot. The horn-rimmed glasses he wears cannot hide the fact that his eyes are always taking things in, scanning every object

19

around him. His mind is always whirring.

He enters one of the movie's sietch sets. The sietches are the cavern homes of the underground-dwelling Fremen and, accordingly, the massive set is earth-colored; gray with streaks of reddish brown flowing through its rough walls. As Dino strides towards the front of the set, photographers in tow, he is greeted by his daughter, Raffaella.

If Dino represents the filmmaker as risk-taker, as straight-talking showman, then Raffaella represents the filmmaker as military strategist. She is a master of organizational skills and seems to thrive on managing the unmanageable. Thirty years of age, she wears her cascading blonde hair in a pony tail. She is most often clad in jeans and casual clothes yet persists in wearing a pearl necklace given to her by her mother for "good luck." She appears and disappears from sets and offices depending on need, an omnipresent earth mother dedicated to mastering this sprawling science-fiction tale and bringing it in on time and on budget.

At the head of the sietch set is the movie's director, David Lynch. Lynch gives the impression that he could not care less about the business end of things and is concentrating all his efforts on making a great movie. Period.

If Dino is flamboyant and Raffaella businesslike and efficient, then Lynch is the personification of "casual-artistic." Usually dressed in baggy khaki pants, long-sleeved white shirt and a leather aviator jacket, the tall, soft-spoken and often bemused director comes across as a new-wave college professor investigating the process of movie-making as a possible art form.

Lynch is utterly calm, quietly humorous, yet very intense. It is his sense of sensible experimentalism that seems to hold things together on the set from day to day. He inspires loyalty with ease.

Posing together for photographers, this triumvirate clearly is composed of three very dissimilar personalities. Yet, for some inexplicable reason, they work perfectly together.

After the *Life* photo session is completed, they all recount their remembrances of how this creative union was born. "After seeing *The Elephant Man,*" Raffaella states, "I knew David was the ideal choice. All those special effects pictures that had been done before, from *Star Wars* to *Alien,* were all very good but they were really high-tech science-fiction stories with characters that weren't humanized very well. In the book, *Dune,* there were so many levels to each character that if we had hired a director who would have only told the story of spaceships and space wars, we wouldn't have

David Lynch, Associate Producer Jose Lopez Rodero, Raffaella De Laurentiis, and Silvana Mangano.

On the blistering desert location near Juarez, David Lynch is given a producer's once-over by Raffaella De Laurentiis.

had a movie . . . at least not the movie that I wanted to make. I called David and we began talking about it. I also started talking to Dino."

"I was looking for a director who was a young and sensitive man, someone who was intelligent and talented," says the elder De Laurentiis. "I looked at *The Elephant Man* and I was impressed. I felt that he was the director to do it. It didn't matter to me that *The Elephant Man* was a small, black and white film. I don't think in terms of big or small or black and white or color. I think in terms of good or bad. His movie was good. Very good."

While the De Laurentiis clan was very gung-ho on the choice of Lynch, Lynch himself had his doubts about the project. "My first reaction was that it wasn't going to work," he grins. "Number one: I probably wouldn't like the book because I had never bothered to read it on my own. Number two: I wouldn't want to work with Dino. I didn't know him but I had heard these stories, you know?" Movie-mogul stuff.

"Dino called me and asked me in for a meeting. I went into the interview thinking that I'd walk into the room and within five minutes I'd know I wouldn't want to do it. After that, I'd just get through the rest of the meeting, leave and that would be the end of it.

"So, I walked into the room—I still hadn't read the book, maybe two-thirds of it—and sat down with Dino and a few people from his office. The strangest thing happened. I felt like I was at home. I just relaxed with Dino. It was great. He told jokes. Fantastic. Still, I left thinking that he was just being nice to me.

"The next meeting, the same thing happened. Dino has this game he plays where he asks you to name three animals and then he comments on your choice. I figured, 'Oh boy, I'm going to name three animals and he's going to figure some way of putting me down.' Everyone in the room named their animals and Dino described our personalities in very poetic terms. It was really incredible. I liked him and I liked the book and that was it."

With Lynch as director and Raffaella as producer, a decision had to be made as to who was going to write the script. Lynch decided to give the assignment to writers he had worked with previously. Once again, however, *Dune*'s complex storyline proved a stumbling block.

"I told Dino that I wanted to write it with Christian Devore and Eric Bergman," says Lynch. "I worked with them on *The Elephant Man* and we had gotten along real well. Not only had we written a good script but we had become good friends. I figured that *Dune* was a giant project and I couldn't write the script on my own.

"We wrote a treatment and a script together. The script was just as long as the book, maybe longer. It just wasn't happening. I think Chris and Eric wanted to go in a different direction than I was intending, so we parted company. I told Dino I wanted to take a crack at it myself. He wasn't too sure about that but he told me to go ahead and start and we'd see how it went."

Before setting off on his assignment, Lynch huddled with *Dune*'s author Herbert. "David and I hit it off right away," recalls the author. "He's a gentleman. He just picked my brains and I didn't hold back anything. I told him anything and everything he wanted to know."

"I wrote seventeen pages," says Lynch, "and took them over to the house Dino was staying at in Beverly Hills. He said they were the best seventeen pages he had read of all the scripts so far and that I had the assignment. So, I started writing. I wrote seven drafts and I went all over the world to script meetings. It was some experience.

"My main goal was to be true to the book and to get the story to be as cinematic as possible."

"That was the biggest challenge," echoes Raffaella, "to turn that book into a movie and keep all that's in the book in the movie. Some

Two <u>Dune</u> fans: Dino and Raffaella De Laurentiis.

writers tried to change it drastically. Others tried to keep some of the characters and eliminate other ones. David was really the first to keep the essence of the book in one, tight script. I think he's gotten the core of what's in the book onto the screen without changing the mood or hurting the characters.

"To be honest, we're *still* nervous about the script. I think we've been faithful to the book but I'm sure that of the millions of *Dune* readers there will be some who will think, 'That's not the way I think it should have been filmed.'"

In any case, Raffaella considers that possible reaction with a shrug. "When you read a book, you interpret things privately. You use your imagination. When you see someone else's imagination, someone else's interpretation, on the screen, you may be upset. You may disagree. But, since I can't be inside everyone's head, I have to do the best I can. I think we've been very faithful to the book. If the movie is a failure," she laughs, not really considering that possibility as a reality, "that means I've screwed up."

Author Herbert is one of those *Dune* fans who is very pleased with Lynch's visual adaptation. "I don't think anything has been lost," he stresses. "I'm pleased with the screenplay. I'm well aware of the fact that film has to use a shorthand process to convey things that are in the novel. It's a translation process, actually, from one language to another.

"When David was done and had a shooting script ready, I actually sat down with him and helped him trim fourteen pages or so out of it. It was a little long at that point. After that, he refined it even more.

"There are a lot of passages of dialogue in the movie that are directly from the book. I think *Dune* readers are going to have fun going back to the book after seeing this and tracking them down."

With a script in hand, a director signed up, Universal Pictures serving as the movie's distributor in most of the world, and her father as the movie's presenter, Raffaella De Laurentiis had to move on to the next giant step. Exactly where would she shoot this massive movie without encountering production expenses that would cripple the movie before it could begin?

A quick trip around the world was called for.

4.
THE REALITY TAKES HOLD

Nobody believed this movie could be made in Mexico.
Raffaella De Laurentiis, producer

It's interesting to ask for a prop, have the request
translated into another language and wind up with an
entirely different object being dragged in.
David Lynch, director

We are quite often surprised on this movie.
Freddie Francis, cinematographer

By the middle of 1982, it was clear that *Dune* was no longer a mere pipe dream. After nearly a decade and a half of sporadic activity, the production was finally a *go*. The problem, at this point, was the size of the film. States Dino De Laurentiis, "*Dune* is my biggest movie. It may be the biggest movie ever."

With a budget in the $40 million range, it was clearly the most ambitious project ever undertaken at Universal Pictures. Aside from its mountainous monetary status, however, the film had other problems that were somewhat staggering to solve.

The story takes place on four different planets, each planet boasting a distinctive look both in ecology and architecture. There are fifty-three speaking roles to be cast, nearly 20,000 extras required, and seventy-five sets to be built.

The question facing producer Raffaella De Laurentiis was basically this: Where was there a studio complex big enough to handle all of *Dune's* requirements?

After an exhaustive search, she decided on Churubusco Studios in Mexico City, a vast complex built decades ago amidst the hustle and bustle of Mexico City, Mexico. Her decision, however, did not come easy.

"It was a very tough choice," she states. "We flew all over the world looking at different locations and studios, all the while budgeting like crazy. We had a lot of problems finding a studio big enough. We couldn't find one anywhere. We also had to find a country that had a good desert location near the studio. We couldn't find one. I tried using England and Spain together. Then, England and India. I tried Italy alone. Then, Italy and Tunisia.

"When we found a desert, we couldn't find the right studio facilities. When we found a decent studio, there was no desert nearby. Churubusco was the only studio that had eight sound stages that were a good size and a desert that was perfect for us only two hours away. It seemed like the logical choice."

Raffaella was aware, however, that filming at Churubusco did present some fairly unique problems. For one thing, despite its size, the complex was badly antiquated in terms of technology. In order to make the *Dune* she envisioned, the producer would have to skill-fully bring the studio facilities up-to-date before a single frame of film could be exposed.

There was also a question of working habits to consider. For instance, because Mexican craftsmen take pride in the detail of their work, many prefer working with old-fashioned tools as opposed to new devices like power saws.

Raffaella didn't let these challenges faze her. "I enjoy chal-lenges," she laughs. "Absolutely. I'm sure that aided me in my decision. Still, it was a very hard decision for me. Nobody believed that the movie could be made in Mexico. Now that it has been made down here, everyone is coming here to film their movies. The same people who told me I was crazy for coming to Mexico two years ago are now staying at the same hotel.

"Sure, I knew that it would be difficult but I never thought that making a movie down here was fighting a losing battle. I never think of fighting losing battles. I only think of fighting *winning* battles.

"Besides, I knew that if I picked a good crew, things would be a lot easier."

Once Churubusco was decided upon, Raffaella realized that she would have to stock the studio with some of the most creative and industrious minds available. In order to get her science-fiction epic produced on time and on budget, she would have to generate a smooth, meticulously planned and executed shooting schedule.

"Smooth shoots just don't happen," she says. "You make a smooth shoot. The biggest challenge a producer has is choosing the crew. You choose the people around you very carefully so that you have a crew you can count on. There can be no fighting or resent-ment between the different heads of departments. That's the first hurdle to clear and that's what I'm best at."

On location in the Samalayuca Desert, the film crew was at the mercy of the elements. Strong winds could delay smoky battle scenes for hours.

An Atreides ornithopter, under construction on a Churubusco set.

"I'm lucky. I've never worked in the United States in a studio. I've always worked with foreign crews comprised of twenty different nationalities. I know who to hire. I know who gets along with whom and who is temperamental."

The production team Raffaella came up with reads like a Who's Who of contemporary filmmaking.

For director of photography, David Lynch insisted on his partner from *The Elephant Man*, Freddie Francis. The winner of an Oscar in 1960 for his work on *Sons and Lovers*, Francis' cinematic credits also include *Room At the Top*, *The Night Must Fall* and *The French Lieutenant's Woman*. As a director, he is best known as a master of dark fantasy, with such films as *Doctor Terror's House of Horrors*, *Asylum* and *Tales from the Crypt* to his credit.

Editor Tony Gibbs won Best British Editing Guild Awards for both *Jesus Christ, Superstar* and *Rollerball*. His skillful style can be seen in a variety of classic British motion pictures, ranging from *Performance* and *The Knack* to *Tom Jones* and *A Taste of Honey*. Among his other credits are such films as *F.I.S.T.*, *A Bridge Too Far*, *Fiddler on the Roof* and *The Loved One*.

For production designer, veteran cinematic conjurer Tony Masters seemed like a natural choice. Nominated by the Academy of Motion Picture Arts and Sciences for an Oscar in 1968 for Best Art Direction on *2001, A Space Odyssey*, he served as Art Director on *Lawrence of Arabia*, and Production Designer on *Papillon*, *Moonspinner*, *The Battle of Britain*, *Buffalo Bill and the Indians*, *The Deep* and *The Heroes of Telemark*. He was a man who, clearly, was not daunted by movies of epic proportions and *Dune* was shaping up to be the epic to end all epics.

As special mechanical effects modeler, long-time De Laurentiis collaborator Carlo Rambaldi was recruited to come up with suitably cosmic creatures for the feature. Rambaldi, who has earned three Oscars for his mechanical whammies in the films *King Kong*, *Alien* and *E.T.*, also provided screen "reality" in such productions as *The White Buffalo*, *The Bible*, *Close Encounters of the Third Kind* and *Andy Warhol's Frankenstein*.

To come up with some truly "spacey" optical work and matte paintings, Hollywood legend Albert Whitlock was hired. Whitlock has won Oscars for his Special Visual Effects seen in *Earthquake* and *The Hindenburg*. His deft hand can also be seen in such films as *The Birds*; *The Thing*; *History of the World, Part One*; *Diamonds Are Forever* and *The Day of the Locust*.

Supervising *Dune's* special mechanical effects, including all its

Francesca Annis, Kyle MacLachlan and Frank Herbert
on the opening day of principal photography.

pyrotechnic phenomena, is Kit West, who won an Oscar for his
Visual Effects work on *Raiders of the Lost Ark*. The talented British
denizen has created eye-boggling effects on over forty films, including *Return of the Jedi, Battle of the Bulge* and *Love and Death*.

To design the costumes for the many worlds found in *Dune*,
Raffaella De Laurentiis turned to Bob Ringwood, a theatrical set and
costume designer who managed to attract critical attention with his
designs for his first feature film, *Excalibur*. His screen debut earned
him a Best Costume Award from the Academy of Science Fiction
and Fantasy.

To coordinate some of the more physical feats of derring-do in
Dune, the producer turned to Japanese-born Kiyoshi Yamazaki, who
served as fight coordinator on *Conan, the Barbarian*. A master in a
variety of martial arts, he has also staged fights in such films as *The
Beast Master* and *The Bad News Bears*.

Rounding out the staff were such film veterans as production
coordinator Golda Offenheim, a master of almost military strategy
in manning a front office; makeup and special effects makeup wizard
Gianetto De Rossi; model-making legend Emilio Ruiz Del Rio; and
construction manager Aldo Puccini.

While some of the production crew were new to the De Laurentiis organization, many of them had worked with either Dino or Raffaella before. "People like to work with us," Dino explains, "for a lot of reasons. We treat people very well. We respect their talent and they respect us. They also respect us because we know what we're talking about, technically. We know movies. We are all professionals in this business, so why not treat each other with respect?"

By the time she had finished her selection, Raffaella knew she had a winning team on her side. "All the people on the crew are great people," she says. "They have to be. Movies aren't made by one person. Movies are made by a lot of people who have to work together under strange conditions to make the best movie they can. Some people think that a crew is just a tool to make a picture. It's not that way in my book.

"Everybody on the crew knew what they were in for. Most knew about *Dune* beforehand. You have to remember that many of them were with me on *Conan* in Spain for two years and heard me talk about *Dune* a lot. When I called them, it was usually, 'Oh, we're finally making it, eh?'"

In spite of her selection, however, Raffaella was aware there were still dozens of technical hurtles to clear, paramount among them settling her crew into their new home at Churubusco. "Initially, some of my people suffered at the idea," she says. "Some of them suffered until the end. Tony Masters was very much against it. He was afraid that his sets would suffer. By the end, I think he was the happiest man in the whole team. His sets turned out beautifully. He was working with people I had worked with before from Spain, Italy and England. He built sets the likes of which have never been seen before. The detail is phenomenal.

"David was very much opposed to Mexico at the beginning. Now, he's delighted. He also realized how much we accomplished here that we couldn't accomplish anywhere else. Sure, we suffered...a lot. Not everything went exactly as we planned. But things got done. I don't think the picture has suffered at all by being filmed in Mexico. A lot of the people have suffered but the picture has gained.

"Had we filmed *Dune* anywhere else in the world, our budget would have been somewhere between $75 million and $100 million dollars."

By the end of 1982, work was already in progress on the Churubusco lot.

A crew of nearly 900 workers would eventually be employed.

David Lynch stands on Arrakis. He had never read about the world of Dune before being asked to direct the film by Raffaella De Laurentiis—and yet he has created it.

Among the ranks would be craftsmen of Mexican, Italian, English, American, French and Venezuelan descent.

As the physical work of creating the worlds of *Dune* began, producer Raffaella and director David Lynch began concentrating on populating their planetscapes with an international cast of acting talent.

If *Dune* was to pack an emotional wallop, actors of the first magnitude had to be chosen.

5.
THE CAST

> *The characters are exactly as I envisioned them...*
> *sometimes even better.*
> **Frank Herbert, author of DUNE**

> *The actors really had to work on this movie.*
> **Raffaella De Laurentiis, producer**

> *This is the dirtiest job I've ever had...*
> *and that includes construction work.*
> **Sting, actor (Feyd)**

The film world of *Dune* is populated by acting talent both familiar and new, a combination of established and fresh faces in the realm of cinema. The casting was done jointly by Raffaella De Laurentiis and David Lynch and, accordingly, is a mixture of De Laurentiis veterans and personal favorites of the director.

"The casting took a long time," admits Lynch. "But it's one of the things that I think everyone is the happiest about. I don't think we made any mistakes in picking people and everyone has been fantastic to work with. A lot of the actors brought a lot of insight into their roles. It was worth the effort and time. It's funny. Quite a few times we were after a specific actor or actress for a role and we just couldn't get them. The same thing happened to me in *The Elephant Man*. At that point, fate just kind of steps in and rescues you. You find someone that you had never thought of that is just wonderful for the part."

With so many speaking roles of importance in the film (although not necessarily lengthy in terms of screen time), Lynch was able to line up a host of big names for *Dune*. Surprisingly enough, some of the biggest stars agreed to take on some of the smallest roles, essentially because they liked both the script and the novel.

One such case was Max Von Sydow, the international star of such films as *The Seventh Seal, The Exorcist, Wild Strawberries* and *The*

New Land. Von Sydow plays Dr. Kynes, a scientist living on the planet Dune who plays a pivotal role in educating both Paul and his family about the realities of the desert planet.

"I am fascinated by the book and by the story," he says, "and I think that the character of Kynes is interesting. Relatively little of him is seen in the film but it remains a fascinating role. Essentially, he introduces young Paul to the Fremen. He also initiates the process of making Dune habitable again. This is the idea that Paul inherits, in a way. I like Kynes. I wish you could see more of him in the movie, though."

One character who is constantly seen on the screen during the cosmic adventure is Lady Jessica, Paul's Mother. British actress Francesca Annis was chosen for the role. Well known for her stage work and for films like *Krull, Macbeth* and *Murder Most Foul,* she found herself intrigued by Jessica's strange mixture of personality traits.

"I see her as a sort of supreme matriarch, really," she explains. "She's a mother, a guardian, a guide and an almost mystical figure, too. And, I mean, let's face it, it *is* quite an achievement to be the head of a religious order *plus* have a coming Messiah as your son."

The role of Paul's father, Duke Leto, was ideal for German actor Jurgen Prochnow, best known as the stalwart submarine captain in the critically acclaimed action film *Das Boot.* "I was worried about Jurgen's accent at first," director Lynch recalls, "but he carried himself with such grace and authority that, after a while, you just accepted him as this great, royal leader."

"I love the character," says Prochnow. "He is a good-hearted man and is military as well. He is a strong man, one taught to hide his feelings and emotions... and he has many of them. He is very much in love with Jessica and could have had a really good life on Caladan. But he has to go to Arrakis. Damn."

As the conniving Emperor, Jose Ferrer took great delight in concocting villainy. A world-renowned stage actor, he has participated in many classic films, including *Moulin Rouge, The Caine Mutiny, Ship of Fools* and *Cyrano De Bergerac,* a film which earned him an Oscar in the Best Actor category.

The Emperor's partners in crime, the evil Baron Harkonnen and his two nefarious nephews, Feyd and Rabban (the Beast) were played by Kenneth McMillan, Sting and Paul Smith, respectively.

McMillan is a familiar face to both stage and movie fans alike, having performed starring roles on Broadway in such plays as *American Buffalo* and *Streamers* and featured roles in films like *Ragtime;*

True Confessions; Whose Life Is It, Anyway and *Heartbeeps*. He saw the Baron as a "megalomaniac...not unlike Adolf Hitler."

As the Baron's evil nephew, Feyd, the rock group Police's lead singer, Sting, represented just the right combination of sexy swagger and savagery. Having already acted in such films as *Quadrophenia* and *Brimstone and Treacle,* the British entertainer admits that, initially, he was not too keen on the idea of doing the science-fiction classic.

"The reason I'm doing *Dune* is largely David Lynch," says Sting. "*Dune* was secondary to me. I really wanted to work with David. I think his previous work is fascinating. David and Raffaella saw me in *Brimstone and Treacle* and saw that I could act—kind of. They sent me the script. I didn't like it. I kept on saying, 'No, no, no.' Then I was asked to a meeting and David asked me why I didn't like the script.

"That was an interesting meeting. I sat with David and Raffaella and, not caring whether I got the movie or not, I was very open and candid. I told them I thought it was humorless and very heavy-handed. I didn't really mean those things. I was pretty harsh. They gave me time to go and read the book. I liked the script a lot better after reading the novel. Now that we've filmed it, I think there is a lot more humor in it and, live, it's a lot less heavy-handed than it was on paper."

As the mammoth Beast Rabban, Lynch cast Paul Smith, an actor who resembles a moving mountain. Exuding evil as Bluto in *Popeye* and the slimey prison guard in *Midnight Express*, Smith has earned the status of being truly hissable on the screen. Fans of his villainy will not be disappointed in this movie. "Rabban does such horrible things...it's unreal," the soft-spoken Smith whispers. "But the nice thing about it is...he enjoys himself so. He's always smiling."

Representing the Bene Gesserit order are actresses Sian Phillips and Silvana Mangano as Reverend Mother Helen Mohiam and Reverend Mother Ramallo, respectively. Mangano, the wife of Dino De Laurentiis, achieved star status in the international screen world for roles in such films as *Bitter Rice, Ulysses, Ludwig* and *Oedipus Rex*. *Dune* marks the first time she has worked with her daughter, Raffaella.

Sian Phillips, best known in America for her appearance in such television dramas as *I, Claudius; Crime and Punishment* and *Smiley's People*, enjoyed her first foray into science fiction. "David had this idea how to play my character. He had me doing extraordinary things. I have to sort of growl like an animal and go barking and do really ugly, horrible and embarrassing things which I've never done before. Well, that's the way he wanted it and I'm sure he's right. Besides, it was fun."

The role of Duke Leto's loyal righthand man Duncan went to Richard Jordan, a handsome actor with such films as *The Friends of Eddie Coyle, Logan's Run, Interiors* and *Rooster Cogburn* to his credit.

The traitorous Dr. Yueh was played by Dean Stockwell, an actor since childhood whose work in films spans three decades and includes titles such as *The Boy With Green Hair, Compulsion* and *Alcino and the Condor.*

Veteran British character actor Freddie Jones of *The Elephant Man, Firefox, Krull, Firestarter* and *Juggernaut* was chosen to play one of Paul's mentors, Thufir Hawat. Distinguished British actor Patrick Stewart was cast as Paul's other key teacher, Gurney Halleck.

Jack Nance of *Eraserhead* and *Hammett* was cast as Nefud. Everett McGill who made a big impression in such films as *Quest for Fire* and *Brubaker* was given the role of the noble Fremen leader Stilgar.

More than any other character in the film, Stilgar guides young Paul Atreides on his journey from somewhat ordinary royal heir to a mystical citizen of the planet Dune. The towering actor enjoyed the chance to play a cosmic sidekick.

"He seems a bit mysterious at first," says McGill, "and I love mysterious characters. But I see him as a man who has suffered enormously, as his people have for nearly a hundred years under the Harkonnens. They have been hunted and pursued. I see him as a worried man, one who fears that he is becoming almost too important. Outwardly, he is a disciplined man. He has to be. But, inwardly, I see a man who is loving, full of life and wants the best for his tribe. He has a wonderful sense of humor. The closer the dream comes to being reality, the closer he sees his tribe moving towards freedom, the greater his delight, the greater his happiness."

Brad Dourif *(Ragtime)* was cast as the Baron's envoy, Piter, and Virginia Madsen plays the Emperor's daughter, Princess Irulan. Seven-year-old Alicia Roanne Witt was chosen to make her screen debut in the role of Alia, Paul's sister and the possessor of extraordinary PSI powers.

Actress Linda Hunt, best known as Billy Kwan from *The Year of Living Dangerously,* was cast as the mysterious Shadout Mapes, the first resident of *Dune* to realize Paul's true identity. "It was a great role," says Hunt, "plus, I got a great death scene out of it. Eyes rolling. Tongue hanging out. The works."

While most of the casting was done in a conventional manner, at least three roles were cast, apparently, by the direct intervention of whatever deity looks over the film community. In the role of Chani, a leader of the Freman and Paul's love interest, David and Raffaella were interested in Sean Young, the willowy heroine of *Blade Runner* and *Young Doctors In Love.*

"I don't think there's anyone who could play her better than me," laughs the actress, "because I'm skinny and elfin." But Sean almost didn't get the chance.

"My agency had set up a meeting with David and Raffaella in New York but never told me about it. (I've since left that agency.) I never showed up for the appointment and they thought I had stood them up. I was on a plane to California that night to test for another movie. It was a seven-thirty flight. David and Raffaella had been booked on a six o'clock flight back to L.A. but they missed it because they were waiting for me to show up.

"The agency I was with told them that I refused to meet with them because they hadn't sent a script over first. I was innocent! Anyhow, I'm on the plane and I begin talking to a stewardess, telling her that I'm an actress and all. A few minutes later, Raffaella walks by. When she returns to her seat, she leans over and says to David, 'I bet that girl's an actress.'

Kyle MacLachlan as Paul Atreides.

Francesca Annis as Lady Jessica.

Jurgen Prochnow as Duke Leto Atreides.

Sting as Baron Harkonnen's nephew, Feyd.

Kenneth McMillan as Baron Harkonnen.

Paul Smith as the evil Rabban.

Sian Phillips
as Reverend Mother Helen Mohiam.

Silvana Mangano
as Reverend Mother Ramallo.

Three members of the Bene Gesserit sisterhood: Reverend Mother Helen Mohiam,
Lady Jessica, and Reverend Mother Ramallo.

Richard Jordan as Duncan Idaho.

Patrick Stewart as Gurney Halleck.

Freddie Jones as Thufir Hawat, a Mentat.

Dean Stockwell as Dr. Yueh,
the Harkonnen spy.

Paul falls in love with Chani (Sean Young), a brave and beautiful Fremen.

The Princess Irulan (Virginia Madsen) with her father, Emperor Shaddam IV (Jose Ferrer).

Max Von Sydow as Dr. Kynes, Imperial Ecologist.

Everett McGill as Fremen leader Stilgar.

Molly Wryn as Fremen Harah.

Alicia Roanne Witt as Paul's sister Alia.

Linda Hunt as the mysterious Shadout Mapes, the Atreides housekeeper on Dune.

"The stewardess leans in right at that point and says, 'She is. Her name is Sean Young.' David and Raffaella look at each other and their heads just go through the roof. They missed their plane because of me!

"Raffaella walks over to me and says, 'Are you Sean Young?' She then tells me what happened. I'm flabbergasted. We go back to her seat and I sit with her and David and we all start drinking champagne. By the time we arrived in L.A. we were roaring drunk. We wound up at Raffaella's house. They gave me the script. I read it later and that was that."

Yet another weird incident in casting involved the role of Harah, a female Freman. The part went to actress Molly Wryn . . . who has never done a movie before in her life.

"I saw a paragraph about *Dune* in the trade papers," she recalls. "I had read the first three books years ago and had liked them. So, I wrote a letter to David Lynch and sent him my photo. He called me. I pretty much knew the day that I walked in that I had the part. David said he had decided as soon as he saw my photo. It was fate."

Probably the most audacious bit of casting occurred in the search for a young man to play the movie's complex hero, young Paul Atreides. After interviewing quite a few up-and-coming actors, David and Raffaella decided upon Kyle MacLachlan, a native of Washington state who, while a veteran of many regional stage productions, had never stepped before a movie camera prior to his screen test for *Dune*.

Recalls Kyle: "I couldn't believe I got the role. I don't know any character I feel closer to. I first read *Dune* when I was fourteen years old. I've read it every year since that time. It's almost been my bible. When I was growing up, I always thought of myself as Paul . . . 'What would Paul do about this? What would Paul do about that?'

"The first time I met David it was at his office at Universal Studios. I liked him immediately. I sat down and I was very excited about the fact that they were doing *Dune* . . . finally. I thought to myself, 'You know, even if I don't get the part, it's great that they're making this movie.' Basically, instead of talking about myself, I talked about the movie. I was saying things like 'What do you think about this movie, David? How are you approaching it? How do you envision Paul?'

"Later, I met with David and Raffaella and I did a screen test. At that point, I thought that I might actually have a chance. David and I clicked right away in a director-actor relationship. So, after two roles of the dice I felt in pretty good shape.

"After a while, it was down to me and two other actors. So, they flew me down to Mexico City for a second test. I thought that was a pretty good sign. I went down, did it and waited around for five days or so. I got the call from Raffaella. Yeeooww!"

Everyone seemed pleased with the final lineup for the film, including author Frank Herbert. "When I first went down to Mexico City, Raffaella threw a dinner party for me. All the actors and actresses were there. I was sitting next to Francesca Annis and I asked her what role she was playing. She told me Jessica. I sort of just looked at her. 'That's Jessica?!' The next day I saw her on the set in costume and, holy cow, that was Jessica all right.

"I went through that a few times when I went down there. I'd see an actor or an actress off the set and think 'They're not right at all.' Then, I'd see them performing in costume and they were all perfect. Once they got before the cameras—Bingo!"

After months of globe-trotting across America and Europe, Lynch and Raffaella returned to Churubusco where, while they continued to cast, the world of *Dune* was physically being designed, built and costumed . . . utilizing a great deal of blood, sweat, tears and multi-national swearing.

6.
DESIGNING DUNE

*As soon as you walk out onto a set,
you're no longer acting. You're living DUNE.*
Molly Wryn, actress (Harah)

*They'd never seen a movie like this down here. If you needed
a saloon built, no problem. That was easy. But an Atreides
spaceship? That took a little bit of explaining.*
Giles Masters, draftsman

*This has turned out to be a wonderfully creative experience.
That pleases me. It could have been a real mess.*
Tony Masters, production designer

When veteran production designer/art director Tony Masters
agreed to accept the assignment of handling design chores for *Dune,*
he was well aware of the enormity of the undertaking. The complex
worlds of *Dune* required that a variety of styles be used in the designs
of the scenery, the weaponry, the furniture, the vehicles and the
architecture.

Seventy-five sets, ranging in proportion from the Olympian to
the Lilliputian, had to be constructed on eight sound stages. Among
some of the more memorable designs required were:

• An immense Emperor's throne room, done entirely in gold.

• The Great Hall of Arrakeen palace, an almost Byzantine-like
structure used by Duke Leto when he assumes control of the planet
Dune.

• Various underground sietches, the living quarters of the
Fremen, carved out of solid rock.

• A spice harvester, a moving factory designed to travel across
the swirling sands of Arrakis seeking melange, a spice necessary for
space travel.

• The Baron's headquarters, a dark and foreboding structure on
Giedi Prime, a cold, evil, overly industrialized planet.

47

Jose Ferrer stands on the golden throne room set,
which took up an entire soundstage.

Add to this laundry list an assortment of spaceship interiors,
hallways, castles and living spaces and you have some idea of what
Tony Masters walked into during the summer of 1982.

"This has been the most challenging project I've ever worked
on," says Masters from his Churubusco office. "It's also been the
most rewarding."

As Masters speaks on this hot, August day, a cluster of workers
are laboring feverishly to complete the Emperor's throne room, a
golden structure that takes up an entire soundstage across the street
from the designer's headquarters. It is the last major set to be built
and the biggest interior design on the whole production. Masters,
although no longer designing at this point, is still on call.

"The throne room has been the set that's taken the most amount
of time," says the tall, thin artist. "It's a gold room with a jade floor
and it's enormously detailed. There's a hell of a lot of draftsmen's

work that has gone into that. Months of detailing. Occasionally, I'd think 'Oh my goodness, maybe you've overdone this.' But, in fact, it will be ready on time."

Masters twists his hawklike visage into a parody of concern. "Everybody is working on top of everybody else—the painters are waiting for the plasterers, the plasterers are waiting for the carpenters. They're all standing on each other's toes now. But it'll get done."

Masters runs a hand through his white hair. "It's been like this the entire time I've been down here. Very productive insanity."

The British master craftsman leans back in his chair and smiles contentedly. His office is covered with papers, the walls transformed into veritable bulletin boards showcasing the various designs found in the film.

A buglike spice-harvester craft sketch is pinned up next to an early, fetal version of the Third-Stage Navigator.

A diamond-shaped Atreides ornithopter is shown both at rest and in the air, its tiny wings spreading out from its sides.

The interior of one of the Baron's oil-stained chambers is casually taped to a wall next to a very sleek but massive Guild Heighliner spaceship.

A variety of styles. A variety of ideas. All arising from one man.

Tony Masters was Dino De Laurentiis' first choice for the *Dune* project. The British designer had worked with him only once previously, on *Buffalo Bill and the Indians*, although he had been approached by Dino to work on other films, including *The White Buffalo* and *King Kong*.

"I would have loved to have done a lot of those movies," Masters says. "But my schedule was never free. This time, I got a call from Dino and he said, 'Hey, Tony. I got a great picture for you.' I said, 'Oh yeah?' He said, 'Yeah. It's so good, you'll pay *me* to work on it.' When he told me it was *Dune*, my reaction was 'Oh my God! That's exciting!' So . . . here I am."

Masters chuckles over the speed with which he was inducted into the world of *Dune*. "He had David Lynch in the office with him when he made that call and he just put me on the phone with him. The next day, David and I met and we were off."

Masters was quite intrigued with the prospect of working with David Lynch, a fellow who was not anyone's idea of your typical showbiz filmmaker. He was even more intrigued after meeting with him. "He is not a passive director," comments Masters.

"David had distinct ideas of his own about how *Dune* should look... he's a former art student. So we'd bat these ideas backwards and forwards between us. He constantly does these strange little drawings which are quite difficult to fathom. But, eventually, I learned to decipher them using a bit of imagination. I built on some of his ideas and worked them in with mine. Between us, we've turned out some rather odd things. If I'd been entirely on my own, the film wouldn't look the way it does now. If David had collaborated with another art director, the film wouldn't have looked anything like it does now, either. The two of us together have produced this... for better or worse!"

Surrounded by sketches and paintings of various sets, Masters is clearly delighted over his participation despite the enormity of his output. "I'd say this is about the same weight, for me, as *2001*," he states. "But it's been much more pleasant because I enjoy working with these people. David is really something. He's very cooperative and he's always available to talk to... but he's not easy at all. He's very hard to please but when you finally get there, he's very appreciative and, so, that's very rewarding.

"He always says, 'Thanks, this is great,' which isn't very often done by directors. But he never lets you relax with a design. He always pushes you further and further. If you make some rough sketches and show them to him, he'll say, 'Great! But how about we have some strange, elongated things going along the wall and some slots here?'

"So you go back to your desk muttering, 'Slots? I don't know.' And you start drawing something and it's kind of interesting and, then, you start making those ideas work and it gets stranger and stranger looking. As a sort of lone designer you tend to make everything work out right... nice. There's a reason for everything. But if someone else steps in and piles a load of new stuff on top of you, the final design becomes this weird hodgepodge of stuff that has a quite unusual look. I quite like that!"

Masters began seriously meeting with Lynch in Los Angeles during the time period when the director was putting the finishing touches on the movie's script. Both men, using the script and the book as a guide, began honing down the different visual styles of the movie.

"We had to come up with four different visual approaches for the four different planets that were easily recognizable... so that the audience knew where they were and who the heroes and the villains were. The first planet we discussed was Caladan, where the Duke and his family live. Caladan is, apparently, a world quite like

Sian Phillips about to make her entrance on the golden throne room set.

our own but more lush. It has lots of rain so the forests are beautiful and plentiful. We figured, well, if we have all these gigantic tree forests, let's make everything on the planet out of wood. In general, the movie was influenced by a number of styles: Venetian, Egyptian and early German Victorian.

"Caladan itself, however, is just a combination of styles. It's sort of Baroque, I suppose, but not Renaissance. It may look that way, initially, but that's just an illusion. We tried to combine traditional styles with styles of the future. The latter, of course, we had to invent. What I was really trying *not* to do was to make anything in this movie look like anything from *2001*.

"When you see any set in this movie, bear in mind that not only did we have to consider the major design elements, the shape of the room or whatever, but all the props that populate the room, from furniture to weaponry. The prop room is filled with weird machine guns and knives and everything. I did all that. It was delightful. It's really thrilling to pick up one of those guns after you've sketched them and actually hold it. You're always quite surprised. 'Did I design this? It looks pretty good.'

"We didn't want any of the props to look spacey. That's a forbidden word around here. Everything we designed for, the Duke, let's say, had to look very functional. Ugly if necessary, lumpy, even awkward but functional."

With Castle Caladan and its environs slated as being wooden, almost Baroque visually, Lynch and Masters turned their attention to Giedi Prime. "The planet of the bad guys," intones Master, "is very black and oily. All the buildings we designed are made out of steel and black metal. They look rather like the inside of Victoria Station with the steam boilers and goodness knows what going on at once. We used a lot of construction-type materials that would be easily recognizable to the audience.

"On Giedi Prime, you're always surrounded by steel, iron, nuts and bolts. The whole planet is as visually alluring as a big fire hydrant. It's devoid of any decoration.

"We mixed the color black with a really bright green to lighten things up a little. The darkness of the sets proved vexing at times. The Baron's shower room was a problem for me. It's dark and filled with steam. Not only is it dark but it's pitch black. Dino visited the set one day when it was being built and he was very worried about the film being too gloomy and black-looking. He wanted everything lightened up. More color. As I was lightening things up and putting more color around, David showed up. He wanted things darker. So, I was stuck between the two of them. Eventually we compromised...a little. Dino has accepted everything now. I don't know if he gave up on us or what."

Giedi Prime, on the screen, is sort of a metallic version of Dante's Inferno. Nearly everything is coated with either steam or oil. The tramways are hard, cold steel. The steps are dull gray. Sweat runs off nearly everyone's brow. The planet is totally corrupt both morally and physically.

"I had to restrain myself from going over the top," Masters admits. "I mean, the Baron is *so* evil, he's almost cartoonish. Interestingly enough, I used to be a comic strip artist. I had to hold myself back designing the Baron's world because it could have been very ludicrous if I really got into his evil nature.

"Basically, black and oily was the order of the day. We stuffed all these strange, strange, evil-looking instruments in the background that could be used for doing *anything*. It depends on how warped your imagination is.

A light-emitting glow-globe (top) floats over the Great Hall of Arrakeen.

Paul studies Arrakis on his filmbook in his room on Caladan.

"We came up with a little machine that the Baron and his men put little rodent-things in, squoods. It looks like a glass cylinder with a straw. When you press down on the thing, it squashes the squood and you can suck its life juices out through the straw. It's sadistic but functional.

"In the Baron's chamber, there's a strange kind of machine that looks like something you'd find in a laundromat . . . an ironing board or something. Heaven knows what the Baron does with that. I have no idea but it looks pretty frightening."

On a more civilized note, to convey the almost corrupt sense of wealth exuded by the high-living Emperor and his minions, Masters turned to the most obviously recognizable monetary status symbol around . . . gold . . . from which to weave his designs.

"His whole planet is made of gold," says Masters. "All the buildings are gold throughout. That's why the throne room has been so much fun to do. We've used some stone with it, a lot of jade. This sort of elegance is quite routine for the Emperor. He doesn't know anything but gold and jade. Even his spaceship reflects that kind of taste. It's a flying palace. A gold ship."

With three of the planets now given a basic design element, wood, metal and gold, Masters focused on Arrakis itself . . . the desert world of Dune. "Rock and earth tones," Masters says in shorthand. "It's a dry and arid planet and its people have tunneled their way into the mountains to make the palace using laser weaponry. They've just cut away the rock in interesting shapes, rather like the inside of the Pyramids. I think the Pyramids influenced me a lot.

"That was bound to happen because I'm fascinated by them. I like the shapes of the corridors. The color of the walls is the natural color of the rock. So, we took those elements and combined them with, of all things, a lot of tiles. The Arrakeen palace is very earthy yet it boasts all these wonderful tiles and mosaics. I think we were influenced a little bit by the cathedral in St. Mark's Square in Venice . . . a little Byzantine as well.

"The Great Hall is one of my favorite sets. The floor has tile patterns that are actually based on the ones in the cathedral in St. Mark's. The castle itself is very powerful. Very sturdy. It's part of the mountain."

Masters took his basic concept of carving living quarters out of the planet's surface one step further to design the Fremen's underground abodes, the sietches. "It's all rock," he says. "The color of the rock, however, is a different color than the palace. The palace is red and black rock but the sietches are green and black. The color

The Duke's men stand guard in the Observation Room.

of the sietches changes the deeper you go. You start off black and, as you go down, the rockface gets greener and greener."

One of the biggest sietch sets, the Hall of Rites, required so much space that it was built outside the sound stages, on the Churubusco back lot. A long hall with large, green-gray walls, it is topped by a steep, three-story flight of stairs and an altar-platform. "It's about five hundred feet long," says Masters. "We didn't build a top to it and the sides of the hall only extend fifteen feet in the air. The rest of the Hall will be matted in by Albert Whitlock. He'll do a matte painting that will show you exactly how intricate these underground spaces can be."

When Masters was busy designing the four civilizations architecturally, he also added small details that showed the worlds' cultural heritages as well. "Aside from the props, the furniture and things," he explains, "we came up with written languages. You'll see examples of them in the background. The Duke's writing desk, for instance, has a machine that translates what he writes into different languages."

"We fashioned different types of script to suit the planets. The Baron's Harkonnen lettering was bold and lumpy. The Atreides and Arrakeen writing was very rectangular and sharp. We managed to work in some circles in it all, too. We have, of course, writing on the walls in English, as well."

Eventually, sketches were made for all seventy-five sets and Masters turned his attention to the vehicles required for the different planetscapes. Giedi Prime's overhead cable-car proved an easy enough feat, a basic trolley with slightly sinister, metallic overtones. But for Dune? A world carved out of stone?

"Well, we couldn't have stone vehicles," Masters laughs. "What you wind up doing is looking at the environment and thinking, 'Now what would work best in that environment?' On a dry and arid planet with powerful dust storms, storms so powerful that they would erode an ordinary car away to a skeleton within a couple of hours if the car was just sitting in the desert, we had to come up with both a functional design and a material to build with that would be believable. So, we came up with the idea of plastisteel, a very powerful substance.

"The flying vehicles, the ornithopters, are made out of this stuff and, during storms, they just fold themselves into neat, diamond-shaped packages until it's over. After that, the pilots push a button, and off the 'thopters fly."

Masters pauses for a moment. "It's quite a delicate situation, you know, working with no limits. It's very difficult. With a period piece, you can buy a few books and look up everything and alter the designs a little. But with a fantasy, you have to make it all up. It's fun but it's time consuming. Most of the details aren't in the script. For instance, if the script says that this character walks down a corridor and enters a room, you have to design both the room and the corridor and also figure out what kind of lighting the corridor would have. And design and build a door. And how does that door open? Does our character use a handle? Is there a machine on the wall that makes the door open automatically? Every single thing must be thought out. Sometimes you come up with marvelous designs.

"At that point, you have to reevaluate your sketches because one thing you cannot do is come up with designs that will overshadow the actors. If two actors are talking in a scene and you've made a sensational background that is causing the audience to go 'Oooh, look at that...it's fantastic!', you've just killed the scene."

Masters flashes a lopsided grin as if to say "It's all part of the turf."

Sketches of the crafts were sent to the model shop for construction, weapons and furniture to props. Because the designs for the sets were the most complicated of the lot, Masters followed their realization the most keenly.

After sketches were made of each and every set, Masters began the actual physical work process. "When you get your sketches approved by the director," he explains, "you then turn them over to a draftsman. We had fifteen altogether on this picture. The draftsman takes your sketch and you show him a rough plan of the layout of the rooms or whatever. He will then start to draw it out architecturally. He comes up with the elevations, etc. You check it with him and says things like 'I think this is too high' or 'We need more room for a camera here,' whatever. After he has finalized his plans, he will then do all the detail drawings; the details of the moldings, the cornices, that sort of thing. These are all full-sized.

"All these drawings are then handed out to the construction department, to the various carpenters, plasterers and painters. From these drawings done by the draftsmen, the actual sets are constructed. On a picture this size, it's always a challenge to keep this work process going smoothly."

It is Masters' nature to downplay the problems connected with his tenure on *Dune*, but problems there were. First and foremost, he had to gather his designs and bring them down to a studio in Mexico to be built...a studio complex not yet equipped with the latest technological advances, where the most intricate outdoor sets still standing were outlaw towns left over from spaghetti westerns and where workers preferred not to use power tools.

"It was a new experience working in Mexico," he explains. "I've never worked here before, although I've worked all over the world. I had to feel my way for a while. But, after an initial period of adjustment, work started progressing well.

"The Mexican workers are wonderful in terms of craftsmanship. Their woodwork is really marvelous. Where we proved a little short-handed was in the area of painters who can do the work well. The Mexicans don't really have much experience in that field and so we had to import Spanish, Italian and American painters. That was the area we always lagged behind in. I wish I had had a few more men and a bit more time on all the sets. I don't consider any of them really finished but, luckily, Freddie Francis knows his lighting and he makes all the sets look wonderful on film. I know where the flaws are, though. But I've hidden them under the carpet pretty effectively."

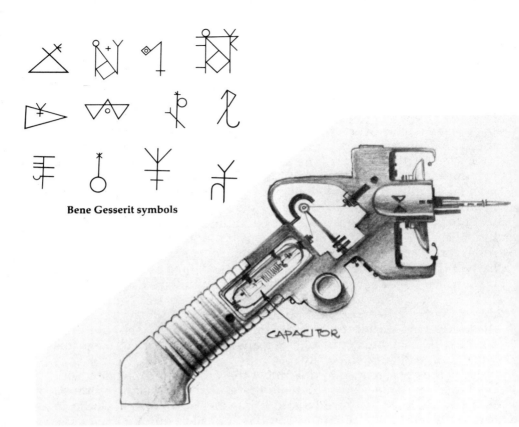

Bene Gesserit symbols

CAPACITOR

Fremen needle gun

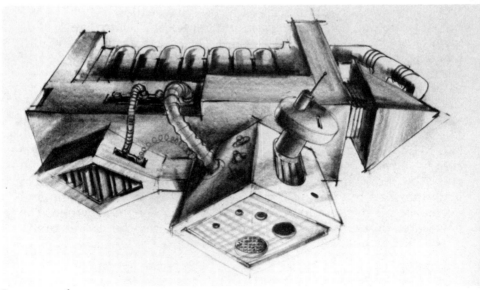

Fremen sound gun

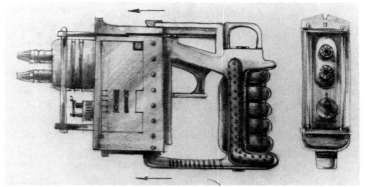

Sardaukar pistol

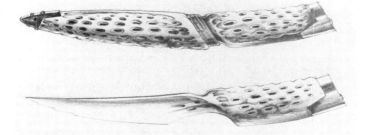

two views of a crysknife

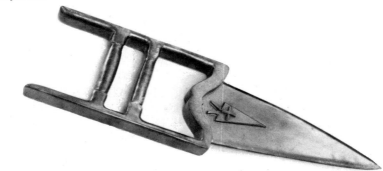

Fremen knife

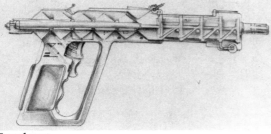

Tarpel gun

*   *   *

While Tony Masters is diplomatic about the problems of gearing up construction for a production the size of *Dune,* in the office next door, his son, draftsman Giles Masters offers commentary that is a bit more frank and definitely more bemused.

"The craziest aspect of this movie has been Mexico," he laughs, a veteran of nearly twelve months at Churubusco. "By the time I got down here, Pier Luigi, the Italian art director, was already working. I came down with an American illustrator, Ron Miller. We walked into this workroom. The studio had just painted it and put down these old carpets.

"That was all there was here. Nothing else ... no furniture, only a few lights, and no telephones. It was pretty difficult getting settled in. We didn't get a telephone for two months, and they still don't work all the time. You get to feel pretty isolated and you wind up laughing about it all.

"I arrived in September of 1982, six months before production began. Tony had done all the designs by that time and we draftsmen just started drawing away. Construction started about a week later.

"Kevin Phipps [the assistant art director] started working first; he began drawing the Great Hall of Arrakeen and I began on the Baron's room in the Harkonnen ship. Jose Luis Barrera [draftsman] began working on Paul's room on Caladan. So, when we started, we were working on three different styles. That was nice because everyone in this room got to be an expert on his planet's architecture. For the first few months, things were progressing in a steady but pretty lackluster pace.

"Things really started happening the day before production. All of a sudden everybody said, 'Wait a minute! What happened to those six months!' When David and the production unit arrived, it finally occurred to people that we were really making a movie down here. Things started humming.

"Wardrobe got down here in December, pretty late. And they still didn't have all the costumes approved. So they were working like mad and we were working like mad. It was crazy."

Giles admits that many on the production staff had serious doubts that *Dune* could be filmed on the Churubusco facility. It was a motion picture that required artistry, teamwork and speed. Frankly, the fact that not many of the local workers had ever labored on a production of this scope before filled the staff with dread. "At first we all had our doubts about getting the sets done properly down here because none of the Mexican workers had ever attempted this before. But it wound up being fantastic. The detail work is amazing. The furniture, for instance, has lacquered leather stuff with inlay. And the floors of the Great Hall? Some of the floors in Caladan? They're all made with real tiles that have been made and cast and put down. There are incredible slabs of tile. For Caladan they put down wood floors. They were beautiful. I felt horrible watching carpets be put down over them. Lovely dyed wood. Very rich."

On a few occasions, however, the multinational makeup of the construction crew did lead to a few noteworthy goofs. "We never had very many *real* problems," Giles states, "just comical stuff. One day I walked onto the Baron's set to see how construction was going. I had designed these big, bulky steel columns for the chamber. They had been made outside of the studio out of fiberglass.

"I walked onto the stage and there were these massive, huge columns and they looked all wrong! My heart sank. I thought, 'Oh dear, I've really done it this time. Mistake. Bad mistake.'"

Giles laughs out loud. "As it turned out they looked wrong because they had been installed upside down. The tops of my columns were on the floor, the bottoms high up on the ceiling. Once they were all turned the rightway-up, it all looked fine. Amazingly enough, considering what we've been up against, the construction on this movie is all incredible."

Outside of Giles' office, in a courtyard situated in the middle of the studio complex, one of the men chiefly responsible for the incredible detail seen on all the *Dune* sets sits down on a stone bench and watches a group of workers apply another coat of gold paint to a honeycombed buttress that will be moved into the Emperor's throne room by the end of the day.

At 69 years of age, Aldo Puccini* has been a master of movie construction for decades, handling the sets for countless films, including *La Strada, The Bible, King Kong, Casanova* and *Orca, the Killer Whale.* He has worked with many of the world's greatest directors including Fellini, Renee Clement, Rosellini, Antonioni, De Sica and, now, he is working with David Lynch.

An old crony of Dino De Laurentiis (his first movie was a De Laurentiis film in 1947, *The Gold of Naples*), Puccini is having the time of his life meeting the challenges of constantly building and striking sets during production. "We build one set and go on to the next and then the next and then the next. Then, we go back to the first set, knock it down and rebuild another one. Time after time after time. I started on this picture in September of 1982. We're *still* building sets and knocking them down almost a year later. But I don't mind. You know? Suppose I was born again. I'd want to do the same job. I love my work. This is important for a man. To love his work."

The amazingly spry Italian leaves his perch and takes a walk through some of the sets. Unlike most movie constructions, which usually utilize large quantities of metal and lightweight plastics, most of Puccini's sets are made out of elaborately shaped wood. "It's pretty unconventional," he admits, "but so is this movie. I was nervous about it but it looks really good."

One of the most impressive interior sets built by Puccini is a section of the planet Dune itself that filled an entire sound stage, a mass of rolling hills and sand dunes constructed out of timber and foam rubber that was 125 feet long, 165 feet wide and 62 feet high at its loftiest point. "That was hard to do," Puccini smiles, his rugged face lighting up when he recalls the set's origins. "Nobody has ever done that before. I took the wood and shaped it, rounded it. Then I covered it all with foam rubber. But before I put the rubber on, I cut it. I created swirls. Then, I colored the foam so it would be the color of the sand. After that, I glued real sand to the top of the foam rubber. When everything was put in place, I then covered the whole structure with real sand; one, two, three or four centimeters of sand depending on what shape we wanted on that part of the desert."

The finished set is a sturdy indoor recreation of the exterior of Dune, solid enough to support the weight of many actors yet fluid enough to allow real footprints to be made in the sand as the characters trudge across this desert "landscape."

Puccini takes a quick stroll through what remains of the Emperor's gold tent, the section of his spaceship blown apart by an atomic blast ("Look at the size of that hole," Puccini marvels. "They wrecked this one good."), before returning to the gold throne room still under construction. He stares at the floor. The gold paint has faint tracks left by some of the lot's stray dogs. "Look at that," he mutters under his breath. "Damn dogs. Look at that."

He passes under a large archway constructed out of towering wood and styrofoam stalactites. Each one of these major pieces is, in turn, composed of smaller stalactites. "There are twenty-four thousand of those," he says. "Handmade."

He stops in the doorway for a moment as a reporter from a national news magazine walks by. Puccini recognizes her from a dinner a few nights before and begins to chat. Within minutes, he is showing her the set. His voice echoes among the stalactites. "If I was born again," he begins. "I'd want to do the same job because I love my work...."

Fremen half dipsticks (far left), Maker Hooks (second from left),
and full dipsticks (third from left).

The massive interior set, housing man-made sand dunes, is sturdy enough
to support the weight of many actors and several tons of sand.

Meanwhile, in his office, Tony Masters is working on a last-minute emergency. A land vehicle has got to be designed quickly for the movie. He is trying to gather as many details about the craft as possible before sitting down at his table. He briefly sums up his feelings on the making of *Dune*.

"We've been able to build a lot more here in Mexico than we could have in any other country. We could never have afforded the sets we've done here anywhere else. We've been filling stages up with sets like mad for the past six months. I mean, there's more acreage here than there was in *2001*. *2001* had a lot of detail to it, but it's nothing compared to what we're doing here.

"Nobody is going to leave the theater after seeing this movie feeling that they haven't gotten their money's worth."

*Shortly after completing *Dune*, Aldo Puccini passed away in his home in Rome, Italy.

7.
COSTUMING <u>DUNE</u>

---

*It's a mixture of fantasy period
costumes and fetish industrial costumes.*
Bob Ringwood, designer

---

*Wearing the stillsuits in the desert
was the next best thing to dying.*
Everett McGill, actor (Stilgar)

I only came close to passing out once...I think.
Paul Smith, actor (Rabban)

The task of designing costumes for *Dune* proved more of a challenge than what is normally encountered on a major film. Since the movie takes place on four distinct locations, at least four distinct dress codes were required.

The House Atreides needed a regal yet military look.

The Baron Harkonnen and his henchmen, dwelling on an industrialized world, required yet another mode of dress.

The underground-dwelling Fremen had to wear clothes that would seem plausible on a desert planet.

The Emperor and his court required a certain amount of pomp.

The spice-dripping Guild Navigators certainly deserved a look of their own as well, as did various lords and ladies, warring armies, spies and members of subcultures.

The man assigned the Herculean task of imagining the unimaginable for the film was Bob Ringwood, a young British costume designer best known for the stylized chivalry evidenced in *Excalibur*. Slight, bearded and wiry, Ringwood descended on the Churubusco studios late in 1982 like a man possessed. Although he brought with him only a small entourage, he amassed a formidable army of cutters and sewers before his fifteen-month stay in Mexico was over.

On this cloud-laden day during the final weeks of live-action shooting, Ringwood sits outside one of the studio's office buildings and reminisces about his involvement.

Dr. Yueh in Atreides Dress Uniform
(far left),
Paul wearing a ceremonial robe
(second from left),
Alia in modified Bene Gesseret robes
(left),
and the Baron in his Suspenser Belt
(below).

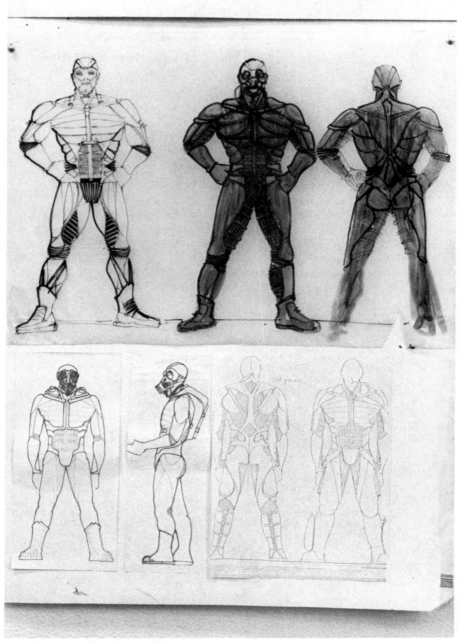

Early designs for the Fremen stillsuit.

"I hadn't read the book when Raffaella first called me," he says. "She had seen *Excalibur* and liked it. I was working in Brussels on a stage show and it took some time for them to track me down. Raffaella asked me if I had read the novel and I said no. We talked for a little while about the movie and she told me she'd ring me back in two or three days."

The designer stifles a laugh. "Six weeks later she rang me back and told me she would be out to see me in three days. And," he motions to the brick building at his back, "here I am."

Ringwood rolls his eyes heavenward as if to say "if only I had known what I was in for." Still, he offers a wry smile and gets down to business. "The big challenge, of course, was the diversity of styles. The movie doesn't have a single, unified look in terms of costumes. I refer to the general style as my transitional look. At least that's my excuse, anyhow. There are four planets to work with: industrial, dignified, military and earthy. I wound up combining a lot of period styles. It's a rather diverse approach.

"The hardest costumes to design were the spacesuits and the stillsuits. David Lynch didn't want anything spacey or anything that resembled a costume you've seen before in a science-fiction picture.

Paul and Jessica in stillsuits.

Jessica in a royal robe on Arrakis.

Sting, appropriately dressed to carry out the Baron's nefarious plans.

The finished costumes ended up being pretty simple, close-to-the-body protective garments. They're almost industrial looking. I must say that I'm pleased to have been able to get away from the standard outer-space stuff. You get bored with that, that sort of NASA look."

One of the most important designs for the film was the stillsuits the Fremen wear. In terms of the storyline, stillsuits are vital to the existence of the desert planet Dune's citizenry. A body-hugging outfit, it allows the Fremen to exist on a water-sparse planet by retaining all the bodily fluids of its wearer and recycling them throughout the suit, keeping the body temperature normal and its moisture intact.

In terms of the film, it is probably the most-viewed costume in the movie's two-plus hours running time. "The costume had to be impressive yet functional," says Ringwood. "I considered a few possibilities before I was finally inspired by hindsight.

"About five years ago, I attended an exhibition of students' work at the Slade College of Art in London. There was a display there by

An Atreides soldier in summer uniform.

Soldier holding a Harkonnen rifle.

a German sculptress who makes these works based on *Grey's Anatomy* out of different materials. The one that impressed me most was of a tall, black man constructed out of leather. The figure had all the muscles exposed. It was really striking. I remembered it when I had to design the stillsuits.

"David told me that he wanted something very dark that related to the body. I went back and looked at the piece. After that, I went out and got a batch of anatomy books and went to work. The stillsuit in the film is actually based on anatomical charts and drawings.

"Design in hand, we went off to Don Post Studios in California. It's a marvelous place that makes masks and things. We did a number of prototypes before coming up with a suit which is basically a muscular body. It looks very good on the men. Really! Anyone who puts on one of these costumes suddenly looks very strong. You're actually putting on a new body. It makes you look quite tough. Just the kind of thing a cave dweller would wear."

Although the snug, rubber stillsuits looked great on the Fremen men, Ringwood found that he had to make subtle alterations on the suits worn by the female Fremen. "The women's suits looked rather unfeminine," he moans, "so we redesigned the suits to have larger breasts. That's also why most of the Fremen women characters have long hair. It softens their looks in the suits. It works quite well."

In designing the Emperor's court, Ringwood took another approach. "The Emperor's court's costumes are basically period pieces. A mixture of late nineteenth century and mid-seventeenth century designs. I thought it would be nice to base them on fact. David was very keen on making the men's costumes look very military, very late-Victorian royal family."

In like manner, since Duke Leto is every inch as royal as the Emperor, his formal dress attire is exceedingly Victorian-regal, while the fighting garb for his men is more functional and modern.

The Emperor's highly trained Sardaukar warriors, the outer-space version of S.S. troops, had to look fierce as opposed to royal. Able-bodied soldiers who could strike at a moment's notice had to be clad in something "active" yet sinister. A sort of space-age, flexible, armored look was the result. "They were made of black rubber," explains Ringwood, "and they're not very sturdy. We've been endlessly repairing them. The stillsuits have had the hell bashed out of them, too. We're always patching them up. Thank goodness the camera doesn't see a lot. The camera is very good that way. To make a costume look broken down and ruined on the screen you really have to destroy it.

First stage Guild Navigators.

"We have people on the set all the time, handling last-minute repairs. People are wearing those suits fourteen hours a day in the sun or under hot lights on the studio and they're fighting all the time. Something's got to give."

Aside from the distinctive planetary look of the costumes, there were several subcultures indigenous to the planet that needed special care, as well as a few larger-than-life figures that required larger-than-life treatment.

"David likes black a lot," says Ringwood, "so, for the Bene Gesserit Reverend Mother, he said he wanted black and yellow. I played around with black and came up with something that is rather nun-ish but much more mysterious.

"The water monks' long, flowing robes are hooded, quite religious (appropriately so since they figure in the Fremen's mystical Water of Life ceremonies in the sietches of Dune) and are wonderful to gaze upon but they weigh about fifty pounds each. They're made out of piped rope tied together by raw silk. They look good," Ringwood chuckles. "I don't care if the actors collapse in their costumes as long as they *look* good on the screen."

Ringwood is very aware that some of the costumes had to be designed for visual impact as opposed to flexibility and, all kidding aside, he was concerned for the wearers. "I've had quite a few people faint," he says. "Actually, considering that many of the extras were wearing full rubber costumes in the sun in the desert for some scenes, we had a pretty good average. Maybe three or four people.

"The most time-consuming element in terms of the costumes being functional was having people learn how to move in them. Everyone today is used to wearing jeans and t-shirts. No one is clothes-conscious in the way that people were in Elizabethan times, when women would wear a hundred pounds of silk and jewels. When we were filming, people would forget that they had ten yards of silk hanging from their dresses in some of the royal scenes and would get very clumsy. We're used to being comfortable today. In the seventeenth century, comfort never entered your mind. It was how you looked that was important.

"Since many of the costumes are based on period designs, people had to learn how to walk all over again. Start from scratch."

Ringwood shrugs. "This has been a very weird film. We've had some problems with all of the costumes. Even the simple ones aren't easy . . . especially when you try to keep your standards high. We've run into problems here, the likes of which you can't imagine.

"For instance, costuming Paul Smith, who is very large in size, in a form-fitting uniform was very difficult. Someone his size! When he expands his back, he stretches out some seven or eight inches. An average-sized person will only stretch two or three. So, you have to come up with a costume that will look good when it's still, yet also looks good when its moving. You can't have it really tight or else it will split. It was finally constructed out of tire rubber. It was plastic quilted over with the kind of rubber that they make the inside of car doors out of."

Ringwood shakes his head incredulously. "I'll work with anything. Finding the right material for the right job is very important. Some designers will find the wrong material and try to force it. If you do that, you wind up losing a lot of time."

Ringwood's design triumphs are all visible on the screen, costumes that were both fun to make and fun to watch.

The Guild members who clean up the spice after it's used by the massive Third-Stage Guild Navigator are clothed in hooded, bulky costumes that give them the appearance of futuristic custodial engineers. The finished designs make them look very much like anti-radiation–suited workers who'd feel more at home at the Three

A water master, wearing a piped rope robe,
administers the Water of Life to Jessica.

Mile Island nuclear facility than on Arrakis. Of course, this effect is
only heightened by the fact that the insides of their helmets are filled
with orange gas.

In terms of sheer artistry, Lady Jessica's costumes deserve much
applause. She wears a variety of shimmering gowns that are never
anything less than ornate. "Francesca Annis was wonderful to work
with," Ringwood enthuses. "She has a twenty-two-inch waist. She
has a very marvelous silhouette. She wears clothes wonderfully. She
moves wonderfully. You know, you can do anything with the human body if you balance everything up."

On the opposite end of the aesthetic spectrum, Ringwood had
to come up with a costume for the evil Baron (Kenneth McMillan),
a fat, scabby, bloated boss man who is so sluglike, he refuses to
walk. Relying on technology, he levitates through life. Not only did

Local Mexican seamstresses demonstrate their handiwork:
Paul's ceremonial robe for the film's final scene.

the costume designer have to create the Baron's outerwear, but he also had to conceive and build the Baron's bulbous body because, for the most part, large wads of the villain's flesh protrude from his clothing.

"The Baron's outfit was fun," Ringwood readily admits. "That was my rubber fetish costume. I loved that. It was easy. The rubber we used for his fleshy parts was made from colostomy-bag rubber. It was the only pink rubber that was strong enough for the outfit." He sighs. "You have to go to some strange places to get things done.

"My biggest challenge was making the Baron's body. It's pretty disgusting. Our final body design is very successful, I think. It's very heavy...about ninety pounds. After we would suit Ken up in his body, we'd then have to put his costume over it. In a funny way, I wish we hadn't covered up his body so much. The body itself is so wonderfully gross it should be seen more.

"The Baron's costume, when it's fully assembled, must weigh close to 250 pounds...as opposed to the Reverend Mother's costume which is light as silk and weighs three to four pounds. Ken

McMillan, who is a small and round man, actually lost weight wearing his costume. We were worried about how hot it would be under there for him, so we designed a second suit that was air-conditioned, water-cooled. It was the kind of setup that NASA uses for its pilots. Kenny didn't want to use it, but it was good to have on standby. We would have pumped cold water through it through tiny tubes which were worked in all over.

"You thought costuming dealt with mere fabrics!" Ringwood snorts. "You have to incorporate technology these days, too. Although it's very nice to use technology a little bit, you can't go overboard. If you're making a costume out of bits of rubber and plastic and you approach people who are experts on the material, they try to get you to make something that is very proper, very sturdy and very complicated. In actuality, you're interested in making something that can be used for four weeks and, then, discarded. They're thinking of it as a car...something that will last for ten years. It's often better to avoid the experts and try to fudge through it yourself."

Aside from the challenges inherent in creating countless costumes in general, Ringwood and his merry band had to clear the additional hurtle of producing them at a rate that could accommodate the hectic production schedule.

"It's been like going to war," he laughs. "I brought over about twelve people with me from England. The rest of the people we hired down here. At one time, I had forty-five people working for me, putting costumes together for three different units filming on three different sets.

"We've had, on the average, twenty people working constantly on the wardrobe. We've made about five hundred outfits down here. There are about four thousand altogether.

"We've been under a lot of pressure to turn out costumes quickly. We actually figured out that, during the last six months, we've been turning out two and a half a day on the average. That's with six cutters [workers who do nothing but cut fabric] working constantly. I've been on the film for fifteen months and we're still making clothes during this, my last week, on the picture."

Aside from the workload, Ringwood's unorthodox designing style has added to the general hilarity. "I'm not a designer who likes to do a lot of drawing," he readily admits. "I'll do a little bit of sketching but I love going to the workshop and actually working things out on a stand. I use the cutters in a way that I suppose other people don't. They have as much input as I do. I throw a germ of an idea out and my team bats it around until it works. I always have an end in mind but I hate just doing a drawing where everything is planned out to the last detail. That doesn't strike me as being very creative.

"I like to play. Sometimes the cutters suggest things that you wouldn't think of on your own. It makes the design one thousand times better. You often argue about it but it usually works."

Ringwood's freewheeling style was not ideally suited for Mexico, either. "It was very difficult setting up here and trying to find the materials we needed," he says. "Most of the materials had to be imported. It took forever to get some of the cloth down here. It was like getting forbidden treasure through customs. The first few costumes, the Caladan things, wound up being done at breakneck speed as a result. We had to work right through the night to get things done on time. There was a period of a month or two when we were just feeling our way around.

"Most of the material was flown in from New York or Los Angeles. You just can't get silks or gold fabrics or anything elaborate down here. You can get leather and cottons but nothing elaborate in great quantities. You can get a few yards of this or that but with our dresses we're talking about *twenty yards* of material for every gown!"

Ringwood slumps on a bench outside the office building. His eyes are puffy and red, the result of too little sleep and a flu bug that has plagued him constantly for the past four weeks. In a few days he will be returning to England and a new assignment. He's been living in Mexico for over a year, cranking out space-age designs like a creative cookie cutter. He has clothed nearly four thousand citizens from four distinct planets. "It hasn't been an extraordinarily difficult task..." he says, "but it's been so *long*."

II.
PRODUCTION

When the director is filming the movie, the producer is worrying about time and money. You worry about the actors. You worry about the crew. Will the special effects look OK? Will the sets get finished on time? Will it rain when you're on location? You have at least one major crisis a day. If the job wasn't so much fun, I would never do this for a living.
Raffaella De Laurentiis, producer

8.
WORK BEGINS

> *I was down there five weeks. It seemed like five years.*
> Sting, actor (Feyd)

> *It's an absolutely giant playpen.*
> *A serious playpen, but a playpen nonetheless.*
> *Francesca Annis, actress (Jessica)*

> *What's it been like shooting in Mexico?*
> *My dear, do you have a day?*
> *Golda Offenheim, production coordinator*

Dune commenced principal photography on March 30, 1983...nearly two years after it had been given the green light by Dino De Laurentiis. By the time the actors arrived at Churubusco in mid-March, the filmmaking team already realized that, no matter how they tried, a certain amount of insanity would reign supreme on the set.

Unit Publicist Anne Strick, a petite blonde who during the course of the picture would serve both as den mother for a host of visiting journalists and dignitaries and as commando leader, dragging her charges through countless sets and locations, pauses briefly in her small, cramped office, recalling the opening days of *Dune*. She is surrounded by filing cabinets, stacks of memos and stray photos.

"Bizarre," she says, "absolutely bizarre. The telephones were late being installed so we couldn't communicate with anyone in the United States. When the phones finally were installed, they proved pretty unreliable. They *still* go out once or twice a week. In general we lose electricity on a pretty regular irregular basis. You know, just when you're getting a head of steam up—bang. There's no electricity. When there's no electricity, I can't use the electric typewriter. When there's no electricity, there's no xeroxing. No sewing. No use of power tools for construction. And," she adds for emphasis, "when there's no electricity, there's no moviemaking."

Strick rests her case. But, because these problems became evident early on in production, producer Raffaella De Laurentiis was able to take certain steps to circumvent shutting the entire movie down every few days. Massive gasoline-powered generators were brought onto the studio complex, providing an alternate source of electricity with which to shoot the entire film. When the electricity now blows, the studio complex may go dark, all extracurricular work may grind to a halt, but the movie itself goes huffing and puffing along. "Imagine making the most technically advanced picture in the world," cracks Raffaella, "in a country that doesn't know too much about modern technology. Fun, eh?"

By March, most of the technical crew members were viewing their next six months with a sense of genuine bemusement bordering on shock. Principal live-action photography was slated to continue until September 6, with second unit and effects work scheduled until January 31, 1984. By the time the cameras were ready to roll, however, enough snafus had occurred to put everyone involved on notice that the shoot was going to be something of a challenge.

Dealing with Mexico's customs department also proved a Herculean task. For no apparent reason, customs inspectors would occasionally hold crucial items needed for the shooting. Cloth needed for costumes. Trunkloads of finished costumes. Materials needed for effects. Film stock. The *Dune* outfit tried every invention to get their materials into the country. In spite of all efforts, however, the customs officials still managed consistently to cripple the movie in small, irritating ways.

"It can be maddening," says Kit West, physical effects wizard extraordinaire. West, a burly, bearded man with a well-developed sense of humor, rolls his eyes heavenward melodramatically as he recalls his first dealing with the Mexican customs crew.

"When I first came down here to check out the facilities, I found that the only way I was going to tackle a movie of this size at this facility was to bring the majority of my workshop down here from my home in England. There simply wasn't enough technology down here to pull it off any other way."

"I packed the whole workshop up. We got a forty-foot container and just loaded it up. I took my mobile workshop and loaded that up. We shipped them both by boat from Southampton. I think the trip across took five weeks. Then the whole works just sat in Mexico City for four to five weeks. Just sat there! We'd send a couple of my boys down there every day to see if there was any chance of getting my equipment to the studio. 'No. No. No.' was all we heard.

An ornithopter on Arrakis.

One of the Arrakeen hallway sets under construction.

"By that time, the main body of my unit was here in Mexico and we all just sat here twiddling our thumbs. I wondered if I should just go out and buy a new set of tools. But I can't stress just how valuable that material in customs was. Hundreds of thousands of dollars worth of machinery that was absolutely necessary to get this movie done. I could have bought it all in America but, with taxes and all, it would have cost the movie four or five times what it should have. Eventually, we got everything out of customs but it was nearly two months late. We found out early on that you just couldn't count on anything happening in a logical manner down here."

To help the actors and actresses get into the country with their luggage intact and on time, the Churubusco office provided the services of a veteran "greeter", whose job was to meet the arriving artists, make them feel at home and move them through Mexico City's airport assemblage of customs officials with the least amount of anxiety.

For the most part, the fellow's style and experience got everyone through in one piece. There were, however, a few notable exceptions. "I had quite a few tapes stolen," says Sting, the world-renowned performer hired to play one of the film's three principal villains. "I had modified a bunch of computers to play music and I had all this digital information on cassette tapes. It got 'lost' in customs. God knows what happened to them. When you play the tapes back over regular speakers it sounds like pigs grunting. I was pretty angry about it. The tapes took days of work to duplicate."

Yet another problem that was soon to be taken as part of the normal routine of filming *Dune* was illness. "I liked being on the planet Arrakis," quips Sting, "but I could have lived quite nicely without the planet Mexico. The smog and the altitude and the food all conspire against you."

Mexico City's altitude—7,200 feet—and its thinner air did cause problems for many of the cast and crew. For some, physical activity was doubly hard. Even the hardiest of the troupe learned, eventually, not to exert themselves. The altitude also had quite a lot to do with those world-famous stomach problems indigenous to the area. All visitors were warned to drink only purified water (since tap water could give tourists nasty amoebas), peel all fresh fruits and vegetables, avoid salads and, to remain on the safe side, eat only in certain, recommended restaurants. In spite of these warnings, however, and all the precautions taken, nearly fifteen percent of the *Dune* entourage was destined to be ill at any given time during the shoot.

"There have been times," said Raffaella De Laurentiis, "when I haven't been sure if I've been running a movie or a hospital."

Aside from culture (and/or physical) shock, many of the movie's crew members had very real technical problems to deal with in getting *Dune* going. Director of photography Freddie Francis was one of them. Francis is an established master of cinematography, one of a handful of film photographers who can truly be called a genius of the medium. A distinguished-looking British fellow with a wry sense of humor that allows him to quietly wisecrack his way out of any impossible situation, Francis is candid about the hurdles he had to clear before exposing a single frame of film on *Dune*.

"I arrived down here Christmas of 1982," he explains, "and most of the sets had already been built or fabricated if not built. All these sets were more or less up and I discovered, to my horror, that they'd been built absolutely *solid*. Normally, you build sets so they break away, so they float, so that sections of them can be pushed and pulled about to allow the camera some movement and the lighting people to do their work.

"Our sets, however, were solid as rocks. Now, at this point, there was no way they were going to tear those sets down. They

David Lynch with Francesca Annis and Sian Phillips, as they prepare for Paul's pain box scene.

were enormous. I just said, 'OK. We're going to treat this film as if we were shooting on location. We'll shoot with low light levels and wide aperture lenses.' That sort of thing.

"However, when the cameras we were going to use arrived for testing, we found that the lenses would not operate at wide-angle speeds. We were really up against it. So, our main battle has been shooting these nonfloatable sets at very, very high light levels. There have been all sorts of problems having to photograph sets which should be lit at very low light levels at very high light levels."

Director Lynch smiles when he recalls Francis' initial reaction to the sets. "Oh yeah, he just said they weren't designed to do any shooting in. But," he adds, "Freddie is great with dealing with problems.

"See, I love those sets. It makes the movie seem more real. When Freddie first saw them he just said, 'OK. There's going to be trouble but we'll make it work.' One of the great things about Freddie is that he is creative on his feet. He's been strapped with sets that you can't really light like regular movie sets. And, still, the look of the film is totally beautiful.

"I mean, we all moan and groan but we always get what we want."

During the first weeks of production, *Dune* would test the mettle of all concerned. Initial scenes involving Caladan went smoothly on the sound stages. While work progressed at Churubusco, however, plans were being made for the film's first bout with location shooting at Las Aguilas Rojas, a rocky site that would double for sections of Arrakis.

The site, which is located within one of the poorer outskirts of Mexico City, is a mass of lava formations and is within sight of the volcanoes Popcateptl and Ixtazihuatl. It has been used before in movies to double for a barren, arid terrain (most notably in *A Man Called Horse*) and seemed ideal to double for a few different sections of Arrakis in *Dune*. The only problem for the movie's location hunters was that, these days, Las Aguilas Rojas is used as a dump.

"The Dead Dog Dump," laughs director Lynch. "That's what we call it now. The first time they took me there, it was an incredible trip. On the way out, I saw about twelve dead dogs. And, then, when we got to the location, there were little kids with dogs on strings. Strings were tied around the dogs' necks. And these dogs were really skinny, their skin stretched tight over their bones. And the kids are just pulling these dogs, running them through the trash.

"And the trash is smoking. You go down there, walk through

the trash, and there are all these dead animals. A pig with a huge slash in it. Dead dogs. Dead rats. And a lot of little live dogs.

"That was quite a day. But the place was pretty ideal for some of our shots and it was close to the studio. So we decided to use it. We sent people in there to clean the place up. First they removed the big stuff, all the bones and debris. What took the longest to clear was stuff like broken glass. We had people rake the site but the glass would just slip through the rakes. So, the dump ended up being very clean except for tons of broken glass. They then had to sift that out of the dirt. When they were done we had bags and bags of broken glass alone. It turned out to be a great location, though. Really beautiful."

As filming progressed, a decision was made to downplay the publicity on the movie for the time being. Because the production would not make it into theaters for at least a year and a half, it was labeled something closely akin to top secret...at least for the first three months of shooting. No sense letting the world know during April of 1983 exactly what it was to be treated to in December of 1984. This decision, in turn, upset some of the local press corps. Why shouldn't they be allowed to visit an American motion picture shooting on their own turf? Fast thinking and diplomacy kept the newshounds at bay for a couple of months.

Carlo Rambaldi, right, and co-worker put the finishing touches on the gigantic third stage Guild Navigator.

Last-minute problems arose and were dealt with quickly. An actor who was cast in one of the lead roles proved unreliable on the set. The part was recast quickly with an actor who, physically, did not fit the character but who, over the course of the movie, brought the role new depth and meaning.

Plasterers and painters would sometimes get in each other's way. Sets were being built as the movie was being filmed. Construction crews would hammer away on one side of a huge sound stage while director Lynch rehearsed his actors on another set some fifty feet away. When the word "action" was yelled, the construction men would patiently wait, their tools at their sides, while a scene taking place on a far-off planet some 10,000 years in the future was filmed on the other side of the paint cans.

Says Lynch recalling his first fragile steps taken in the cinematic realm of *Dune*, "I remember sitting in Freddie's apartment one day after we'd been shooting. We were doing night work. It was the third week and we were really tired. We sat there looking at each other, totally in shock. 'We've got twenty-one weeks to go. It's just too much to think about.'

"We discovered then that you can't really think about the whole movie. You'd go nuts. You think about the next week. The next hour. And you just roll along. Pretty soon, we found that the movie was halfway done. Even then, we couldn't face the prospect of twelve more weeks. Pretty soon, there's only two weeks left and you find yourself feeling really buoyant. I mean, we've done some really hard work on this movie and there's still a lot of hard work to go but, when you look back on what you've done and you find yourself being really pleased with it...you just get really happy."

A wide grin spreads across his face. "Of course, getting through it, present-tense, can be pretty tough."

9.
THE FIRST FEW WEEKS

David has no regards for the rules, which is rather good.
And as I have no regards for the rules of cinematography,
I suppose the two of us get along very well together.
Freddie Francis, cinematographer

Getting through a movie like this is survival.
It's adaptability. It's the dinosaur principle, isn't it?
Francesca Annis, actress (Jessica)

I'm curious as hell to see what this is going to look like
with all the stuff we are supposed to be imagining in our
minds actually put in the film.
Kyle MacLachlan, actor (Paul)

The first month of production transforms the Churubusco lot into a beehive of activity.

On a sound stage which will eventually metamorphose into the Baron's shower room, actor Kenneth McMillan is hanging, suspended by a wire harness. His character, the Baron Harkonnen, is so bloated and disgustingly fat he floats from place to place in a formfitting black suit, activated by a gravity-defying belt. McMillan will have to act while being manipulated, marionette style, by a technician positioned high above on the scaffolding, operating a series of controls housed on a moving platform.

McMillan spins round and around the half-completed shower stall, spouting the lines that will eventually be delivered to his beloved nephew, Feyd (Sting).

David Lynch walks onto the half-completed set to watch the run-throughs from the sidelines. He is followed by a two-man video crew. A decision has been made to tape most of the making of *Dune* for publicity/promotion purposes. In essence, for the next six months, there will be two movies being shot simultaneously: a science-fiction fantasy and a documentary of a science-fiction fantasy being filmed.

McMillan is cavorting in the air as the wires pull him around the shower stall like an obese Peter Pan. He spots the video crew. "Now I'd like to sing *Over the Rainbow*," he smiles impishly.

Another circular pass. This time he screws his face up into a mock grimace and yells, "I'm dying, Egypt, dying."

Someone asks Lynch if he is a vegetarian. The video crew trains their focus on him. "I eat fish and chicken. Little animals," he says. Nobody can figure out if he is kidding.

McMillan keeps on spinning. Lynch exits. Sting walks in to watch his partner-in-crime soar. "This is really fun," McMillan shouts. "You wanna try it?"

Sting smiles. McMillan crosses his legs in midair and places a finger delicately below his chin. "I'm a cherub," he announces. Sting and McMillan banter for a few moments before the British singer leaves. McMillan is keeping both his own spirits and that of the crew up during the flight test. The mood is zany as he continues his flybys. Suddenly there's a crash from above. McMillan is yanked violently backwards. His face goes pale. A wire has gotten snarled somewhere overhead. A crewman rushes forward to steady McMillan's suspended body.

The wire is repaired, while McMillan is still dangling. Someone asks him if he would like to call it quits. He wants to do a few more flybys before departing the set. "It's like falling off a horse," he reasons. "You have to get back on right away or else you'll never get back on at all."

Kyle MacLachlan is bound and gagged aboard a Harkonnen ship. It is part of a scene wherein Paul and his mother have been kidnapped by the Baron's brigands and are being taken into the desert to die. Paul is required to free himself from his bonds and battle one of the Harkonnen military men, debilitating him with a kick or two before killing him with a well-placed heel to the heart. After this final kick, blood is supposed to pour from the Harkonnen warrior's lips.

The scene must be filmed several times. One version will catch all the vital kicks, another version will emphasize the blood spurting effects of the fight.

The cameras roll and Kyle delivers some excellent kicks. The Harkonnen meanie, however, doesn't land correctly. A second fight is filmed. And a third.

The Harkonnen actor is getting the living daylights kicked out of him. He is weary but finds the whole process quite fun. Before

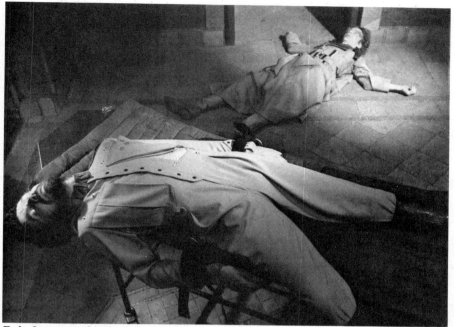

Duke Leto meets his death, but not before dispatching the villainous Piter (Brad Dourif).

a fourth round of kicking, he turns to Kyle. "I'll be a good boy. I promise," he smiles. MacLachlan obviously doesn't trust a member of the Baron's team because he kicks the tar out of the actor yet another time.

"We're going to do the same thing but with blood in his mouth," Lynch announces.

Between takes, Kyle and Lynch confer. "What's the best angle for rupturing the heart?" Lynch wonders aloud.

Blood is poured into the Harkonnen villain's mouth. When he is kicked on this go-round, he will spit out the blood and make his injuries look most grievous. The actor takes a sip of "blood" from a cup. He lifts the cup up towards the camera. "Here's to you," he toasts.

Kyle returns to his position on the floor. The actor resumes his stance above his captive. The cameras are about to roll when Lynch suddenly comments, "Look. His lips are too red. They look like little rosebuds!"

A makeup artist is dispatched to powder down the actor's lips. The omnipresent video crew is focusing on his face. The actor's cheeks are now puffed out, hamster-style, filled with fake blood. He is trying very hard not to laugh as the camera closes in and a makeup man bats away at the pursed pair of ruby-red lips.

Seeing that the actor is really trying hard not to spit the blood out prematurely, Lynch casually announces, "OK. Let's have lunch." He turns to the actor. "Stay here."

The actor nearly chokes himself laughing. When the kidding subsides the bloodied fight is staged perfectly. Paul Atreides kicks the Harkonnen smack in the middle of his chest cavity. The Harkonnen reels backwards, his life fluid spurting from his lips. He collapses on the floor in a heap, dead. Paul springs to his feet, victorious.

All in a morning's work... with time to spare for a hearty lunch.

At the Dead Dog Dump, night shooting has commenced. Things are going slowly. Several scenes are to be filmed there, initially, tracing Paul and Jessica's flight through the sands of Dune and their arrival at a Fremen stronghold. Once there, the twosome encounter Stilgar (Everett McGill) and Chani (Sean Young).

The filming is moving at a snail's pace at the former dumpsite. Sand is being blown about with large fans. The air is filled with grit. The crew is wearing goggles and surgical masks. The actors are covered with grime.

The mood is tense and, in order to survive, a lot of kidding around is done.

Two crewmembers walk out onto the location site wearing old-fashioned World War II gas masks. "They're more effective than those little things," says one, pointing to the masks worn by his peers.

Before the actors are allowed to go before the cameras, a makeup artist stands before them with a gunlike device that, when cranked, emits thick clouds of dust. The cast members are, in effect, being dusted down; covered with extra grit to make their appearance seem even more woeful before the cameras.

Bored by the waiting, actress Sean Young does a Charlie Chaplin imitation before the video crew.

Freddie Francis is talking into a walkie-talkie to colleague Roy Larner. He is trying to position properly the large lights located on the opposite side of the dump. "Swing it left," he says. "No, now swing it right."

Before he can complete another sentence, Francis is bathed in darkness. Noting the obvious, Francis clutches the walkie-talkie. "It's gone out, Roy."

The walkie-talkie burps out a reply. "The genny (generator) has gone."

"The genny's gone," Francis repeats unbelieving. "Lovely."

Dust continues to blow everywhere.

Crewmembers work feverishly to restore the generator needed to provide power for the spotlights.

Sean Young preens before the video crew, covered with grime and wearing a dust-laden stillsuit. "It's the epitomy of fashion, my deah," she says dramatically.

She inserts nose plugs into her nostrils. Standing in the middle of the Dead Dog Dump, caked with grit and with the long rubber hoses stuck up her nose, Young enlarges her saucer eyes and slowly advances on the video camera. "I'm ready for my closeup now, Mr. De Mille."

In a playful mood, Kyle MacLachlan coaxes Everett McGill into an impromptu dance routine. The pair, in stillsuits, kick up a storm

On the Churubusco lot, the massive "bottom" of a Spice Harvester. Rocks will be tossed down from the platform to simulate the attack of a gigantic sandworm.

of dirt. "The dancing Fremen!" Kyle announces.

There will be some explosions called for this evening and director Lynch is conferring with pyrotechnics ace Kit West, getting into some detail. Freddie Francis sits patiently next to the camera. "I let him blow out two candles on *The Elephant Man* and now he thinks he's a special effects expert." Lynch hears Francis' crack and begins laughing.

Somehow, the cast and crew keep their spirits up and make it through the night.

They return to their hotels, gagging and wheezing, every exposed pore of their bodies caked with dirt.

Sean Young is exhausted. In her role of Fremen heroine, Chani, she must be both fierce and feminine, warrior and seductress. After a few nights at the Dead Dog Dump, Young reflects on the more physical aspects of her character. "She's very strong," the actress laughs. "She is in *shape*. She doesn't mess around.

"Chani is interesting because she has so many different facets. She doesn't say too much. There are a lot of shots of her reacting to things. Her commentary is visual half the time. I like that. When the camera just closes in on your face, that's when the real acting goes on."

Young traipses into the makeup room before her next shot. Her body goes limp as the makeup artists slowly transform her from a sophisticated New York resident to a headstrong Fremen warrior. She is almost totally silent during the preparation.

"The more I do movies," she explains, "the more I realize that the makeup room in the morning is where half of your head comes from the rest of the day on the set. You develop a very personal relationship with your makeup man, your hair guy, and vice versa. You learn how not to offend one another and how to get your point across. You learn how to say things like 'What do you think about this eyebrow?' It may sound strange but when you're together in there creating the way you look, you're also helping create a character."

An hour later, Young is on a sietch set. Both her character and her makeup are being doused with red dirt before she is allowed to step before the cameras.

Paul Smith is a heavy in *Dune,* both figuratively and literally. As Rabban, the Baron's mountainous nephew, he resembles the Michelin tire man, a massive amount of human flesh encased in an even more

At right: The Lady Jessica dressed for her Water of Life ceremony scene

massive black rubber outfit. Smith is having problems dealing with the rarified Mexican air. He is breathing heavily and sweating both on and off camera. He is also having the time of his life.

Seated, between takes, in one of the *Dune* dressing rooms, he gleefully talks about his finest moment to date. "I had a great scene with Max Von Sydow," he says proudly. "He's Doctor Kynes. In the script, he's being held prisoner by my men and I order them to take him into the desert and let him die. We were getting ready to film it and I said to David, 'David. What would you think if I picked him up and threw him over my shoulder?'

"He was already bloodied from a beating. So, we put blood on my hands so it's clear that I'm the one who did the beating. We then did this sort of bloodlusty sort of crazy stroll back and forth. David liked it. Then he said, 'What if you stroke his cheek lovingly?' We got into this weird conversation about this affectionate sort of strange, sadistic game Rabban was playing. I loved it. 'OK,' David said. 'Let's do it. Let's try it. Let's see what happens.' There was real communication there. David communicates. There are many directors who don't say anything or they'll say something like 'Something's wrong and I don't know what.' Well, if the director doesn't know, then I sure won't. But with David, there is an energy there. I just love the energy. I felt this hum going on the set that day. It was like a buzz."

Smith wipes a river of sweat from his brow. "It was a pleasure working with Max. Max didn't have any dialogue in this scene but he was just such a nice man. I said, 'Max. Do you mind if I carry you around a little bit?'

"He said, 'I'm heavy.' I said, 'Don't worry about it.' The costume weighed a hundred pounds. I had three hundred pounds on me, counting Max. It didn't matter. Whatever. I was *acting*!"

During the course of the House Atreides' first few days on the planet Dune, Paul and Duke Leto are introduced to the concept of spice-mining by Dr. Kynes. To illustrate the practice, Kynes accompanies Leto and Paul, in an ornithopter, into the desert where a spice harvester, a mobile factory, is busily digging in below them.

From out of nowhere, a mountainous sandworm appears and heads for the harvester, attracted by the whirring vibrations made by the machinery. The miners panic and flee the large vehicle as tons of rock and grit tumble down upon them. The Duke and Paul rescue many of the men as the worm destroys the harvester in a scene of both savagery and majesty.

On the back lot at Churubusco, there is considerably less majesty evident as an important part of the sequence is filmed. A section of the harvester door, part of the side of the vehicle and two large support pods, have been built and positioned on a piece of desert landscape.

A large group of extras, clad in mining outfits, is slated to run out of the harvester's door as the avalanche caused by the oncoming worm begins cascading down the side of the vessel. The word "action" is yelled. The men tumble out of the craft.

And the spectacular avalanche? What will be seen in the finished movie as a thunderous wave of rock and earth is, today, being supplied by a dozen workers positioned above the harvester set on scaffolding. On a command, the men gleefully reach into large, cardboard containers situated before them and toss handfuls of dirt and rocks off the side of the scaffolding onto the extras below.

One of the avalanche crew becomes so involved in his work that, when he runs out of rock and silt, he picks up his box and raises it above his head to hurl it down upon the fleeing miners. A quick thinking comrade restrains him. Spice miners may be eaten by sandworms, pummeled with rock but never, repeat, never, be beaned by cardboard boxes. Something about verisimilitude.

Sean Young (right) and Fremen, covered with grit on the Dead Dog Dump location.

* * *

Jurgen Prochnow, as Duke Leto, is held prisoner by the Baron and his men. The Duke is sprawled on a black stretcher at the Baron's headquarters on Giedi Prime; he is drugged and only semiconscious. Sting, playing Feyd, is hovering by the bedside. They are surrounded by crewmembers. David Lynch is in the middle of filming the scene when what sounds like a gunshot shatters the quiet of a take. Lynch watches, dumbfounded, as chaos rears its head.

"We had an open 5K bulb," he says, amazed. "It was pointed downward. We had a screen up to protect it because when they burn down and they're open like that, they're dangerous. I think they heat up more. The bulb just blew up. There was this huge explosion. There were a couple of seconds of total silence. Then hot glass started raining down on all of us.

"Jurgen was tied to the stretcher with these straps. I don't know how he did it. *He* doesn't know how he did it. But he got off that stretcher. And where he was lying? Hot glass just rained down. It burned into and fused itself to the plastic of the stretcher.

"A piece of glass fell down one of the dolly grip's pants and burned his back...just sizzled the skin. We were all really lucky. It was miraculous that we all escaped and nobody got hurt really badly on that one."

"That was one of the most frightening experiences in my life," says Sting, "Jurgen almost getting killed. I was right next to him. It was chilling. There was hot glass flying all over."

On the set, the damage is assessed. The glass is cleaned up. The cast and crew chill out for a few moments. The scene is shot with a new bulb. It's filmed without a hitch, but nerves are still on edge at the end of the day.

In the Arrakeen palace, the beast Rabban is staring slackjawed as, outside in the desert, a battle is raging between the Fremen and his Harkonnen troopers. Rabban's men are getting the cosmic stuffing knocked out of them by the Fremen troops, desert dwellers galvanized by a new leader known as Paul Atreides. At this point, a wounded Harkonnen warrior is scheduled to run into the castle and yell: "They're screaming Muad'Dib...Muad'Dib...making sounds...They're killing us."

A Mexican extra is being very carefully made-up to look exceedingly ravaged and trod-upon.

Actor Paul Smith, as Rabban, wears half of his bulky suit and readies himself for a rehearsal.

Lynch gives the go-ahead and the Harkonnen extra dashes into the room, screaming at the top of his lungs: "Deer screaming Moob Deeb...Moob Deeb...makeeng sounds. Deer keeleeng us. Dave cootout Suttis' eyes!"

Lynch doesn't know whether to laugh, cry or perhaps seek another line of work. Whatever is running through his mind, he does not show it. He smiles slightly and very calmly, gently and patiently approaches the actor and tries to clue him in as to the correct pronunciation of the lines of dialogue.

The actor nods in understanding and, then, for the next twenty minutes, proceeds to mispronounce nearly every word he has to deliver. Lynch displays enough compassion to qualify him for sainthood in most major religions. He is getting nowhere, however.

Finally, it is Smith who speaks. "Couldn't I just kill him when he runs in...before he gets to say anything?"

Kenneth McMillan sits in the makeup room. He is in the midst of one of the first applications of the Baron's makeup. It will take over three hours. His hairline is altered. His skin texture is changed. Large, pus-filled sacks are glued onto his face and neck. Scars are laid on. Scabs and sores are carefully grafted onto his skin.

"Anything I do after this is going to seem so easy," he mutters.

The video crew arrives to carefully record his painful transition.

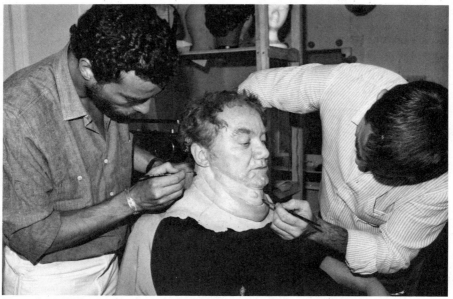

Kenneth McMillan begins the long and painful makeup transformation that will turn him into the repulsive Baron. Makeup chief Gianetto De Rossi, right, will add layers of flab and boils.

McMillan is bored to tears sitting in the makeup chair. "Next time you visit," the actor cracks, "bring me a toy."

During the application, Sting drops by. "You've got to stop eating that greasy food for breakfast," Sting admonishes, staring at the boils on his co-star's neck. "Tomorrow morning, it's fruit."

On his way to his own dressing room, Kyle MacLachlan also stops by. "You're looking lovely today."

McMillan purses his lips. "Thank you, dear."

Later, McMillan will be filming a very dramatic bit of dialogue, in which the Baron sits on his throne and vows revenge on the Duke and his family. Halfway through his speech, the biggest of his neck boils works itself loose and hangs from the actor's Adam's apple, transforming the Harkonnen meanie into something resembling an angry turkey.

McMillan, not realizing the situation, continues to rant and rave and growl. At the end of the scene, he looks at director Lynch hopefully. A 'how was it?' look plays across his face. A faint chorus of giggles arises from behind the camera. McMillan fingers his neck and figures out the rest. The giggles turn into laughter.

"You think it's easy doing this?" McMillan asks no one in particular.

For many of her scenes in *Dune*, Francesca Annis is called upon to either wear an ornate gown or, during her period as a Bene Gesserit Reverend Mother, walk around wearing a skintight bald wig topped by a black habit.

Resting between takes on one of the Arrakeen sets, the actress, wearing both her headpiece and her flowing black robes, sits very straight while "relaxing." "It's not difficult for me to dress like this," she smiles, balancing the tiara-like habit on her chrome-dome.

"Since I've worked a lot with the Royal Shakespeare and National theaters in England, I've gotten used to wearing period clothing. I don't find it at all difficult or alienating. Oddly enough, it's more difficult for me to rehearse without the costume on. The costume helps you get into character, somehow."

As for her partially hairless look, she says, "The strangest part of it all for me is pulling the bald wig off. Putting it on is a slow process. It happens so gradually that you hardly notice it at all. The weird part is taking this off. It takes much less time. You just reach in the back of the bald cap and lift up the latex rubber. It's like a top layer of skin coming off. It's strange to see your real self suddenly appearing in the mirror.

On the industrial world of Giedi Prime, the Baron "floats" down
a stairwell, actually suspended by an intricate wire and pulley system
that is out of view of the movie camera.

"The bald cap is quite an amazing accomplishment. It looks very real. It's very impressive."

Francesca's bald look doesn't impress *everyone*, however. Her two small children visiting her on the set are amazingly indifferent. "They're not into all these externals yet," she says. "For them it's just a case of, 'God. There's Mummy in a fancy dress and funny makeup again.'"

On the backlot of Churubusco stands a massive, man-made cliff. During the course of the film, Paul Atreides will scramble across this mountainside. A large boulder will come loose and tumble towards the ground, sending the Atreides heir flying into space. The boulder will slam onto the sandy ground with a resounding thud.

The boulder is actually a mechanically controlled apparatus that can be hoisted into position and, then, with a flick of a lever be sent slamming down onto the desert.

"It's all pretty cut and dry," says one crewmember. "When you release the rock it just falls. There's a stopper on the thing so when it falls it doesn't shake. It just grabs onto the ground and sits there tight. The first time the thing fell it didn't have that stopper. It hit the ground and bounced up and down again and again. Boom. Boom. Boom. Boom. A big rock like that hitting the ground like a cartoon thing. We fixed that pretty quickly."

A couple of hundred extras, dressed as Fremen, Harkonnen villains and loyal soldiers of the Duke stand outside one of the Churubusco stages in the sun. The old army adage of "hurry up and wait" is a rule to live by on *any* motion picture set but on a special effects–oriented movie it is written in gold. And on a special-effects film being shot at a facility where *anything* can and often does happen to slow down production, the waiting time in between shots can seem like a small eternity.

"Getting the extras together initially isn't much of a problem," says one crewmember. "*Keeping* them together is. When you have people sitting around for an hour, they get bored. When they get bored, they start playing around and when they start playing around...there can be problems getting them back in line."

As he speaks, two Atreides guards point their large stun guns at each other.

"You dead," says one.

"No, *you* dead," replies the other.

Kenneth McMillan is waddling across the lot wearing the beginnings of the ballooning Baron outfit. He looks a bit like a scaled-down version of a Macy's Thanksgiving Day Parade balloon figure. Bob Ringwood and two customers trail reverently behind. McMillan spots the videotape crew and waves merrily as he waddles onward, slowly but surely shifting his weight from one side to another.

"I must weigh about five hundred pounds in this thing," McMillan explains. "It's silicon, soft leather and rubber."

He points to his flabby pseudo-self. "It's funny how you can get used to anything. When we first started shooting, they used to have to wheel me to the set. Then I found that I could actually walk in this. I'd rather walk. It only takes me forty-five minutes to get dressed now. When we started it took well over two hours. Makeup was longer at first, too. It took about three hours. Now, we're down to about two."

He waddles down an alleyway. "The tough thing is steps. I still need help with steps."

*   *   *

Two weeks after the exploding bulb incident, Jurgen Prochnow is back on that same black stretcher on the same set. It is part of a nightmare sequence being used to add extra impact to the Duke's drug-induced period.

The scene calls for the evil Baron to sneak up behind the sleeping Duke and, after fondling the left cheek of Leto's face, to dig his fingers into the right. At this point, the Duke's face is to be torn open and green gas is to billow out of the wound.

To film the scene, a bogus cheek is made out of rubber and makeup. A small tube is attached to it. The tube runs down the back of Jurgen's ear and down the side of the stretcher. Off camera, at the other end of the tube, a technician pumps green smoke into the device. Eventually, it will make its way to the phony cheek. When McMillan tears into the Duke, the technician will pump and the smoke will flow.

Hopefully the scene will be done one off (on the first take). The makeup process for Prochnow for this scene is tedious and complicated and everyone is hoping that things will go smoothly. McMillan is carefully instructed how to hold his hand, how to dig into the substance and how to position his arm.

"Action."

Cameras rolling, the Baron approaches the fallen Duke. He digs his hand into Leto's skin. Smoke pours out on cue. Then, without uttering a cry, actor Prochnow suddenly leaps from the stretcher, clutching his cheek. He pushes McMillan aside and runs off camera, his cheek still smoking. "Cut!"

Everyone on the set is dumbfounded.

McMillan stands, stunned, next to the stretcher. "What happened?" he repeats over and over. "What happened?"

"I'd better go see if Jurgen's all right," Lynch mutters, darting off into the shadows.

Jurgen isn't.

Dune has just had its first accident.

"First- and second-degree burns," Lynch comments later. "I can't understand it. The smoke that was supposed to come out of the cheek...We rehearsed it. It was tested on a dummy and on a real person. We even tested it on Jurgen."

During the tests, however, the makeup appliance wasn't sealed as securely as it would be during the take. And, so, while the cameras rolled, the smoke built up in the cheek before McMillan tore into it, heating up all the while.

Comments Lynch, "It was one of those things that was tested

and the smoke was very cool in the test...'cause it goes through this long pipe before it gets to the pouch. There were zero problems. When we filmed, it just heated up like crazy."

The sequence was Prochnow's last scheduled shot in the picture. It was filmed. It was usable. But it left the cast and crew quite shaken.

10.
FREDDIE FRANCIS

Working with Freddie isn't work. It's fun.
David Lynch, director

Freddie's diplomatic, unintimidated and secure about what
a good director of photography he is. He enjoys that.
He also has a loony sense of humor.
Sean Young, actress (Chani)

I really was looking forward to working with him. I mean,
he directed DR. TERROR'S HOUSE OF HORRORS. Great film.
Sting, actor (Feyd)

Freddie Francis is unflappable. Day after day, sitting next to his camera, the well-known cinematographer manages to find solutions to seemingly unsolvable problems dealing with lighting, sets and pyrotechnic puzzles. From a distance, the compact gentleman looks fairly placid. He seems constantly fatigued, his eyes giving off a sort of world-weary look. He seldom gets angry. He doesn't seem to smile too often.

As one draws nearer to Francis on the set, however, one discovers that he is a master of the dry one-liner. Surrounded by a camera crew composed of old friends, Francis is constantly making caustic comments about the travails being faced from moment to moment. He manages to crack up both the film's cameramen and director Lynch. Occasionally, if a quip is really on the nose, he'll make himself laugh aloud as well.

Today he is perched at the back of a simulated stone platform on one of the movie's brooding sietch sets. The shot is to be part of a sequence wherein Paul slowly walks forward to address a group of assembled Fremen and demonstrate the power of his "weirding way." It's a simple setup, the camera photographing actor Kyle MacLachlan from behind. In the finished film, it will be intercut with other footage featuring Fremen warriors beating on strangely shaped drums.

105

For this short bit, there are no Fremen drummers afoot. Director Lynch is rehearsing the walk with Kyle, trying to get a sort of casual yet militaristic gait out of the young actor. He calls for a drummer.

There are no drummers.

Lynch then asks Directors Guild trainee Ian Woolf to beat a drum so that Kyle can get the feel of the scene.

Woolf, a bearded New Yorker, grabs a drum, hangs it around his neck and beats it, tom-tom style in a steady rum-tum-tum march mode. Lynch turns around. "Uh, I wanted something neater. Something like. Ba-da-bump-bumpidybumpidybumpidy-bump."

Woolf gapes at the director. A second rehearsal. Ian begins playing again. Rum-tum-tum.

Lynch turns around and explains what he'd like to hear, a drum beat with more "bumpidys" than "rum-tums."

Freddie Francis rolls his eyes heavenward. "David. For the amount of money we're paying the poor boy, don't expect Buddy Rich."

The set is reduced to laughter. Lynch accepts a solid rum-tum-tum.

David Lynch and cinematographer Freddie Francis working on a scene for <u>Dune</u>.

On set and off, Freddie Francis is relentlessly polite and effervescent. "I'm not exactly a practical joker," he explains. "But I do have a sense of humor and I like to have fun in my life...and if one is on a movie, that's my life twenty-four hours a day. I've got to have fun on the set because the hours that we're working here are ridiculous. I don't have the time to have fun anyplace else so I might as well have fun on the floor."

Because of the enormous scope of the film, both Francis and Lynch and most of the top crewmembers do with very little sleep, trying to deal with both technology-spawned delays and unexpected bouts with nature on a location shoot. "The hours! The hours!" he whispers in mock horror.

For Francis, this is his second teaming with director Lynch. Their initial collaboration on *The Elephant Man* earned critical praise and raised quite a few eyebrows as well. From a distance, the twosome just didn't seem like a workable team. Francis was a wise-cracking British veteran of the movie business and Lynch appeared to be an intellectual neophyte.

"I think we work well together because our philosophies jibe," says Francis. "I have this philosophy that it's the cameraman's job of doing everything the director wants and never saying no to it. When I was young, I used to be amazed at the way the cameramen on the floor used to rule everything. When they were saying, 'No, I can't do this,' what they were really saying was 'I won't do this because I can't make it look pretty.' I decided that was wrong. When I became a cameraman I decided that the most fun would be to try to do everything the director wanted, to try to do things that are virtually impossible. I'm sure that's why I get along so well with David. He's the most unorthodox director in the world. He gets an idea in his head that may be impractical technically but he likes it. It's my job to make his vision a reality. I like that.

"This is a very difficult film for both David and me. Personally, when I go on the floor with a director, I like to shoot a scene or a sequence knowing that that's *it*. *That* is what the public is going to see. On this film, you can't do that. You've got to leave quite a bit for the special effects people to add later on. It's hard to work with those kinds of restrictions.

"We manage to work around them. David and I are sort of a united force. He backs me up and I back David up. On many occasions we just have to say, 'Well, this is all we can do here. Let's make the best of it.'"

While *Dune* is undoubtedly a bona fide science-fiction adventure, the nature of the story dictates that it have a different cinematic look to it than any of the more recent excursions in science fiction, from *Star Wars* to *E.T.*

"We're trying to make it look very strange, very alien," says Francis. "We want you to know that you're living on another world here. We're making a lot of the sequences very dark, but seeable. You'll see this huge desert planet with brown skies and little people running about below on the sand. Normally, when you see a desert scene in a film, you see long, black shadows. In our film, you won't have black shadows. You'll have brown shadows. And our desert will be this white-yellow expanse, almost like the sea. I mean, if you go to see this movie you're not going to want to see one of those ordinary Arabian-type deserts.

"Our basic reality is very different. I don't think the audience is going to readily understand why. I hope they don't realize this while they're watching the film because, then, they'll start paying attention to the photography. *None* of our shadows are black. They have a black base but they all have a sort of colored hue to them. That hue varies from set to set. I'm getting that effect by using my little magic box, the light flex.

"It was invented by a cameraman friend of mine, Jerry Turpin, for a movie called *Young Winston*. On that movie, Richard Attenborough said to Jerry that he'd seen some copies of a very famous old London magazine called *The London Illustrated News* which had wonderful photos that were strangely tinted. He thought it would be great to duplicate that tint in his picture.

"Jerry did all sorts of tests with filters and nothing ever quite worked. He was sort of pondering that problem at home, sitting in his study. He was gazing at his lawn through a closed window, just staring at a silver birch tree. Inside the room were green curtains. The sun hit the green velvet curtains and reflected back onto the window. The window turned green. Looking through it, Jerry saw that the green affected everything but the highlights. In other words, the shadows were tinted far more than the main objects. Jerry set to work and came up with a primitive version of what we're using today.

"It looked like a large cookie tin with a light at the top and a pane of glass on the front. The light illuminated the glass with a certain tint and the camera shot through it. It colored the shadows and gave the film sort of a pre-fogging effect. I used it in *The French Lieutenant's Woman* as a sort of contrast control on the film. With *Dune*, however, we're really furthering the light-flex system. We're

Francis frames a shot using the lightflex system.

using it constantly to subtly alter the reality you're experiencing. Little oddities."

Aside from the light-flex system, Francis has devised another way to heighten the reality of *Dune* by inventing a device to make the fierce desert sand storms appear even more horrific on screen. "We've come up with a portable foreground sand storm," he says. "We put it right under the lens. It looks a bit like a goldfish bowl only it's square. We blow sand in one side and blow it back from the other side so the stuff is always circulating in front of the camera. This helps us a lot if we're filming a sand storm on a sunny day and we want to kill all the shadows. This does everything for us."

Inventions notwithstanding, Francis has had to grit his teeth quite often to get through some of *Dune*'s more complex shots. "There just isn't the technology down here for this sort of film," he explains, "so we've had to jerryrig a lot of things. The workers down here are lovely people but they're not experienced. The two elec-

tricians I brought with me from England have been virtually running
a film school here to get the movie going.

"We've had some awfully, awfully difficult shots to do. We've
filmed a lot of things down all these labyrinths of corridors which,
because of the way they were built, were almost impossible to reposition to let the light in. It's been very, very hard to shoot some
of the more difficult stuff on these sets. We might as well have gone
into a coal mine and done it."

Aside from the shadowy sietch sets, Francis has found a few of
the physical effects tricky to shoot around as well. "Some of the
Baron's scenes were unusually difficult," Francis admits. "The wires
he was hanging from had to be reasonably thick...otherwise you'd
have lost the Baron. I kept on muttering to David, 'If we do this
scene without seeing the wires...I want extra money!' We had
about six major scenes which—by all known photographic meth-
ods—should have revealed the presence of those wires. But they
didn't. Miraculous. So, David told Raffaella about my extra money.
She gave me an extra dollar a shot. Hmmm. I think she owes me
six extra dollars a week for the rest of the film.

"The Baron's scenes were very troublesome. More so because
David doesn't care about getting rid of the wires physically; he just
expects them not to be there when he sees the footage. David is
constantly coming up with wild things. He is sort of new on the
scene and doesn't understand any limitations. That's great for a
director. He always asks for the impossible. It's become a joke now.
When he asks·me a question I start saying things like 'Well, this is
definitely the end. This is where I get the sack!' But that's the fun
of it. I suppose that I've been around so long that I can always pull
something out of my bag of tricks and make the shot acceptable.

"To get the Baron to fly and not see his wires, we did it all
through lighting. We took into account where the wires happened
to be at a particular time and balanced the amount of light from the
background and foreground until the wires just blended in with the
colors. It was very tricky."

Francis watches the crew set up the next shot. "One of the best
things that's happened on this picture is that everything, nationality-
wise, has gelled. There hasn't been any dissension on the floor at
all. That has surprised and delighted me tremendously. When we
first started the picture I would have put money on the fact that so
many nationalities present would have been harmful. But it's been
wonderful. Everybody loves everybody and that has made the picture a lot easier than it might have been."

He stares out at the moody sietch set. "Now if we could only get this to look a little brighter."

11.
THE SAGA CONTINUES

*I think David likes the Harkonnens, who are the most
hideous band in the film. I think he likes the nightmare
sequences. The movie should reflect that. It'll be
a wolf in sheep's clothing. That suits me.*
Sting, actor (Feyd)

*I think this script is terrific. I can't believe
it's remained as complex as it has. That's difficult to do
with film. Film is dumb, you know? It really is.*
Brad Dourif, actor (Piter)

*There are days when so much is going on, I feel that
combat photography would be easy by comparison.*
David Lynch, director

Within the first two months of production, it became clear that
something very special, albeit strange, was going on down at Churubusco studios. An international crew was somehow functioning
more smoothly than anyone had expected. Construction was pro-
ceeding on time. For the complicated special effects shots requiring
actors to be composited with strange and exotic optical backgrounds,
the largest blue screen in the world, 35 feet high and 108 feet wide,
had been positioned perfectly across an entire wall of a sound stage.

And it was during the first few months of production that many
of the stellar names appearing in smaller roles entered and exited
the world of *Dune*: Max Von Sydow, Linda Hunt, Richard Jordan,
Freddie Jones, Brad Dourif and Sian Phillips. As a result, there was
always a sense of excitement on the set. A sense of newness. Says
Sting: "I'm working in front of the camera with some great people.
And when I'm not working, it's great fun watching."

Brad Dourif has played many celluloid oddballs in his time, but
the Baron's emissary Piter may be the most outrageous character he

has portrayed to date. With flaming red hair spiraling upward from his high forehead and eyebrows slanted precariously enough to put most ski slopes to shame, Dourif's Piter is a figure to be reckoned with on the set.

On this day, Dourif is called upon to step from a Harkonnen cable car and walk down a long, metal stairway while wearing a cumbersome coat. Dourif must make the trip a few times until director Lynch decides it's right. The actor does not seem to mind the huffing and puffing at all, however. He finds his role quite fascinating.

"This is the first real villain I've ever played," he says proudly. "And, since it's a science-fiction story, a lot of the character is left to your imagination. I've been sort of racking my brain, creating a whole. Peter's a Mentat. They're military espionage people; trained to kill people, to stab people in the back, to lie, to cheat, to poison people. They've been trained since birth, really."

A smile appears on his wild-eyed face. "This is a fairy tale for me. Very, very dark. I mean, no one here lives happily ever after. *Never.*"

It is decided that, during the filming of *Dune,* the video crew will tape certain messages from director Lynch to the audience. Selections of the taping will be edited into a presentation to be shown at science-fiction conventions.

Lynch is covered with dirt and grime on the backlot when the video crew approaches him. He nods his head and agrees to their plan.

He stops preparing a scene for a moment. He faces the camera and smiles. "Hi. Welcome to the convention."

"Francesca's had a few close calls," says one crewmember. "We were filming a scene where Paul, Jessica and Duke Leto are leaving Caladan. They walk into their spaceship and take off for Arrakis. There was a huge door leading to their ship that was supposed to slide up when they approach it and, then, close when they're inside.

"We did one shot and then it was time to slide the doorway panel up and get the actors out for another try. The door came up a little bit and, as the three of them were walking out, something happened in the back and the door just came down. It grazed the back of Francesca's head. It knocked her down. She wasn't hurt but it was a pretty surprising way to start a scene.

"It's been a strange shoot in little ways. One night, Francesca was trying to light a gas stove in her apartment and it blew up. It singed her eyebrows off. I guess you'd call stuff like that hardcore blooper material."

Francesca Annis is seated in the cockpit of a 'thopter with Kyle MacLachlan. In the story, Jessica and Paul have just barely escaped with their lives after Harkonnen treachery has driven them out of their new home on Arrakis and snuffed out the life of Duke Leto.

Francesca, as Jessica, suddenly realizes her husband's fate. Tears well up in her eyes. They cascade down her cheeks. "Leto! He's dead! He's dead," she wails.

"Cut," director Lynch cries, obviously pleased.

Francesca continues to cry. "Do you think we can try that again?" she asks Lynch between sobs.

Lynch is obviously surprised but delighted. "You bet we can," he says. "You bet we can."

The actress stops crying as the lights are lowered between takes. Her makeup is adjusted. The cameras roll and, once again, Lady Jessica suffers a dramatic emotional breakdown on cue.

"It's hard for me to think of this as a big fantasy," says Annis later, "because the fantastic elements are not visible when you are actually making the film. The director fills that in for me before we do the scene. He tells me about the worms and the Heighliners and the 'thopters.

"For example, in this scene, we're stepping out of a prop space-craft set up on the studio's back parking lot and David is telling us that there are millions of water cannons and fountains and thousands of men and women standing there in front of us, but we are actually staring at the back of the electrician's van. It is also difficult for me to realize the special effects element of the picture because I'm so caught up in the human values of the story.

"The movie, by and large, is very down-to-earth and humanistic. It's about losing a husband, losing a father, risking damaging your newborn baby. There are a lot of emotional values and contemporary issues in this. I imagine that accounts for the success of the book.

"There have been times, and I suppose this is inevitable on a special effects film and especially for me since I haven't done a lot of them, when I've walked out and said, 'God. I just can't see how they're going to do this!' But you put your trust in Freddie and David. They know what they're doing. Later, you see the finished scene and you're amazed.

"When we were at the Dead Dog location, I thought it looked

miserable. Later, when I saw the finished scene, the location looked entirely different. That is the power of making films, you create complete illusion. On film, the Dead Dog location looks nothing like it did to the eye. When you're there, everybody reassures you and says things like 'It won't look like this on the screen. We're using bright lights but we're going to stop down the camera.' I think I know what they mean, technically, but I don't realize what the end result will be. Of course, the end result was absolutely wonderful. On the screen, the Dump looks incredibly hazy, and reddish. Very atmospheric and awe-inspiring.

"When things do get difficult on a movie like this, it's comforting to know that, in the end, you're taking part in a grand illusion. It has nothing to do with real life whatsoever."

Molly Wryn slowly walks down a set of stone sietch steps. She is surrounded by large, foreboding walls that stretch clear up to the stage's ceiling. Without the presence of camera or crew to destroy the illusion, the sietch set does actually seem to be an Olympian underground structure carved from rock. "Nothing is everyday on Dune," Wryn comments. "Everything is *ultra*."

A studio nurse is prowling around the set, checking the blood pressure of some of the crewmembers. Sickness is on the rise and it seems like a good idea to monitor the health of some of the prime movers of the production.

David Lynch rolls up his sleeve. The nurse wraps the blood-pressure tourniquet around Lynch's extended arm. She begins pumping the attached rubber bulb furiously as Lynch watches her warily, waiting for her to announce his blood pressure to the world. He pops a lozenge into his smoke-inflamed throat.

Lynch glances up and notices the video crew hovering nearby. "Hi," he smiles. "Welcome to the convention."

Freddie Jones stands on one of the Arrakeen castle sets. He is in the middle of delivering a speech when a lightbulb pops with a bang. He finishes the speech before looking up and commenting, "Well, that didn't sound too good, did it?"

The speech is filmed again, successfully.

A few moments later, his entrance into the room is being staged. A number of the Duke's soldiers are supposed to quietly march out of the room, holding their riflelike stun guns over their shoulders. The young extras are having trouble concentrating on their foot maneuvers while simultaneously balancing their weapons properly.

Lynch patiently waits for the young locals to get their military act in gear. Finally, an exasperated assistant director runs over to the line of uniformed men, yanking their rifles into the proper positions one by one.

He approaches a soldier who is holding his weapon at an angle that will certainly spell death for the soldier walking directly in front of him.

"He doesn't know what it is," the assistant director bellows, "a rifle or a salami!"

The guns are positioned. The men march off the set. By the time they march back on for another take, their guns are all out of whack. The assistant director starts making guttural noises in Spanish.

"Thank goodness I don't understand Spanish," Freddie Francis comments.

Richard Jordan is having the time of his life. Although his role of Duncan has been reduced to a near-cameo, he quite enjoys run-

The Baron's twisted envoy, Piter, menaces the captured Jessica, with Paul in the background.

ning up and down the corridors of the Arrakeen palace during the
fierce battle between the Duke's loyal men and the Baron's evil
henchmen. Unfortunately, Duncan does not emerge from the skirmish intact.

"This is my attitude," says the actor. "It's a great way to make
a living. I mean, this morning on the set...I have this crazy gun
in one hand and this knife in the other. I have a rubber suit on and
I'm soaking wet. The sweat is just running off me. I've got this weird
belt on and if you push a button it's supposed to protect you from
everything.

"And I run out and I kill this big, huge guy by shooting with
my gun. But the guy isn't quite dead. So he grabs my gun and I
stick the knife through his helmet, into his brain. And, then, he
dies. Then, I just run off some place. And I thought, 'By God! This
is terrific. I'm getting paid for this. I'm playing like I did when I
was five years old.'"

Later on that day, Duncan will have his head blown open by an
enemy gun. "Still," Jordan says. "It sure beats working."

On orders from Baron Harkonnen,
Piter is about to reward Dr. Yueh for his treachery.

Valiant Duncan Idaho prepares for his last stand
against the Harkonnen horde invading the Arrakeen Castle.

Tony Masters is walking across a half-struck set on a sound stage. When this set is completely removed, the golden throne room of the Emperor will be constructed. It will take three months to assemble. Half of Masters' job, apparently, is to patrol the studio grounds like a school teacher, checking out the condition of his charges.

"Sometimes you are a bit surprised when you see a set under construction," he smiles. "When you do your sketches of the set, you try to make it into an interesting shape. Then, it gets drawn by the draftsmen and built on the stage. At that point, you walk on the stage and snoop around and discover that there are angles and shapes that you didn't ever dream would appear. Thankfully, that doesn't happen too often.

"So far, we haven't had any major disasters with the sets. There are always little things that you never really think of that somehow get blown up out of proportion and hold up the production. It's usually a stupid thing like a door handle. The actor walks up, pulls the door open and the handle comes off in his hand. Then, they can't screw it on again. The set has been made with handles that don't work. It's the stupid stuff that no one really gives any time to that winds up costing time.

"I'm always on call. Quite often I'll be called down to a set after it's been lit. Someone will say, 'We think this scene will really look nice if we shoot it from up there, a high angle looking down. Unfortunately, there's a piece of ceiling up there. Now, what can we do about that?'

"I'll say, 'If you give us a half-hour, we'll cut that away and we'll replace it with something else and we'll make the job work.' And, so, we work quickly to improvise. We make the sets larger or smaller or move a piece this way or that every day."

Masters walks off the soon-to-be throne-room stage back towards his office. "We're building a set on stage four that's going to be interesting. It's the training room that Paul is going to use, a place where they train soldiers the art of combat by using robots. That's going to be interesting to see completed. I think they're going to make the robots out of *wood*."

He shakes his head ruefully. "In Mexico, I suppose that makes sense."

On a night shoot at the Dead Dog dump, several dozen of the Duke's loyal soldiers are supposed to charge across the barren terrain. They are being pursued and fired upon by Harkonnen troops. The soldiers on both sides are being portrayed by somewhat overzealous local extras.

Eventually, explosions will be set off but, for the next hour and a half, the armies will simply rehearse their battle while, up on a nearby ledge, the camera crew lines up their shots.

Time after time, the Duke's legions run, yelling, over the hills. They are so excited, however, that when the Harkonnens attack, many of Leto's followers hit the dirt in true John Wayne western fashion.

Ian Woolf, the DGA trainee who is supervising the run-through, is appalled. He stands amidst the chaos, bellowing through a bullhorn. "No one dies, damn it! Quit falling down!"

David Lynch, Sting and assorted crewmembers are hovering around a camera on one of the Arrakeen sets, setting up a shot. The video crew approaches. Lynch turns around and faces the all-seeing documentary camera.

"Hi," he smiles. "Welcome to the convention."

The Beast Rabban hears that a mysterious figure is successfully leading the Fremen against the Harkonnen conquerors of Dune. Paul Smith, as Rabban, sitting in water and surrounded by light bulbs, had to overcome concern about his possible electrocution.

Sting casts a suspicious eye at the video setup. MTV this isn't. "What's that for?" he asks.

"This is for a science-fiction convention," Lynch explains. "They want to know what's happening with *Dune.*"

"Hah!" one crewmember laughs. "*Nobody* knows."

By the second month, it is clear that, in terms of health, filming *Dune* is going to be quite a challenge. Those who aren't sick to their stomachs have the flu, those who don't have either have sore throats from the various smoke effects used almost daily.

Kyle MacLachlan is a little under the weather today. Sitting on a sietch set, he stoically describes the Mexico City experience. "I've had a real tough time getting some of the foods that I like here. I wouldn't say that I'm a health food nut but I do enjoy natural foods. There's a tremendous amount of sugar in the foods down here.

"The altitude was a problem for me for weeks. Then, that went away. The pollution, of course, is a constant problem but you get used to that, too. I guess your lungs get black enough that they just don't notice the air. The water is a constant problem. In that respect, it's pretty hard to relax down here."

Later that month, one of the crewmembers is sent home with severe internal problems caused by diet.

On one of the Harkonnen sets, director David Lynch demonstrates exactly what the shoot has done to him. He puts his thumb and forefinger around his belt buckle and pulls out his khaki pants away from his stomach. They are quite baggy. "Look. I've lost twenty pounds since I've been down here. I look like a bum!"

Freddie Francis casually looks up from his perch next to the camera. "Personally, I think that look will come back, David."

Paul Smith is seated in a large tub in a steam-filled Arrakeen castle room. The tub is filled with water. A strange, elongated lamp hangs above Smith's head. The scene calls for Rabban to hear bad news about the ongoing battle between the Fremen and his Harkonnen soldiers. Rabban is being beaten by the desert dwellers and beaten badly.

He orders his men to alter the death toll so that his uncle, the Baron, will not suspect that the planet Arrakis is in a major state of revolt.

At the end of his speech, with steam rising from the "hot" water of the tub, Rabban is to form a fist and send it hurtling up into the light. The light will rupture and a shower of black oil will drip down onto the Beast Rabban.

The light above Smith's head has a real bulb in it. It's taking forever to position it correctly so that the actor can casually reach up and smash it. Smith is a little apprehensive about sitting in a tank full of water while shattering a real, live, exceedingly lit lightbulb.

The voltage is nearly nonexistent and every safety precaution has been taken but Smith is *still* understandably skittish. After all, it is a well-known fact that water and electricity just don't mix.

Director Lynch does his best to calm the man, coming up with appropriate small talk. "Have you ever noticed that when an electrician screws in a lightbulb he keeps one hand in his pocket?" Lynch begins. "That's so if something happens and he gets a big shock, he doesn't fry his heart. The surge will bypass his chest and go right down through his leg. If he had both hands on the bulb, though, the power couldn't be routed and..."

Smith nods, stunned, as Lynch continues his enthralling tales of electricians at work.

Two members of the second-unit crew are watching two "glow-globes" float across a set. In reality, the floating globes, suspensor-buoyed illuminating devices (in the script, self-powered by organic batteries), are winged constructions suspended and manipulated very carefully by wires worked from overhead scaffolding. The entire day has been set aside to practice the movements of the props so that, when they are called upon to interact with actors, the flying lightbulbs will go through their motions without a hitch.

"So," one technician says to the other, his mind leaving Caladan for thoughts of the commissary, "do you like macaroni salad?"

Paul Smith's character of Rabban, the Baron's beastly nephew, is a fascinating study in pure evil. No matter what terrifying deed he is doing, Rabban always has a cheerful smile on his face.

"He's got a great grin," says Lynch. "There's no two ways about it, Rabban is happy in his work...and his work is killing. He's a big, happy crusher."

Smith agrees. "There's a little bit of the sadistic guard from *Midnight Express* in him and a touch of Bluto from *Popeye*. He's an interesting sort of maniac. He loves what he's doing. I mean, he just loves killing. The fact that they let him do it all day long is just heaven for him."

Smith is seated in a large chair before the cameras. To his left is a tableful of squoods in see-through cannisters. On cue, Smith will pick up a squood (a small rodent) in a jar, squeeze the top part of the jar down in a viselike motion, squash the squood and drink its life blood out of the bottom of the jar through a straw.

The scene takes a while to set up. The squoods all have to be placed in a certain configuration on the table before Smith picks one up. Then, there are practical problems.

"We have a leaky squood there, David," Freddie Francis comments, looking at the rubber rodents on the table.

"Get me another squood," Lynch says, "that one is leaking."

A new squood in a jar is brought forward. "He doesn't look too good," Lynch comments. "Stick him in the back of the bunch."

The cameras roll and Smith starts squashing squoods, sucking up the resulting mush with gusto. One squood works. And the next. And...

Smith squashes. The squood is squished. Not too much gunk oozes out.

"Too dry," Lynch says. "Cut! We have some dry squoods here."

"Much too dry," Smith comments, quite the connoisseur at this point. "Much too dry."

Rabban takes a squood break.

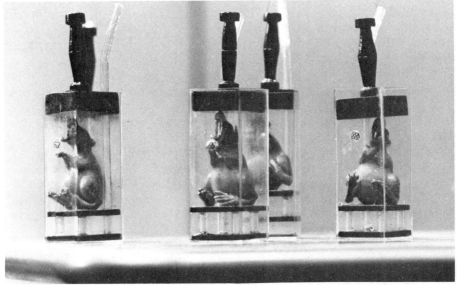

The squoods were, in reality, rubber creatures filled with blood-colored "juice."

After a half hour of squooding it, Smith is finally let go by Lynch. The director has what he needs. Smith is ravenous. He orders a sandwich. The sandwich is slow in coming so he eats DGA trainee Ian Woolf's. "Now *this* is delicious," Smith says, between bites. "I'll never eat another squood again in my life."

Linda Hunt is getting ready to leave the *Dune* location. Her role as the Shadout Mapes has been completed. Although *Dune* is only the second film for the veteran stage actress, she feels that it has been one of the most eye-opening experiences of her long show business career.

"I've never been near anything as big as this," she marvels. "It was fascinating to watch.

"Kyle and I had a scene with this floating weapon called a hunter-seeker. It's like a large syringe. I just watched him with it. He practiced for hours to get all the moves down. The amount of planning before the actors actually got onto the set was remarkable. You would think that there would be a lot of delays and a lot of waiting on this film because of all the effects but, actually, all the physical effects were planned out meticulously before we stepped onto the stage. Things moved very quickly.

"It's quite remarkable how a movie this size used some very old-fashioned stage tricks in extraordinary ways. There's a scene in a hallway where Paul's father, the Duke, is stunned. That was very amusing. Someone shoots a weapon at Leto while I'm in the middle of my death scene. All sorts of wires were used with explosive effects."

Dune marked Hunt's first excursion into science fiction. "I felt like a child in a toy store at times," she says. "The first day, when I took a tour of the sets, I was mesmerized by it all. In the costume shop, way in the back, they had a little museum with miniature renderings of all the costumes. It was magical.

"It was such a joy to act in this. Everything we handled was just so exquisitely made, so wonderfully detailed. I use a weapon called a crysknife. The detail of the carving that was done on its ivory handle—I'm sure it wasn't ivory, probably plastic—was amazing. It seemed so real. The weight of it. The feel of it. I felt instinctively how I should use it as soon as I touched it.

"It was endowed with the power of a real weapon by the care with which it had been made. I think the audience will have a sense of this throughout the movie. There is a sense of realism to this fantasy that I don't think is present very often in movies. This isn't

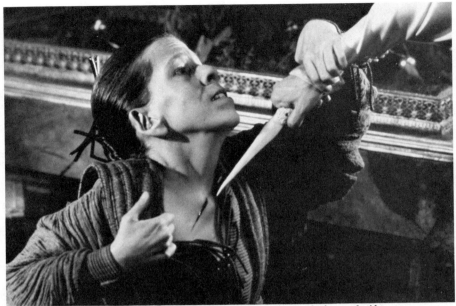

The Shadout Mapes puts her loyalty to the test at the wrong end of a crysknife.

special effects in the sense of 'how can we outdo what's been done before.' It's special effects in terms of 'world building.'

"Special effects in this movie could be defined as *the passion of creating*. How can we bring this world to life? How can we create a detailed fictional environment? How can we create entire societies that are believable?"

Hunt readies herself for her trip back to New York. Within the next few weeks, at least a half-dozen other major names will enter the Churubusco lot, doing their stints on *Dune*. Hunt reflects on this particular aspect of the hectic production schedule with a smile. "This is the first time I ever really drifted in and out of a movie. I feel like a transient, really, because people like Kyle and Francesca will be down here for the entire movie. They've created a world of their own down here. I feel like I'm intruding.

"I'm sorry that I'm missing out on the whole experience. I realize that, after a while, you get warped staying on a film for six months but, I think, that warped feeling actually helps your performance. They're going to film *Dune* straight through. I don't know how anyone will get through the experience. I would have loved to have given it a shot, though. It's a very nice world to visit."

12.
THE SWIRLING SANDS
OF DUNE

What was it like filming in the desert?
Let's just say it was unique.
David Lynch, director

I was unprepared for the purity of the desert
and its elegance and its great, classy beauty.
Patrick Stewart, actor (Gurney)

Boy, was it hot!
Paul Smith, actor (Rabban)

From day one of production, *Dune* was a movie that consumed an amazing amount of space. It needed eight complete sound stages to house its over six dozen sets (with some stages housing three and four sets at a time).

Even more desperate was its need for proper desert locations to simulate the vast expanses of the barren planet Arrakis.

During the course of the film, Paul and Lady Jessica are stranded in the desert and are seen meeting Fremen allies there. Battle scenes occur on the sandswept plains. Worm-riding sequences. 'Thopter rescues. While the Dead Dog Dump would suffice for some of the sietch scenes and, later, serve double duty as the land located directly outside of Duke Leto's Arraken headquarters, an actual desert was needed for the more majestic shots.

The Samalayuca desert, outside of Juarez, was chosen. Before the crew journeyed to the location, however, two hundred workers spent *two months* crawling on their hands and knees over a three-square-mile swatch of the land to clear it of scorpions, rattlesnakes and any traces of plant growth.

By the time the cast and crew of *Dune* journeyed there for the first week of location shooting, a section of the desert had been transformed into a totally dead, totally barren slice of planet.

David Lynch is sitting patiently next to Freddie Francis in the middle of the location shoot. A fierce battle is set to be filmed in which Paul and his trusted aide, Gurney, are reunited after having been separated for years. The smoke billowing across the sky is the result of a pile of old auto tires being burned out of camera range to simulate the chaos of warfare.

It's quite a trick to get the smoke to billow correctly. It often comes in thin wisps, which are followed by dense layers. Not only won't the smoke cooperate in terms of consistency, but also the desert wind alternately blows the smoke away from the actors and, then, into the eyes of the crewmembers. Everyone is wearing surgical masks and goggles. The thick, rubber-based smoke has transformed the crew into something resembling the cast of an old-fashioned Mississippi minstral show. Faces are black. Eyes are white. Tempers are getting short.

Juan Carlos Lopez Rodero, assistant to the director and known to everyone as "Kuki," is frowning as he gazes out upon the columns of listless extras who are waiting for the smoke to flow correctly. "As usual," he mutters. "There are fifty people in the wrong place."

"The smoke is thinning," Lynch notes.

"Put a couple of more tires on!" Kuki yells to one of his workers. A few more tires are tossed onto the bonfire, causing thick clouds of black to roar upwards into the sky. The wind sucks them straight up. None of the clouds make their way to the spot where the in-

Stilgar and Paul Atreides stand in the middle of their Fremen army. On location near Juarez.

terplanetary armies are just waiting for the chance to do celluloid battle.

Everyone is bored. The cameras cannot roll until the smoke engulfs the soldiers. Freddie Francis stares at the clouds spiraling heavenward. "Get this wind going properly, will you, Kuki?"

Eventually, the wind does gibe with the wishes of director Lynch and the battle and reunion scene is staged. It is clear, however, that the location shots scheduled for the desert are not going to be easy to complete.

At the end of the second day, a very exhausted Patrick Stewart reflects on the experience. He has arrived on the production relatively late. A British actor best known for his stage work, Stewart is in awe of the production both in terms of its scope and its deranged shooting schedule.

"It's hard to get into the rhythm of things," he concedes, "coping with the huge periods of inactivity and then having to focus and concentrate your energy and skill into a very few brief moments before the camera.

"This morning is a good example. We got a very early start on the day, arriving about 8:30. I showed the director my costume at about 10 o'clock. He had never seen it before. Then, I waited another couple of hours while another scene was completed. Then I talked about my scene with the director. Then, I waited for another three-quarters of an hour for the smoke to flow properly. And all this is in fairly uncomfortable conditions, the heat and all. And because of those conditions, everyone is exhausted before we begin. Then, suddenly, a lot of clouds appeared from nowhere. We had to pack

Juan Carlos Lopez Rodero, known to all as Kuki, finds that even
the best can't order the desert winds around.

Hundreds of burning tires were used to create the smoke
for the desert battle scenes.

all of that into two takes of forty seconds each. Now, that's what I mean by a difference in a rhythm of work. There was eighty seconds of work for me today, compared with an average of twelve hours of just being here."

Although he wasn't required to work on the first day of the location shooting, Stewart went out with his fellow actors "as a show of solidarity." He found the desert breathtaking. "It's got terrific style and elegance. David and I talked about that a little during that first morning. We both agreed that what is so appealing about it is that everything is so clean. Clean in the sense that its lines and outlines are so clearly defined. Nothing is blurred. I found that absolutely thrilling.

"But being here is misery, in fact. The day I spent working today was the most uncomfortable day of my life. It's harder for everyone who's wearing one of these rubber stillsuits. The suits just concentrate the heat. And today we were coping with thick black smoke as well, burning only a few yards away from us. They say that, in the sun, the temperature is between 120 and 130.

"It may seem as though I'm complaining but I think all those distasteful elements added to the strength of the scene. The heat, the discomfort, the intensity, all that terrible smoke. Coupling that with the fact that the director was expecting us to do everything within eighty seconds and you find yourself in a situation that's quite stimulating. We did two takes. That's it. Tomorrow we shall go back and do close-ups on the same scene.

"We never could have done that scene in that way in a rehearsal room or even on a stage. It wouldn't have been possible. Maybe after weeks of rehearsing we could have gotten that free. But, you see, reality was imposing itself on us today. Some of the time, Kyle and I were unable to speak during our reunion because of the clouds of black smoke. I was happy to have that to contend with, though. It was exactly the quality we needed for the scene. It's a moment where I come face to face with a man I've thought dead for two years. It was exciting. But, I will admit that I was jolly glad when it was over. Those eighty seconds of work left me more drained than anything I've done in a long time.

"Kyle and I rode home in the car together and we barely spoke for the hour's drive. Neither of us could really summon up the energy for conversation. It was a case of just withdrawing, drawing back inside yourself and conserving your energy."

The shooting in the desert puts a strain on everyone's stamina. When it is hot, it is scorching. When it is windy, it is fierce. When the sun sets, the air turns bitterly cold. If it rains, the desert sand is turned an entirely different color, causing a change in the shooting schedule and a week's postponement of some shots. Suffice it to say that everything that can go wrong, does.

Even Paul Smith, a veteran of desert landscapes, finds the going tough. "I live in Israel," he says. "I've shot in the desert. I know what deserts are like. But this film has wiped out all of my fantasies of ever working in the desert again. You know, the *Beau Geste* type of desert with oases and things? Forget it.

"David came up with some extra scenes for me to film out here. I wasn't sure what they were. They took me to the location on a three-wheeled buggy. It was the only thing that could take the steep upgrades of the dunes. We went down a dune and way across this expanse to where David was. He tells me that there's a battle scene that's going to be filmed and I'm part of it.

"I asked David, 'What do you want me to do?' David says, 'You see that sand dune over there?' It's about three hundred meters away and *everything* leading towards the camera is uphill. 'Now, what I want you to do is to come up over that sand dune. Behind you will be your army. You walk up to within eight feet of the camera and you will say this line of dialogue.'

"'Dialogue?' I said. 'Oh yeah. You have dialogue.' He pulls out a piece of paper and gives it to me. I'm still looking at that sand dune. 'David, that's an awfully long walk.'

"David looks at the sand dune. 'Can you make it?'

"I shrug. 'We'll see.' So, I go off to put my costume on. It's a killer. Have you ever tried to put your hand in a rubber glove when your hand is wet? The fingers just won't go in. It just pulls and pulls but nothing happens. Well, I put the first four layers of my costume on and got soaked. Like *that!*" He snaps his fingers to dramatize how little time had elapsed.

"I was, in fact, stretching the plastic. There was no give. There was no slide. I couldn't bend. Every time I moved I was pulling the material apart. I was covered with sweat. Anyhow, I get behind that dune and they finally call, 'Action!' I hop over one dune. I hop over another dune. I'm halfway to the camera when I stop for a minute. I look around.

"All my men have stopped, too, because they're all supposed to key in on my movements. I've had it. I'm halfway to the camera and I've had it. I bite my lip and go on. I get to about twenty-five steps from the camera and I know that there's not one more step left in me. I do the dialogue. I do it right. They love it. 'Cut.'

A wind machine will create a man-made sand storm.

The glamor of movie-making proves a myth as Paul Smith and his men
must move through the heat in heavy rubber suits.

Paul and Gurney are reunited during a desert battle.
At the end of the first day of desert shooting in extreme heat,
both actors were left completely exhausted.

"David comes up to me and says, 'Paul. It looks really good. I'd like to get you within eight feet of the camera. So, stay where you are. Just tell me when you're ready to go again. Catch your breath and say, "When." I need twenty more steps.'

"I'm pouring sweat. 'David. I'm not sure I can give you *ten!*' OK. I stand there for a few moments, resting. We start up again. It is excruciating. I bit the inside of my lip so bad that it bled . . . because I knew David needed it. I got twenty-three steps out of myself, not ten. I got there and did my lines. They printed it and applauded.

"I stood there, weaving. 'Get me a chair, quick.' I don't know whether you've ever had the feeling where you want to vomit and go to the bathroom at the same time and you just know that you're going to pass out? Well, I was determined this wasn't going to happen to me. They didn't get the chair in time so I just lay on my back in the sand and began unzipping my suit. People crowded around me. I just told them to leave me alone, I wasn't going to pass out, I just had to stay there for a while.

"They wanted to take me to the truck. I told them I'd go after a rest. After a few moments, I went down to the truck and they drove me over to my caravan, my dressing room. About two hours later, we came back for a close-up. The close-up was neat because they only needed me in the top half of my costume. I was standing there with the top half of this rubber suit on and my shorts. It was lovely. They're shooting the close-up and, suddenly, I toppled over on my back. Ever see a tree roll backwards? Everyone thought I had passed out. It wasn't that. I was standing on this incline on the side of the dune and the sand just started sliding from under my heels. I couldn't move because they were shooting my close-up so I was trying to balance as best as I could. Then, I just did a back flip. Man, did I laugh.

"That day two or three people fainted. They had real trouble that day."

"I feel sorry for the guys who have to wear those outfits," says Ian Woolf. "The Sardaukars and the Harkonnens. They're covered from head to toe. We're talking about 120 degrees at 12:30 in the afternoon and being dressed in rubber suits. Everyone was a real trooper, though. The funniest thing is that some of the extras we worked with came down from El Paso, Texas. They were all rowdy college kids. They were used to the heat. They had a great time. They just kept yelling, 'When are we going to kick some Harkonnen butt?' We were really lucky. Not many people passed out at all."

The cases of smoke inhalation, heat exhaustion and dehydration made the Juarez outing more of a lesson in survival than movie-making. Aside from the physical discomfort there were some very basic technical problems to cope with. "Things would have been more difficult for me, personally," says Freddie Francis, "without the light-flex system. I wanted certain textures, different colors to be seen on our desert. The light flex helped out tremendously. In terms of getting lamps or generators out to the location...that was fairly horrible."

The violent sandstorms and battles not filmed on location at Juarez were done at the Dead Dog Dump. Although a more geographically convenient location for most of the actors, it proved every bit as hellish as the sand dune locale. "We were there for nearly three weeks," says Everett McGill, who plays Stilgar, a Fremen leader and close comrade of Paul's.

"To simulate the sandstorms, they just pumped dust and dirt all over us. We're talking about tremendous volumes, too. Great

Between takes, the film's Fremen find no place to hide from the desert sun.

bags of dirt pumped across the set. So much that it gathered on rocks a full half-inch deep. They had to clean off the rocks in between shots. We were all just consuming this dust. Breathing it in. We weren't really prepared for it. So, I took a shampoo bottle and emptied it out. I put a wet t-shirt in it, cut out a hole in one end of the bottle and used it to breathe through. The dust was filtered away through the t-shirt. The t-shirt turned brown."

McGill's ingenuity impressed many of his fellow actors, who made do with conventional surgical masks. "I come from a family of farmers," he says. "We're a practical-minded people. We had a lot of wherewithal and we're always doing something with baling wire or string or glue.

"The most ironic aspect of shooting those sandstorm scenes with the Fremen was those stillsuits. The Fremen have designed those suits to be super-efficient. They're body air-conditioners and fluid recyclers. They keep you at an even temperature all the time and you never have any water loss. Well, when we were out in the desert and shooting at the Dead Dog Dump, the real-life suits were killing us. When we weren't sweating, we were freezing. If it wasn't for those Fremen suits, we all would have survived a lot better."

"Acting at the Dead Dog location wearing my stillsuit was pretty weird," states Kyle MacLachlan. "It's like wearing a big rubber band. Any movement, going from the normal body posture of standing erect with your arms at your sides, like raising your arms, is like pulling against a rubber band. There's a constant tension you're working against. After a while, you don't notice it because you're moving all the time. But when you finish for the day, you're twice as tired. Add to that the tremendous amount of dust being poured on top of us at 4 o'clock in the morning and the fact that we're wearing nose plugs and you have some idea of how much fun we had a lot of the times."

By midsummer, the actors breathed a collective sigh of relief. Most of the toughest desert scenes had been filmed, the Dead Dog Dump would be converted to a second Dune location and, for a while at least, the cast and crew would retreat to the relative luxury afforded by Churubusco's sound stages.

13.
THE SPECIAL EFFECTS
OF KIT WEST

The best special effects are the ones you don't notice.
Kit West, special visual effects

There are times when I look at things on the set
and I can't believe my eyes. The impossible
becomes possible almost every day.
Kyle MacLachlan, actor (Paul)

Sometimes we have to do things that, under normal
circumstances, would strike you as quite idiotic.
Francesca Annis, actress (Jessica)

Dune is not a special effects picture per se. Very little of its storyline actually relies on a single effect, weapon or creature in terms of dramatic impact. Its special effects are not constantly in the spotlight. Rather, they are subtly interwoven into the complex plotline to heighten its dramatic intensity. The characters and their adventures are the real focal points of the picture, while the special effects are used liberally to create a sense of realism.

Although many moviegoers are familiar with spectacular optical effects techniques such as stop motion animation (bringing an inanimate object to "life" by moving it a fraction of an inch at a time as the film is exposed one frame at a time), blue screen shots (combining live action with new backgrounds through the use of blue backing) and rotoscoping (tracing live action movements with animation techniques), not too many people think about a film's special physical effects: ingenius "little" tricks that, quite often, prove the backbone of a movie. For example:

When Paul tells his Fremen colleagues of the power of his weirding way, they are impressed not only by his words, but also by a very visual demonstration of its effects on solid matter.

When Duke Leto's loyal followers are caught unaware in the Arrakeen palace by Baron Harkonnen's minions, they embark on a space-age firefight using guns and other weaponry that reduce half of the castle corridors to pock-marked collages of smoke and fire.

When Paul is taught to heighten his fighting skills by his mentors, he is pitted against a multi-armed fighting robot which descends from the ceiling and spins and whirls, parrying and thrusting every movement its human opponent makes.

Special physical effects.

The man responsible for all the physical effects of *Dune*, from explosions to weird weaponry, is Kit West. A bearded, rotund British artist, West started out as a cameraman at a documentary company before gradually becoming adept at visual wizardry by working for a television commercial house in England.

Eventually, he abandoned his normal camerawork and, after serving an apprenticeship on dozens of low-budgeted horror, science fiction and adventure films, graduated to major features. He has concocted, over the years, virtually every kind of bizarre on-set effect imaginable. Most recently, West won an Oscar for his work on *Raiders of the Lost Ark*.

Basically, it is West's job to create a host of eye-boggling stunts that can be carried out "live," while the cameras are running. Spaceships, laser zaps and larger-than-life monster worms will be created using different optical effects in post-production, long after live-action photography has been completed. West's brand of magic, however, is one the actors can see in the here and now. It's an almost mathematical endeavor, requiring technical savvy, imagination, ingenuity and an uncanny sense of timing.

Kit West is sitting at his desk in his small office when one of his assistants trots in to tell him that David Lynch needs him on the set immediately.

"Oh God," he moans. West scurries over to a sietch set where several extras dressed as Fremen are standing in front of an earth-colored wall. In the scene, they will be testing their use of the "Weirding Way" with Fremen sound guns. When they point their weapons at the wall, the earth will shake (thanks to a jiggling camera), and a large overhanging section of the wall will explode after being bombarded by the sound rays.

This apparently simple plan is complicated immensely by the fact that the scene has only been added to the script that week and the wall to be blown up was not originally built to explode. Fortunately, the structure is, by and large, made of packed styrofoam.

Kit West carries the discarded tires used to create the fires during <u>Dune</u>'s battle scenes.

West is all over the set. He supervises the boring of deep holes into the structure of the wall. The holes have to be placed strategically so that, when the charges placed inside ignite, the wall will blow up both harmlessly and dramatically.

Steel rods are driven into the wall. Lengths of explosives that will be set off by remote control are then planted.

West backs off as Lynch rehearses the actors. Lynch wants to see them react to the sound of a starter's pistol going off in order to gauge their physical reaction to a sudden, violent explosion. Lynch hands Kuki the gun. Kuki points it carefully in the air. He squeezes the trigger. Everyone holds their breath. The gun doesn't go off. After a few false tries, the gun works. Blam! The actors react fairly well. Lynch coaxes them in terms of acting startled and actually jumping without leaving their assigned positions before the camera.

Earplugs are handed out on the set. The crew and all bystanders either use plugs or hold their fingers in their ears as Kit West pre-

An elaborate pyrotechnic set-up was required to stage the
invasion of the palace of Arrakeen by the Baron's Harkonnen horde.
This fight scene was staged at the Dead Dog Dump.

pares the charges. Lynch has to get the shot "one off," filmed on the first take. If something goes wrong, either on the acting or effects end, a whole new section of wall will have to be reattached to the set—a big time delay—for a second try or the shot will have to be dropped altogether.

The cameras roll. The Fremen point their weapon at the wall. They begin to tremble. A lever is thrown. The explosives ignite. The wall blows apart in a smokey roar. The actors don't have to pretend to be startled. . . . they *are* startled. . . . as are most of the cast and crew on the set. Shards of styrofoam wall fly everywhere as huge hunks of the sietch collapse onto the floor scant inches in front of the extras. The smell of sulfur fills the room.

It's a flawless take.

West tarries on the set for a moment, watching the workers carry the larger hunks of the wall off the floor while the camera angles are switched for the close-up reaction shots.

West turns and walks back to his small office. He plops himself into a chair. Outside the glass wall lining one side of his cubicle, local workers create new weapons and props.

"A tricky movie," he states. "Tricky. It's a very big challenge in terms of scope. There are some very unusual effects that won't be apparent on the screen.

"Our battle scenes, for instance, are very big but they won't resemble conventional battles, the ones you see in war films. Many of them will be a massive combination of all the effects departments on this picture, the opticals and the model people and the blue backing. We've also got quite a few live-action battles. We've tackled some already and we've still got a lot to go.

"I have to go back to the desert in a month or so because when we went up there the first time, we were rained out. We had some very heavy storms and the sand changed color completely. It didn't look like the same location. It certainly didn't look like a hot desert. It almost turned to mud."

He shrugs his shoulders and grins. "Everything is a challenge on a movie like this. Like that scene we just did, the blowing up of the wall? Not really simple at all. There are a lot of explosions and fires and people blowing up on this movie and we are trying desperately to give the pyrotechnics a different look; something different from either the World War II–type movies or the *Star Wars*–type films which, usually, add a lot more sparks to their explosions.

"But, as you just saw, our weapons aren't laser guns and things. Most of the weapons use sound waves. The weapons will be pointed at an object and, then, the object will blow. There won't be ray-gun effects added later, just sound effects. Our explosions, as a result, have to be sudden, and, uh, *explosive*."

What intrigued West most about the script for *Dune* was the fact that some very extraordinary occurrences are treated very ordinarily. "You're just expected to accept all these weird things on the screen as commonplace," West states. "So, we have to come up with ways of accomplishing these tasks that look *un*spectacular in a movie sense."

As an example, West cites the flights of fancy literally performed by the bloated Baron. Whereas other villains may stalk or waddle or march across a room, the Baron simply glides, floating above the surface of his oily techno-realm.

"We've had to make him do incredible things," West says. "You see, the Baron floats about eighteen inches off the ground throughout the entire picture. But, he has to float in conjunction with talking and walking, too. It has to be smooth.

"That's not an easy job to accomplish under any circumstance. The sets of Giedi Prime were no help, either. We have a thirty-five-foot-high row of steps that the Baron comes down while talking to someone. When he gets to the bottom, he turns and goes down another flight of steps. That was a big problem inasmuch as we didn't have a lot of height in the ceiling on that stage. We were restricted into what kind of overhead rigging we could build.

"I had the help of the boy who did the wire web for me on *Return of the Jedi*. I was pleased when he agreed to work on this movie with me. His name is John Stirber and he's been a tremendous asset.

"Basically, to get the Baron to fly we used a body harness suspended by wires and guided by an overhead tracking system. Because the sets were designed to be very enclosed we had to monitor everything over closed-circuit television. There are about a half-dozen people working controls, pulling ropes and wires to get him to float smoothly down the stairway without touching the stairs. It's a diagonal angle, too, so it was tricky. Everyone had their own monitor in front of them and had to watch certain points. Again, when you see this on the screen it won't be a spectacular effect, like a building blowing up. You'll just accept this fellow floating about."

Although wire harnesses have been used in films and stage productions for years, West believes this is the most intricate usage conceived to date. The rigging proved a real challenge to set up. In designing and construction, West had to worry not only about the Baron's varied movements, but also the villain's weight.

Kenneth McMillan, in his floating harness, with wire expert John Stirber.

The Baron slowly rises to the ceiling during a conversation with his "doctor."

The Baron, laughing maniacally, flies through the air,
thanks to an elaborate overhead tracking system.

Says West, "We had to be very careful. When the Baron is finally
all suited up, he weighs something like three hundred and fifty
pounds. We wanted to use the thinnest possible wires to make
things easier for the camera's point of view but, for safety's sake,
we had to use wires thick enough to support that weight.

At least fifty percent of the finished harness movements' realism
depended on the reaction of actor McMillan to the setup. If he hung
from the harness like a large, round, inanimate object, the Baron,
in the finished movie, would not seem so much a villain as a human
water balloon poised to drop on an unsuspecting hero's head at any
moment.

"Ken was wonderful," West says. "We met in Los Angeles months
before he went down to the set. We talked and he got a sense about
my devotion to my work. He was pretty confident of my being able
to pull this off so he wasn't really scared when he first stepped into
the rigging. We hung him quite a few times in his harness up in
Los Angeles while they were fitting him for his costume. He was
getting more and more used to it. We had him down here for about
three or four days before shooting and gave him daily practice ses-
sions. By the time we were ready to shoot, he was confident enough

in the harness to concentrate on his acting. He was marvelous. He concentrated on being evil and he left moving himself about to us. There are some movements there that could have been frightening, too. At one point, we fly him very quickly from eighteen inches up to twenty feet and, then, fly him backwards across the set at great speed. He loved it all."

For some of the Baron's more intimate shots, in which he is seen only from the waist up, West was able to "cheat" a bit. "For the close-ups, we didn't want to risk showing the wires so we had a special trolley built. He's not standing in it, exactly. He's suspended in it around the waist, like a big roly-poly doll. It gives him a sort of back and forth floating movement. The bit around his waist is really like a cradle. For the close-up scenes, we had someone manually pull this trolley around off-camera. All you can see on the screen is the Baron apparently gliding across the room, swaying slightly."

West believes that the flying scenes will be one of the movie's highpoints. "It's absolute choreography," he says. "You see, every movement required overhead rails for the rigging. David and I rehearsed everything with a stand-in a month before we actually filmed. We had to have all the moves plotted in terms of the Baron's relationship to other people, props, et cetera. It had to be worked out in tremendous detail. It was one of the major problems of this picture and I'm very pleased to say that I'm delighted with what I've seen in the dailies."

West resorted to wires and other traditional "live" effects in another dramatic section of the film. When Duke Leto and his family first land on the planet Dune, they are confronted by a people that may or may not be hostile to the newcomers.

At one point, Paul is readying himself for sleep when the headboard of his bed slides open and a floating weapon, a hunter-seeker, emerges. This device, which resembles a free-floating hypodermic needle, is supposed to hover around the room. Motion-activated, it will puncture its victim if the hapless human makes the slightest move. In the film, the Shadout Mapes [played by Linda Hunt] blunders into Paul's room and the flying weapon aims straight for her. As it does so, Paul, in a bravado showing of catlike reflexes, snatches the lethal satellite from its path, midair, and smashes it into a wall. It explodes and disintegrates.

"That had to be plotted very carefully," says West, "because, again, it was a sequence where we were creating a very strange effect without reverting to any opticals at all. The hunter-seeker is a quite menacing-looking device. We had to sit down with David before the shot and say, 'Now, where do you want this thing to go, because there will be actors in its path and we've got to use various techniques.'

"In the scene, the thing is supposed to leave the headboard, float, turn, focus on someone, turn away, float a bit more and, then, when the door to the room is opened, turn and dive at the door at a tremendous rate. It is during that final pass that Paul snatches it out of the air and smashes it, breaking its poisonous nosecone.

"We finally worked it all out using fine wires. We projected the weapon along wires using compressed air. In other shots, we had it suspended from wires, marionette-style. For the shots where it has to move along, rise and, then, move along again, we had it mounted on a special white sheet of glass that was, in turn, placed on a frame that was motorized. The frame moved the glass up and down and from side to side. Paul is seen standing there next to this thing so this simple trick looks really effective."

The glass frame couldn't be used in the long shot in which Paul is required to snatch and smash the evil projectile, however. "That's

Paul is threatened by a hunter-seeker,
a murderous needle-like device built by Kit West.

when we used the compressed air and the wire," says West. "We had Kyle rehearse with the setup a few times to get his timing down. A thin wire ran by him and we just shot the hunter-seeker past him via compressed air. As it zips by, he grabs it. And the moment he grabs it, we cut this very thin wire loose so the hunter-seeker is now free and Kyle can carry on and smash the thing against the wall. That took quite a bit of timing."

Many of the effects generated by West for *Dune* require the actors to participate directly. If they are not physically handling devices that are part of the effects process, they are reacting to various examples of pyrotechnic wizardry. West realizes that, no matter how dramatic the effect may be technically, if the actors react inappropriately, the scene will lose all of its cinematic clout.

For that reason, he tries to meet and discuss the scenes beforehand with all the people involved, whenever possible.

"Some actors get very nervous and overreact to physical effects," he says. "You find some that get so petrified that they miss their cue or mess things up. At that point, you find yourself with an explosion that's gone off and a shot that's ruined.

"For that reason, I try to rehearse as often as possible. Sometimes, however, time just doesn't permit that or some other technicality arises that prevents a lot of rehearsing. Take this morning. That's just one example of a lot of the explosions we're doing. They have to be done one-off because you're blowing up part of a set that would take a week to rebuild.

"I don't fault any actor who is frightened of an explosion. That's quite understandable. Some actors have never been in a picture where there's even been a gun fired. I did one film where they handed an actor a machine gun filled with blanks. He pulled the trigger and the whole gun just flew out of his hand. He didn't know anything about the vibrations or the kick.

"The trick is to talk to these people as much as possible about what they're going to do. Now, in this movie, Kyle has been subjected to quite a few squibs [small explosive pellets that can be set off to simulate a variety of effects, from bullet holes in wood, to ricochets off rock, to gunshot wounds in the chest] and quite a few explosions so far. We chatted with him about everything and he's come through it quite well.

"This morning, we blew a section of a robot off. Kyle was on the set again. He's quite used to the robots by now and that, in itself, is a show of his determination."

West points to a drawing of a strange, cylindrical machine hanging from a wall. "That's one of our little creations," he chuckles.

David Lynch watches as a group of Fremen blow up a sietch wall, thanks to explosive charges installed by Kit West.

Before departing Caladan, Paul trains with a fighter robot.

"One of the training robots. In the movie, Paul is taught how to fight using these things. He has to match it by using his bodily skills and, later, his voice.

"The robot is supposed to be fully mechanized. Spears fly out of it, swords and stuff. It lowers itself down from the ceiling and then rotates to and fro, following Kyle. It's his job to outwit it.

"We built the thing out of wood and ran it with radio controls and compressed air. It was quite complicated. Again, Kyle's scenes with the robots had to be choreographed because, if he or one of the operators was a little out of line, one of the spears could have gotten him. We built a couple of models. The one used for the fighting scenes was fully mechanized.

"We had about five operators working the thing simultaneously. The trick was that the battle had to take place within this fighting circle. It was sort of like a miniature bull ring. We really worked hard at coordinating the moves for that sequence. David then came in, turned on the cameras and we got the whole master shot [the main shot] in one take. We were very lucky on that one.

"For the sequence we did this morning, with part of the robot blowing up, we used a less mechanized, balsa-wood model."

The bearded effects expert begins to grow animated in his chair, gesticulating as he recalls one of the biggest scenes in the movie he has filmed thus far.

"At the end of the movie, there's an explosion that takes place outside the Emperor's steel tent that's sort of like a thermonuclear blast," he reveals. "We filmed a scene inside the tent that was supposedly taking place at the same time as this blast is going off right outside. The Baron is left alone with Paul's little sister, Alia. She's quite a little devil. She grabs the tubes that activate his suspensor belt and pulls them out. That sends him into a sort of dizzying spiral because his flotation device is now totally out of control.

"At that point, with him spinning wildly, the atomic explosion goes off outside. That creates an implosion on our set. In other words, the explosion doesn't blow *in* to the Baron's room. The entire wall is sucked *out* into this vacuum caused by the atomic explosion. The Baron is then just sucked right out."

Kit West chuckles to himself. "Now *that* was a tricky one because we couldn't actually use any explosives. Explosives would wind up blowing everything *into* the room. We had to have the complete wall prepared with a series of air rams and wire rigs. When the 'explosion' goes off outside, the whole wall is, thus, sucked away from the camera and out into the void across the stage. We, literally, just yanked the thing off the stage.

The crew plants explosive charges in special
lightweight models of the training robots.

"In the movie, you will see the Baron spiraling into this explosion
outside. That will be done using blue screen [a process wherein one
element in the frame of film—in this case, the spiraling Baron—
will be placed onto another background optically, via the use of a
neutral, or blue, screen]. In a separate setup, we filmed the Baron's
body twirling. We had him spinning on wires. The camera was
mounted on a special rig which made the camera whirl round and
round. The camera was spinning in one direction and we had Ken
spinning in another. The camera, then, trucked quickly away from
him. So, when you print that over the shot that I did with the
implosion, you will see the wall blow away first and, then, the
spinning Baron going after it. Then, he will be swallowed by one

of the large sandworms approaching the tent from the outside.

"Now, during our actual implosion setup, after the Baron goes flying through the hole, little Alia is also sucked towards the wall. She doesn't get sucked out, though. She gets tangled in a section of the tent left intact. So, we had to do a shot of her being propelled through space. She zips across the room, hits a wall and slides down. We couldn't use a real person for that so we actually made a small articulated dummy. We rigged it on a wire with a shock cord. When we hit the release she was shot straight across the room at the wall. The moment she hit the wall we cut the wire and she slid down naturally. Because the dummy was so articulated, it had a collapsing movement which worked quite nicely. We filmed it very quickly. She was really snapped against that wall. All her joints just quivered with the impact. We filmed at twice the normal speed to bring it back to reality when the film is projected. Anybody hitting that wall that hard would kill themselves, of course, but, as I said, this kid is pretty strange."

Another call from the set and Kit West is off and running yet again. Another sietch set. Another explosion. En route to a date with pyrotechnic destiny, the master craftsman describes his work on *Dune* thus: "Of all the movies I've ever worked on, this is the first that I've gone through all the cards for. I've used very nearly every trick that I have learned, or am learning, that exists in the book. And," he adds stepping onto the sound stage, "quite a few that don't."

14.
D-DAY AND
SUMMER MADNESS

*There were sometimes two hundred people
on the other side of the camera while
you were doing your scene. It never really bothered
you, though, because of David.
His concentration is never broken.*
Linda Hunt, actress (Shadout Mapes)

*We've had so many visitors on the set that, in a sense,
we've been previewing the movie as it's being made.*
Anne Strick, unit publicist

*It got to be pretty funny, at times. You'd be filming a scene
and in would march all these people with DUNE tote bags.*
David Lynch, director

The month of June brought a certain brand of hyperkinetic insanity that had, heretofore, not been seen on the Churubusco lot. The movie was approaching the halfway point in live-action shooting. Construction was at a frenzy, with workers beginning the building of large, wooden structures that would, eventually, be fashioned into sections of towering sandworms.

The Mexican summer weather showed itself unsympathetic to the filming, offering hot and dry mornings, cloud-littered afternoons and, more often than not, rainy evenings.

The production schedule called for one of the most grueling on-the-set scenes to be filmed, the final combat in the Great Hall between Paul and evil Feyd. Most of the movie's principal characters as well as a few hundred extras had to be assembled for the confrontation. The climactic scene took over a week and a half to complete because it featured, among other things, a blood-curdling battle,

155

the Emperor's ceremonial entrance and pages upon pages of spoken dialogue.

June would mark the departure of such actors as Sting and Kenneth McMillan from the project. It would also mark the arrival of magazine writers, marketing executives and movie exhibitors to the lot. *Dune* was finally available for inspection by V.I.P.s who would eventually tout the movie, either in theaters or in print.

As a result, a certain sense of (barely) controlled pandemonium reigned for the month. The lot was always crowded with costumed extras, curious visitors, harried construction crews and hungry stray dogs. Not exactly a glamorous environment, but a productive one.

Sting is lying, sprawled on his back, on a small platform that has been made to resemble a section of the floor in the Great Hall. A knife is embedded in his neck, the result of a battle with Kyle MacLachlan filmed a day earlier. In this close-up shot, the results of Paul Atreides' deadly aim will be seen.

On cue, both Sting's chest and the ground beneath his body will split open with a hideous "c-c-c-c-crack." It is a time-consuming scene and a tricky one. The actor/musician must remain in position,

**In the Great Hall of Arrakeen, Paul and Feyd
face each other for the film's climactic fight scene.**

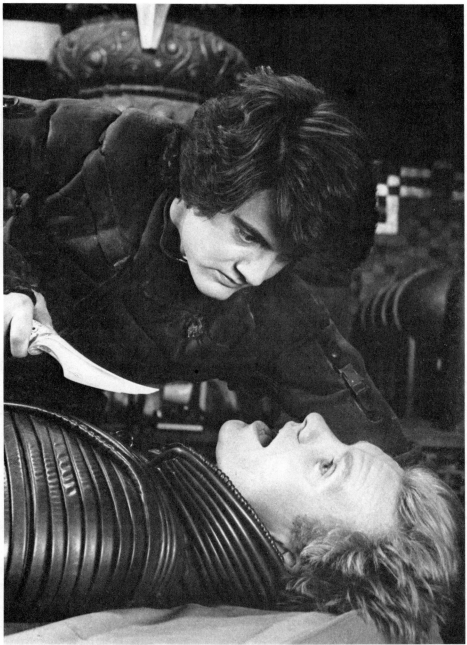
Paul watches as Feyd breathes his last.

patiently, while workers place towels beneath his neck and torso to
give his body the proper angle needed for the camera.

David Lynch supervises it all. "Could we have a little more
blood?" Blood is poured in the actor's mouth and over his lips.
"Now you're talkin'," Lynch nods, grinning.

The knife is carefully placed at an angle that, while seemingly
exaggerated to the naked eye, will look perfectly normal albeit lethal
on the screen.

"Action."

Feyd's body lies motionless. Suddenly. Splat! His chest explodes.
The ground trembles and splits open, thanks to a crew of technicians
pulling it apart from below.

It's a take. Sting sits up slowly and wipes the foul-tasting artificial
blood off his lips. Tomorrow, he will be in the Great Hall, on the
ground, while Kyle MacLachlan delivers a speech to the assembled
multitudes who have just "witnessed" the fatal encounter.

Sting will leave the following day to rehearse with his rock group,
the Police, for a tour that will take them into every major city in
America. It will be difficult for the actor to shift mental gears, returning to the world of rock from the world of rottenness. His character, Feyd, has proven himself to be a virtual renaissance man when
it comes to aberrant behavior. During the course of the movie, he
has tortured and he has killed. He has carried around a shaved cat
in a cage just to please the Baron. He has frolicked in a steaming
shower wearing nothing more than a green leather codpiece and a
smile while planning world annihilation. He has fought and he has
plotted. In short, he has graduated with honors from Screen Villainy
101 School.

Understandably, Sting is now exhausted. He is, however, pleased
with his stint in Mexico.

"It wasn't a difficult role," he explains. "It wasn't a large part.
It wasn't like playing the lead role, with a lot of emotional ups and
downs. My character is pretty consistent. I have one thing in mind
throughout the movie . . . me.

"Feyd is a villain. But he probably thinks he's a hero. He probably
considers himself perfectly honorable and wonderful. There is a side
to the evil psyche that allows it to think it's good. Feyd is certainly
perverse . . . but only in our viewpoint. He's quite normal in terms
of his environment. He comes from a pretty weird planet. God
knows what his mother is like. His uncle is certainly a bit off."

Taking into account his own bloody demise as well as the carnage
he causes throughout the movie, Sting confesses, "I don't know

Sting models one of his
more eye-catching outfits.
Says Sting of his character:
"Feyd is evil...with a large jockstrap."

about anybody else, but I'm pretty squeamish about those kinds of things. I think David is using the violence. It's part of his vision to bring us to a sense of reality. So, we're caught between wanting to entertain an audience and wanting to remind them of reality.

"I'm quite happy being mean. I don't particularly want to do nice roles. I really don't. I think we've got enough of those around."

With McMillan and most of the key villains ready to depart the studio, the mood on the lot right now is almost like that of a graduation exercise. The Baron is in the process of being sucked out of a huge hole in the wall of a vast, golden spaceship set. Sting, for one, will mourn his passing.

"Ken McMillan is probably the best actor I've ever worked with," he marvels. "He's totally believable and professional. When he's floating down the stairs on wires, when he's flying, you don't think twice about it. When he's grinning at me licentiously, he means it. Acting with him is a dream. All you have to do is look into his eyes and tell the truth. Our scenes are very strange ones but, then again, I'm not interested in acting in movies that are mundane.

"The hardest part of the movie for me has been the waiting. Ken had to spend hours and hours on end being made up. I had all my musical equipment with me in my dressing room so I'd amuse myself for hours on end playing with that while waiting to be called on the set."

Sting acknowledges that acting in scenes with close to a thousand extras can get a bit out-of-control at times but he adds, "I was never really discouraged. It takes an elephant gun to stop me from doing anything...and they couldn't get one of those through customs."

With only a day left in character, Sting reflects on his intergalactic villain role. "Feyd is evil...with a large jockstrap. I think Feyd is the product of inbreeding within the ranks of the Harkonnen upper classes for a few hundred years. He's intense, rotten and quite deadly...but he has a good side."

Sting smiles diabolically. "But you don't see that in the movie. I think he likes...animals."

Molly Wryn, who plays the Freman Harah, is awaiting her cue to enter the Great Hall, to take her place in the massive, final scene. She, too, remembers the Baron with fondness. "It was really frightening watching the scenes with the Baron. Ken stays so intense between shots. He's a madman.

"Offstage, he's a lot of fun. I was really amazed. He's taking people's pictures in the hall and messing around. He's wonderful. But when he's before the cameras, he is so *evil*.

"Ken's generous, too. When he dies, Alia (Alicia Roanne Witt) has to walk up to him and rip his belt off. She pushes him away and he just takes off into space. That scene took a lot of time to film because Alicia was afraid of falling over. They did it over and over again. But Ken was very patient. He just stayed right in there and he worked. He really coaxed the scene out of Alicia."

The mood on the Great Hall set is tense. The movements of a few hundred people have to be coordinated, but their costumes make it exceptionally difficult. The elderly men playing the Fremen monks have a rough time handling their turns.

David Lynch tries to be philosophical about the time it takes to set up certain portions of the scene. "Those robes must be murder," he says. "I bet you could kill yourself trying to negotiate a flight of stairs."

Later, one of the monks leans back to sit in his canvas chair. The chair, however, is not there. Because of his robe's thickness, the monk does not realize he's sitting on air until he is halfway down to the ground. He lands with a thud.

Alicia Roanne Witt, looking almost as devilish as she does when in character as Alia, bursts into stifled giggles.

The monk mutters something in Spanish. It is not "Have a nice day."

There are long delays on the set as extras are lined up and positioned and repositioned. Actors stand in front of huge fans to cool off. This, in turn, musses their hair. Hairdressers are brought in to recomb the offending locks. When the scene is delayed again, the actors step in front of the fans again. When the scene is ready to be shot, the actors are not, because their hair is mussed anew. And so it goes. For an entire afternoon.

Sean Young undoes the top of her stillsuit and begins doing limbering-up exercise. An avid dancer, Sean jangles her arms out at her side in the stifling heat. "I do this so I don't let the energy die...ever," she explains. "That's the power. That's the force. If you keep that energy with you then you'll have it as soon as they start that camera going.

"We all get through these delays in different ways. We all prepare for our scenes in different ways. Everett McGill doesn't say a word. He is the quietest person on the set. He meditates. He gets so quiet, it's incredible. That's what works for him.

"Me? I try to get my energy level revved up so I have that extra kick."

At one point in the scene, Alicia as Alia, dressed in a miniature version of the Reverend Mother's robe, must "walk" out to meet her brother, Paul. Right before the scene is to be shot, the little girl is hoisted on top of a small, skateboardlike platform. Alicia kneels on the platform. Her robe is spread around her feet so they won't be noticeable under the gown's train. When "action" is yelled, the young actress does not actually walk to her brother but, rather, is *pulled* towards Paul by a technician out of camera range.

Explains Sean Young: "When David first saw Alicia, he knew she was perfect for the role...and she is. When she's in costume, she *is* Alia. She has the most wonderful face. The only problem is

Juan Carlos Lopez Rodero places a kneeling Alia on a platform that will be pulled and rocked across the set to simulate a walking motion.

Alia gets the best of the evil Baron.

that Alicia is eight years old and a little too tall for the height Alia really should be.

"So, for all the faraway shots, David hired a double for Alicia who is maybe three years old. Real young and real short. For the close-up scenes, Alicia kneels on her little platform. They dress her down while she's kneeling. There's a wire connected to the bottom of the platform and a fellow behind the camera pulls her along. You never really sees her feet in those shots. When she's pulled along, she just sort of rocks back and forth like she's walking. She's gotten really good at it."

As the activity on the set increases, the behind-the-scenes action heats up as well.

Publicist Anne Strick is preparing for D-Day...*Dune* day. Actually, D-Day will last three days, during which over eighty movie exhibitors (the people who book films into theaters) will be flown down to Mexico City to experience, firsthand, the Universe of Dune. They are to be greeted at the airport by special *Dune* hostesses. There will be a large *Welcome to Dune* banner unfurled at their hotel.

They will be given *Dune* tote bags. *Dune* tequila. They will be taken on a tour of the entire Churubusco complex, and shuttled onto stages while David Lynch is filming scenes. They will dine with the stars and the production executives. They will be given demonstrations of explosions and special effects on the Churubusco back lot. For three days, a sound stage will be turned into a *Dune* memorabilia display, showcasing props, paintings and costumes. Skits will be performed on empty sets using fully costumed extras.

The person responsible for the logistics of this invasion is Anne Strick. She is taking it all in stride. "It's a business unto itself," she acknowledges. "But it's harmonious with the making of the movie. Although the big tour is screwing up the schedule a little because we've had to stop one set from being destroyed."

Strick is being characteristically nonchalant about the whole affair. In effect, she has been asked to turn the *Dune* location into a theme park for the three D-Days while the film continues to be made. Whipping the studio into shape while constructing various displays and juggling her duties as publicity chief is not easy. There are myriads of foul-ups to circumvent. The visit by the exhibitors is top priority because, if they can be excited by the premise of a *Dune* movie now, they will be even more excited when the finished film is actually released, approximately eighteen months down the line.

The pressure is on.

Five beautiful transparencies selected to be blown up into huge photographic posters to hang on the stages for the grand tour arrive from the printers two days before the tour is scheduled to commence. They are the right size but out of focus. The situation is tentatively remedied when it is decided to hang them, mounted, above eye level. Hopefully, visitors gazing *up* at them will not notice the fuzziness, just the crick in their necks.

A hundred assistants are recruited to help coordinate D-Day. They turn out to be of less help than expected. Two assistants volunteer to help the art department organize their displays. The art department is very pleased, of course, and ask their newfound assistants what they do best. Could they help paint? No, they reply. Could they use a hammer? No. Could they mount pictures? No. Well, then, what *could* they do? The pair smile beatifically. "We *assist!*"

In the week before *Dune* Day, bizarre requests become commonplace. One hundred fifty plain umbrellas are called for. The worker sent out on this mission, returns empty-handed, stating that in all of Mexico, there are only umbrellas with floral prints.

Two days before the big day, a memo is sent out reminding all relevant personnel that it is imperative that all bathrooms be supplied with toilet paper and towels by 9 a.m. on Friday, D-Day.

D-Day arrives. So do the exhibitors. They are wined and dined and given the grand intergalactic treatment. They leave impressed, secure in the knowledge that *Dune* will, indeed, be a very special motion picture event.

Their visit marks a dramatic change in the routine of making *Dune*. Because the movie will no longer be kept a top-secret project, a small but steady stream of reporters, magazine writers and merchandising executives will be allowed to wander about the set. The *Dune* set tours will continue, in one form or another, for another two months. In essence, *Dune* will be *sold* as it is being shot.

"Pretty strange, eh?" David Lynch smiles. "Exciting, though."

15.
A CONVERSATION WITH PAUL ATREIDES

The young actor who is playing Paul? It's fascinating.
He claims that DUNE has been his Bible.
He's read it every year since he was fourteen.
Frank Herbert, author of DUNE

This is Kyle's first film. He seems to be doing very well.
He's done stage so he knows what acting is all about.
Max Von Sydow, actor (Dr. Kynes)

I'm awed by the newness of it, coming into a movie having
never done one before. Then again, I'm an old friend of Paul's.
I feel like I know him. In a sense, I am Paul.
Kyle MacLachlan, actor (Paul)

Kyle MacLachlan stands on the platform positioned at the front of the underground sietch set. Dressed in a dirt-spattered stillsuit, he stands at attention in front of a large "stone" pyramid. MacLachlan has just delivered a speech to the Fremen troops, explaining to them that they have at their command a powerful weapon virtually unstoppable by any technologically advanced army...the organic weirding way.

In the script, Paul turns to the pyramid, crouches in a martial arts pose and, using only his voice (modified via the use of an amplification device, a weirding module), shatters the stone structure into thousands of pieces.

On the set, Kyle MacLachlan is facing the rubber molded object bravely. Every crewmember behind him is wearing earplugs. Those closest to the pyramid are wearing goggles as well. The triangular structure has been wired with explosives. A huge, compressed-air gun has been placed beside the camera. On a given signal, the

Paul prepares for his first worm ride, maker hook in hand.
In the foreground is a thumper, a pulsating device that attracts worms.

charges will go off and the air cannon will roar, blasting the pieces
of the fragmenting pyramid off to one side.

Kyle braces himself for the scene to begin. Director David Lynch,
cameraman Freddie Francis, effects supervisor Kit West and the rest
of the crew are having trouble communicating verbally because they
are all wearing earplugs. They rely on hand signals.

"Action" is both called and signaled.

Kyle stands motionless before the pyramid.

The charges are set off.

The air cannon roars.

A flash of light. A peal of thunder.

The pyramid explodes...sort of. Actually, it *im*plodes. The
structure expands and contracts. Several large hunks of it fly into
the air. Shards from the top shoot everywhere. A small fleck of the
hardened rubber strikes the actor under the eye. He does not flinch.

Clouds of sulfur fill the small set. The base of the pyramid remains stubbornly intact. "Cut. Cut."

Paul uses the weirding module to set off an explosion that was actually created by a combination of pre-set explosive charges and an off-camera air cannon.

The scene will have to be redone with another pyramid. But, first, the set has to be cleaned up.

Kit West is not too pleased. "We tried blowing one of these up before and it worked. I know exactly what happened. You see, we used this special material so that when it blew, if it hit anybody, it wouldn't hurt them. It was a special expanding polyurethane. To paint it, they had to surface it. We told them not to surface it in glass because, again, if it hit someone it would hurt. So, we surfaced it with something called whitewash. It's a thick powder that you put on the outside of walls. You mix it with water. If you don't mix in enough water, however, it stays really thick. I guess the coating on this was just too thick. It acted like an elastic. We'll add more explosives to the next one. Maybe fifty percent more."

MacLachlan traipses off to a small dressing room located outside the stage, next to a large generator. He attempts to relax for a few minutes. The generator belches steadily not ten feet away, sounding like a World War II fighter plane just hit by enemy fire. MacLachlan

Paul and Stilgar in their stillsuits.

eases his stillsuited body into a rickety, wooden chair while several crewmembers struggle by, a second black pyramid in their hands. MacLachlan notes their passage and grins.

The young actor is anything but discouraged. This is his first starring role. Coincidentally, this is also his first film...ever. He is understandably excited by the experience. Even more so because he is an unabashed fan of the Frank Herbert novel. The entire experience is striking him as a phantasmagoric excursion into sight and sound. When a scene gets flubbed, as has just happened, he just shrugs it off.

When asked how it feels to stand unprotected before a pyramid that is supposed to blow up while the rest of his peers are protected with earplugs and goggles, he just shrugs. "What goes through my mind?" he smiles. "Well, mainly, I just try to be as smooth as I can. I don't want it to be my screw-up that causes us to do the scene again. I make sure I do my job. I let the technicians take care of theirs. I don't even think beyond what I have to do. I just let them blow it up and then whatever happens happens.

"It was a little frightening just now. I saw this thing just taking off and I felt that shard hit my face. I closed my eyes really quickly."

Despite *Dune*'s pyrotechnic displays, eye-boggling special effects and internationally famous cast, the focal point of the entire film is the character of Paul Atreides, the son of a Duke who is transformed into a space-age Messiah by film's end. In a sense, a lot of the movie's effectiveness is resting on the performance of rookie film actor MacLachlan.

"That aspect of the movie hasn't really hit me yet," he says. "I'm too caught up in the story. I'm too caught up in the fact that, finally, *Dune* is being made into a movie. I mean, as a fan, I've been waiting for this for years. Now, as an actor, I want to make sure that Paul Atreides is everything that a *Dune* fan expects."

More than any other person in either the cast or crew of this production, Washington-born Kyle MacLachlan has a very solid emotional attachment to the subject matter. "It's difficult to sum up how I feel about Paul," he begins. "What makes it hard is the fact that I first read the novel when I was fourteen. Paul immediately became a heroic figure for me.

"When you're thirteen or fourteen, you're going through all these little changes. You're looking for a direction. And Paul happened to be one of the 'people' I latched on to for direction. He steered me for a while until I went on to something else. But, for a while, he was a hero figure for me.

"He's well trained physically and mentally, which makes him a real role model. But he's also complex. There are two people in his personality. There's Paul Atreides, who is a life supporter, and there's his mystical other self, Muad'Dib, the one the Fremen call their leader. Muad'Dib is the one who can be the angry god...who can kill a small number of people so that a larger number will survive.

"The one thing that David and I are trying to get away from in the movie is the concept that killing is good, that absolute power is good. There's a line in the movie, Paul says, 'Whoever can destroy a thing controls a thing.' That's scary to me. I mean, in this day and age, with nuclear warfare a possibility, whoever can destroy the world controls it. That's not really a positive statement.

"David and I are trying to concentrate more on the life-affirming elements of Paul and less on the fact that he is now the leader of the universe. Paul is really a prisoner of his destiny, you know. He's the kind of person you look up to but feel sorry for at the same time."

This basic sense of humanity might seem a fragile gem to try to preserve in a movie the size of *Dune*. "The size of the movie doesn't intimidate me at all," Kyle laughs. "I mean, I've never done a movie before, right? So this seems quite natural to me. This is the way movies are done. The size of this movie seems normal to me. What do I know? Maybe when the movie finally comes out, I'll be awe-struck. But not right now. All I worry about is the camera and the director and the actors. We're just going to put a good story together. That's the way I think about it."

For MacLachlan, the making of *Dune* has been a learning experience in a number of ways. Besides having to acclimate himself to moviemaking techniques, he had to train in martial arts under the guidance of Kiyoshi Yamazaki, the fighting expert who helped put the clout in *Conan, the Barbarian*.

"We had a pretty extensive training period," says Kyle, "but it wasn't too grueling because, coming into it, I had a brown belt in karate. So, when Yamazaki came down, we immediately spoke a similar language. He taught me weaponry, some of the samurai techniques and akido. I was able to pick up what I needed fairly quickly.

"I've done a lot of fight scenes with humans that were pretty tricky. Nothing's gone wrong, although they *have* been pretty uncomfortable. In most of them, I've been wearing a rubber stillsuit. When you hit the ground in those things, you find yourself bouncing.

"The robot fight was the most difficult scene." In that sequence, Paul is placed in an enclosed area with a mechanized robot-warrior and asked to battle it to the finish. Either he dismantles the robot or the robot will dismantle him.

"I trained and trained and trained on a certain series of moves to use against this robot. The robot would work in synch with me. By the time I got in the ring with the thing, all my training just disappeared. I mean, I *remembered* all my training and everything but as soon as they turned the robot on, it was every man—or machine—for himself. They told me, 'Don't get killed,' and then turned the cameras on.

"It was scary but it was fun. I suppose I could have gotten bruised up but I wouldn't have gotten mangled or anything. It was me against the guys operating the robot. We paid very close attention to each other so we wouldn't hurt each other. At the same time, we were trying to make the fight look real. Talk about thinking on your feet. It was really crazy but it looks great."

Even for a seasoned professional, working with some of the physical and optical effects in *Dune* would be a challenge. For newcomer Kyle, it's been a combination nuisance and game.

"The most difficult effects scenes are the ones where you have to work with opticals that won't be matted in until months later. We've been climbing up rocks and looking over our shoulders and reacting to nonexistent giant worms chasing after us. In reality, you're looking at the crew. A lot of thoughts run through your mind. You hope that you're gauging it correctly in terms of your physical movements, your eyeline. You also try to get inside Paul and figure out how he would react. Then, you try to visualize just what it is you're reacting to. You just keep your fingers crossed and trust David's eye and hope that it's going to look OK.

"Most of the regular effects have gone off OK. There've been some surprises, of course. During the hunter-seeker scene, for instance, I snatched the thing out of the air and smashed it up against a wall. They had rigged two explosions in there for sparks. When I rammed the thing against the wall and those two explosions, one in the wall and one in the weapon, collided, the force was so great that my hand just bounced back, recoil. That really shocked me.

"There have been little things that have slowed us down. Pieces of costumes have fallen off. Or someone will pull one of these crys-knives out"—he points to a weapon securely fastened to the side of his stillsuit—"and mess up.

"There are ones that are made out of hard plastic like this one

Having disposed of their Harkonnen captors,
Paul and Jessica escape from a disabled ornithopter.

and ones that are made of rubber. You'll be fighting with someone with a rubber knife and the blade will just bend over. Stupid things like that."

The role of Paul has often been physically draining for the young actor, replete with desert battles, rolling and tumbling and various other physical stunts. But Paul Atreides is also a complicated role, one that has often taxed MacLachlan's emotional stamina as well.

"The scene that sticks out in my mind as the most difficult," says Kyle, "is the scene in the desert where I fight and kill a Fremen, Jamis. I fight him reluctantly...to the death. Now, Paul has never killed a man before. I have to make a quick transition between being a victor and being guilt-ridden. Jessica comes up behind me and says 'How does it feel to be a killer?' I turned back to face Jamis' body and tears are supposed to start running down my face.

"In the book, there was a period of time between the killing and the actual funeral for Jamis. There was a real ritual surrounding the death. In the script, I was sort of put on the spot in terms of the transformation. That was really hard on an emotional level."

To alleviate the inevitable pressures that arise while waiting on a set, the young actor sometimes resorts to humor. More often than not, his partner in crime is Everett McGill, who plays Paul's loyal Fremen compatriot, Stilgar. The image of MacLachlan and McGill

Paul and Chani with Alia and Jessica.

Paul, armed with his weirding module and sound gun.

quietly cutting up is an odd one. MacLachlan is a very eager, determined young actor and the towering McGill a quiet, introspective one.

"Most of the things we've wanted to do we've chickened out on," MacLachlan admits.

"After a while, you find yourself thinking in silly ways. I think we're all pretty silly people down here but when you throw a whole bunch of silly people together, we become very serious. We've been really serious about the movies and we've really worked hard . . . but we're capable of some pretty funny stuff to break the tension, too."

As a *Dune* aficionado, Kyle realizes the differences between *Dune*, the book, and *Dune*, the movie, and is sympathetic to those fans of the novel who may be worried about how the movie is going to treat their treasured source material.

"I had a hard time dealing with the differences between the two forms myself," he says. "When I first read the script I was disappointed. I came in saying, 'I want *Dune.*' It took me a little time to get used to the differences. I finally said, 'It's not going to be *Dune* by Frank Herbert. It's going to be *Dune* by Frank Herbert, adapted by David Lynch, put on film and conveyed by actors.'

"Whenever I say something like 'I was disappointed when I read the script,' I feel kind of strange because I really like David Lynch a lot. I think most of my problems arose from the fact that I hadn't read many scripts before and the format change was difficult for me. Scripts are like books in shorthand. I didn't consider that. Later, when I read a lot of other scripts, I realized how strong ours was and got really fired up to do it.

"I think all the fans of the book should realize that they're not going to see the book on the screen. I think this movie is going to stand on its own merits. It's also going to shake people up.

"They've got to be touched somehow."

One of Lynch's assistants runs up to the trailer. It is time for MacLachlan to try exploding the pyramid once again. The actor walks briskly back towards the set.

"I'm really curious to see what this is all going to look like when it's finished," he muses, "with the effects and stuff. After I'm finished acting here, I'll just become another observer. I'm not going to know what to expect. I'll become like everyone else in the audience."

MacLachlan, just another typical moviegoer, marches back to the sietch set, shouts at a large black pyramid and blows it to smithereens.

16.
OF WORMS AND MEN

One of the things I'm looking forward to most is seeing one of those sandworms. If they're anything like the designs, they're going to be great.
Kyle MacLachlan, actor (Paul)

Filming the worm footage on the backlot was quite difficult.
Freddie Francis, cinematographer

Watching them film the worm footage out back was one of the funniest things I've ever seen in my life.
Francesca Annis, actress (Jessica)

The single most memorable image in the original novel, *Dune,* the event that triggered the most imaginative flights of fancy on the part of the reader, was the appearance of the sandworms of Arrakis. Titanic creatures which burrow deep within the recesses of the planet, surfacing up through the sand dunes like great whales smashing through ocean breakers, the sandworms are known as Shai-Hulud to the people of Dune.

Roughly translated, the title means "Old Man of the Desert" or "Old Father Eternity" or "Grandfather of the Desert." Sandworms grow to enormous size (Fremen insist that specimens longer than 400 meters have been seen undulating through the deep recesses of the desert) and live to a great age unless slain prematurely or drowned in water, which is poisonous to them.

In the story, the great worms are connected directly to the creation of melange, the spice of spices, the crop for which Arrakis is the unique source.

Going into the picture, both David Lynch and Raffaella De Laurentiis realized that the valid visualization of these mythological beasts was an integral part of their story. At times, the screen would have to be crawling, literally, with the worms.

179

Early working sketches of the Arrakeen Sandworm—Shai-Hulud, "The Old Man of the Desert."

Main characters would have to be chased across the sand by the creatures. One or two people would have to be consumed by the worms. Spice harvesters and spice mining machinery would also run afoul of them. Still another aspect of the film called for key characters to harpoon and, then, mount one of the sandworms during the Fremen custom of sandriding.

Early in pre-production, it was decided that several different types of special effects worms would be used for the movie. For the wide-range, optical shots, mechanical effects wizard Carlo Rambaldi would design and work worms of different sizes that would be shot against miniature locations and/or matted in with existing footage of live action.

For the many live-action shots, different sections of worms were to be built with Kit West and Carlo Rambaldi working on different aspects of the oversized props.

On the back lot of Churubusco studios, Kyle MacLachlan is patiently waiting on the sidelines while Carlo Rambaldi and one of his assistants inspect a large section of worm that has been built. The section, roughly fifteen feet high and about as long, is mounted on a wheeled base. Its rough, rubber exterior will represent a small piece of a single section of the worm. A truck stationed on the side of the lot will pull the prop along a track, giving it the illusion of rapid movement.

The scene calls for Kyle, as Paul, to run alongside the worm

On the Churubusco backlot, Kyle MacLachlan chases after a section
of sandworm that is mounted on a track and pulled by a truck offscreen.
A camera, mounted on a parallel track, records his moves.

with a harpoonlike instrument, a maker hook. He is to plunge the
weapon into the side of the beast, hook a ring into it and, later (in
a scene filmed separately), climb aboard the beast's back.

A section of the planet Dune has been created in front of the
swath of track. Tons of desert sand have been trucked in and dumped.

Carlo Rambaldi and his assistant are supervising a few last-minute details. When Kyle plunges his hook into the side of the worm,
a flap of skin will be ripped open. A section of gooey worm tendons
and entrails will be seen. Rambaldi and company are applying a
slimy substance to the inside of the worm. "Latex and gelatin,"
Rambaldi explains. "I will explain no more. We must not destroy
the illusion."

The sheer, fragile tendons themselves were made out of thousands of prophylactics ("Boy, did that order look good being sent
down here," laughs David Lynch. "What a manly movie.") by first
cutting off the tips of each and every one of the condoms. The sheer
rubber devices were then cut in half, lengthwise. Each piece of the
membrane was pasted in individually, creating a fragile network of

Paul (MacLachlan) uses his maker hook to attack a section of worm which, in reality, consists of thousands of carefully placed rubber condoms.

webbing. The finished assemblage was then doused with a slimy substance to give it an appropriately moist sheen.

The membranes, already covered with the manufactured slime, are now being covered with an extra coat of gelatin before the shot. Rambaldi backs up. The section of tendon is to be closed. There is a problem. The skin flap will not shut properly. Finally, it is forced shut.

Lynch is worried about the scene. "It's a one-off thing," he explains. "There's so much gelatin in there that the condoms won't stick together again if we screw it up."

Work on the worm is finished. The crew backs up towards the camera. Workers come in and rake the sand, eliminating the footprints. Rehearsals begin. It is difficult to get the speed of the truck pulling the worm and Kyle's running speed synchronized. Adding to the difficulty is the fact that pounds of red earth are being blown into the actor's face by large fans. The deserts of Dune are never tranquil...not even for fledgling worm riders. Rehearsal after rehearsal after rehearsal takes place. Kyle is exhausted but still game.

"Hold it. Hold it." Someone notices that the red earth has seriously changed the color of the worm's surface. It is now too dark for the shot to be done. Bags of white fuller's earth are sent for to dust the worm down, lightening its skin tone.

Finally, the worm is ready. Kyle is ready. The man-made dust storm begins. Kyle races alongside the great worm and plunges his weapon into the creature's side. A flap of skin tears open. The pointed object slices through a mass of gooey tendons. The weapon sticks. The tendons tear.

A collective sigh of relief goes up on the other side of the camera.

The following day, the worm shot is the topic of discussion around the lot. "It was very difficult for my camera operator," says Freddie Francis, "because the section of the worm was exactly the length and width of his frame. So, if he wasn't a very fine camera operator, not only would you have seen the worm on the screen but some very nice advertisements on the wall of the local cinema behind the worm as well."

Francesca Annis found the scene symptomatic of the nonglamour connected with effects film. "I have to take some snapshots of that to send to friends back home," she says. "They won't believe it. When I stood out there watching that scene, that just about summed up the film industry for me.

"I mean, there was this section of what is going to wind up being a gigantic monster worm that cascades through the sand. So, there is a bit of this old worm and there are some actors there, complete lunatics running alongside this thing when someone yells 'Action!'

"The worm is being pulled along on a bit of old string by an old truck. A couple of tacky old umbrellas are set up with about eighteen people trying to get underneath them because it's so hot. A couple of old blankets are strung up between two trees so the actors can sit underneath them. And there, right next to this scene, is a motorway. The lot is right on the edge of a motorway. There are hundreds of cars zooming by. Beep. Beep. Vrrrooom. Vrooom. I mean you just couldn't believe the scene unless you were standing right there."

Meanwhile, back in reality, construction of an even bigger section of worm is in progress. Outside of the administration offices, large, curved wooden surfaces are slowly being covered with large swaths of foam rubber. Eventually, these will represent the top of the worm that actors such as Kyle MacLachlan, Sean Young and Molly Wryn will be photographed straddling.

In his cluttered workshop, Kit West prowls around diagrams of the large slice of worm. "There will be three segments of worm shown, sort of like three large ribs. But it's being built in six pieces. They're made of wood and covered with foam rubber. Then, using heat, blow lamps, we'll etch into the rubber surface, creating a mottled effect. And, then, in one of the sections, the section that is supposed to be nearest the head, we'll have blow holes, like a whale's. We'll have blowers in there shooting out air and sand when the actors do their riding."

The sections, when completed, will be brought into massive sound stage two and placed in front of the movie's blue screen. "All of these sections have to be mounted on a mechanical rocker because we have to create an undulating movement," continues West.

"The rocker itself is composed of a large metal rectangle on a ball base. The frame is forty feet square with enormous springs on shock cord. The frame's ball base allows it to go back and forth and side to side simultaneously, creating a sort of freewheeling riding movement. The worm won't be moved using hydraulics. It will be manually operated. We will have half a dozen people around those springs prodding them with huge bars. It's a very crude method but it really works. You see, that large rectangular area stabilizes itself on the ball. All it needs is a slight push to start it rocking."

West relaxes in his chair and smiles, a contented man. The effect is obviously going to work and work well. Outside in the courtyard,

Two views of Carlo Rambaldi's mechanical worms
thundering across a miniature desert set.

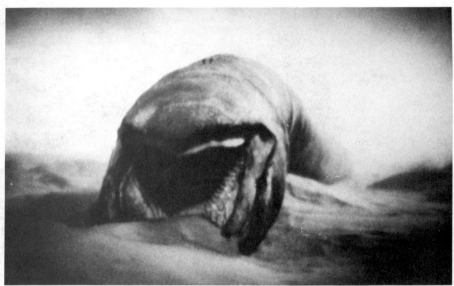

The mechanical worm strikes again.

dozens of studio workers are attaching the foam-rubber padding to the wooden frames. West's smile takes on a slightly cockeyed angle. There's only one small problem nagging at the back of his mind. "We have to have them done by next Tuesday," he says.

He has less than five working days to turn the slabs into worm skin. It will take a miracle to squeeze so much work into so little time.

Five days later, the result of that miracle is being filmed in front of the blue screen.

Paul Atreides is taking his first worm ride.

At right: No longer in the film, this photograph is of the original version of Paul's Water of Life scene. In the final version of <u>Dune</u>, this scene occurs on the open des

17.
A LONG, HOT SUMMER

Now that the end is in sight,
I feel a little sad. This has been magical.
Molly Wryn, actress (Harah)

We've been down here so long
that we're getting a little punchy.
Kyle MacLachlan, actor (Paul)

Everyone else goes home in September. But I stay down here.
After principal photography, we start the special effects.
Then the fun really begins.
David Lynch, director

For the cast and the crew of *Dune,* August proved itself a very schizophrenic time period. On the one hand, the atmosphere on the lot relaxed somewhat in that the end of principal photography was in sight. Yet, during that month, some of the movie's most dramatic scenes had to be filmed. Key cast members would fly in for certain effects sequences. The daily and/or weekly bouts with sickness could now cause crucial delays in a shooting schedule that was being changed constantly. In short, everyone was under the gun now that the movie was drawing to the end of the principal-photography phase of production.

Production coordinator Golda Offenheim's office functions as a crisis control center. Located directly outside producer Raffaella De Laurentiis' headquarters, Golda's quarters act as a buffer zone. When problems arise, they are first routed to Golda. It is then her decision to either handle them herself or pass them along to the appropriate parties.

A longtime member of the British movie scene—she began her career back in 1944 and has, over the years, worked with such producers as Cubby Broccoli (on the Sean Connery *Bond* films), Norman Jewison (on such films as *Rollerball* and *Fiddler on the Roof*) and Dino De Laurentiis *(Ragtime* and *Flash Gordon)*—Golda is not particularly impressed that the live-action portions of the movie are near completion. She is still up to her neck in moment-to-moment dilemmas.

She takes a deep breath and rattles off a few of the knottier problems she has to tackle today. "Fourteen thousand feet of film stock should get out of customs today...we hope," she says. "The full-size model of the Guild navigator has just arrived...damaged. I've still got wardrobe delayed in customs from four and a half weeks ago. We've had camera equipment delayed seven weeks. We've had some equipment stolen. The suitcases arrived empty."

The matriarchal figure heaves a sigh. "Oh well, at least they left us the suitcases. They are very nice suitcases. We have little bits of camera parts from London inside. Little pieces of ground glass and the like. Charming."

One of Offenheim's biggest challenges has been getting film stock and props in and out of the country on time. It hasn't been easy. "It's very difficult getting things done promptly," Golda states. "It takes a week for our dailies (the footage shot on any given day) to get through customs. So, in order to get the film in and out of the country faster, we arranged to send it out via courier. Then, the customs agents got wise to us and impounded one shipment. We changed couriers. The customs officials found out and went after that courier so we switched back to the original one. We've been pretty successful with this practice. After today, we'll only have three thousand feet of film stuck in customs.

"Getting the costumes into the country without delay was impossible. People wound up bringing in finished costumes in their luggage. We're going to have a lot of suitcases left over at the end of this picture. People were arriving from all over the world with suitcases containing costumes. If they were coming down here, we'd ask them to take an extra suitcase with them as luggage. They would just walk through."

One of the crewmembers sticks his head inside Golda's office. "You wanted me?"

Golda rolls her eyes melodramatically. "Air bags! Air bags! The stuntmen are going mad. Is there any way we can get them out of customs today?"

"I'll do my best."

The crewmember leaves and Golda simply shakes her head.

Producer Raffaella De Laurentiis with production coordinator Golda Offenheim.

"How can we do stunts without air bags for the stuntmen to land on?"

The phone rings. Eight crates of large models have arrived from Los Angeles. The problem is . . . there's no place to store them. The delivery men have just left the boxes out in the middle of the studio lot. In the hot sun. "Where are we going to put all those boxes?" Golda wonders.

Golda herself has personally entered into the customs game, helping a small, preliminary model of Carlo Rambaldi's third-stage navigator get into Mexico. The navigator is a strange, fetuslike creature that looks half-human, half-worm. "I carried it through customs in a trunk," explains Golda.

"I was stopped by officials. They opened the trunk and asked me what was inside.

" '*That* is a Third-Stage Navigator,' I declared.

"They let me through." Golda Offenheim can't help but laugh. "I didn't know what to expect working down here . . . and I haven't been disappointed at all."

Legions of journalists are arriving on the set during the movie's last full month of shooting. Unit publicist Anne Strick's cubicle looks like a World War II command post, its small amount of space usually filled with large clusters of journalistic bodies.

One writer is disgruntled because Max Von Sydow and Jurgen Prochnow are no longer on the set. A photographer has made the mistake of not carrying his equipment through with him on his flight. He sent it down separately. It has now been swallowed by customs. His problem will eventually wind up in Golda's office.

Another writer, expecting to see a dramatic moment being filmed with some of the movie's top actors, is instead led onto a stage where Kit West is sending his small dummy version of Alia hurtling against the ruptured wall of the Emperor's steel tent over and over again. The little girl-doll smashes into the wall with a resounding "whooommmp." One. Two. Three times. Finally, the writer turns to his tour guide and deadpans: "The kid is quite a little trooper, isn't she?"

Throughout it all, Strick keeps smiling. The entire year has been one fraught with misadventure and unintentional hilarity. "I carry a flashlight around at all times," she says. "Because the electricity *still* keeps going off. We've pretty much gotten used to the irregularities connected with the studio."

Strick brings some of her magazine writer visitors with her to the studio commissary, a cafeteria-style affair that resembles a casual New York bistro more than a studio restaurant. When the De Laurentiis Corporation journeyed down to the Churubusco location, they decided to revamp some of the complex, including the food services for the cast and crew. Recalls Strick, "Raffaella built the restaurant down here and she wasn't happy about the pasta they were serving. So, she ordered pasta from Italy through her father, who owns the DDL Foodshow in New York and Los Angeles. The pasta was impounded in customs for three months. When it finally was released, we had it for lunch."

According to Strick, one way the entire *Dune* troupe has survived is by constantly expecting the unexpected. "Some of our most aggravating moments have also been our funniest," she says. "For instance, we once needed a few thousand extras for a night scene at the Azteca Stadium. We hired them all from the Mexican Army. They were told to show up on a certain night. At the last minute, however, we had a schedule change. On the day before, we notified the general in charge that the date had been pushed back.

"No problem, right? Well, on the original night the shoot had been scheduled for, there was one, lone painter at the stadium. He hears something. He turns around and sees a few thousand soldiers...very angry soldiers...showing up. It turns out that the general had never informed his men.

"Let's just say our problems down here have been *different*."

The sietch set is overcrowded. Dozens of stillsuited Fremen male and female extras are being herded into the back of the cavern. Kyle MacLachlan is to address them from the elevated front of the earth-colored stage. For some odd reason, there are more spectators than usual in the background, huddled around Lynch, Francis and the crew.

"I don't even notice the crowds anymore," Lynch says, matter-of-factly. "It was horrible, at first, feeling that people were *behind* you when you were working, when you were talking to an actor. You've got to feel free to say whatever you feel like to the people you're working with. Little by little, I just started forgetting other people were there. Unless we're on a really small stage, there are three or four hundred people standing back there. You just block it out. I don't notice the difference if it's a studio tour or if it's our people or whatever. It's like Freddie says, 'Dino, if you want five thousand extras, all you've got to do is turn the camera around.'"

In the Fremen Hall of Rites, a call to arms.

Ladders litter the area where the visitors stand, gawking. It is a hot August day. The number of people squeezed onto the set make the sietch seem twice as hot as it is outside in the blazing sunlight.

Freddie Francis is trying to frame the shot carefully. The camera will focus on Kyle but, in the foreground of the screen, will be the backs of the Fremen crowd.

On the side of the sietch, a worker narrowly misses knocking over a row of Fremen spears that stretches some fifteen feet alongside a wall. In front of the spears, rows of handguns are hung precariously.

"Pheeewwww," he whispers to no one in particular.

A little girl standing amongst the visitors begins to cry. A Fremen woman runs to the child and begins soothing the little girl in Spanish. DGA trainee Ian Woolf walks over to see what the problem is. The Fremen extra has brought her daughter onto the set for a visit. The child, a toddler of perhaps three years of age, is not impressed. In fact, she's petrified. She does not like the set. She does not like the lights. She does not like her mother's rubber suit. And, most emphatically, she does not like the fact that mom has to wander off and get lost in a crowd.

Ian looks at assistant director Kuki. "Did you tell that Fremen extra she could bring her kid to the set all day?"

Kuki sets his eyebrows in classic Vincent Price–arched position. "No."

"She said you did."

Kuki looks at the little girl. "So what am I going to do now? Stuff her in a trunk?"

The extras are being positioned and repositioned. David Lynch is having cup holders attached to his director's chair so he can place his large cups of soda conveniently at hand. The holders are attached. They are too small for the soda cups.

"Watch the haircuts, please," Freddie Francis cautions. Gordon Hayman, the camera operator, carefully scrutinizes the Fremen lines. The Fremen are repositioned. Those with styled haircuts, signs of the 1980s, are moved forward towards Kyle. The men closest to the camera must have unkempt hair. "We can't have good haircuts showing," Freddie states in mock seriousness.

Fremen men, it seems, do not know the pleasures afforded by a blow-dryer.

The shot is almost ready for the cameras. At that point, Dino De Laurentiis, on a visit to the studio, enters with his daughter, Raffaella. Work stops. Dino, Raffaella and Lynch chat. Photos are taken. Dino leaves. Activity resumes.

The Fremen mother's child starts wailing again. A female visitor to the set consoles the child and reduces the wailing to a whimper.

Things are beginning to gel. Suddenly, a worker bumps into one of the spears leaning against the wall. That spear topples over. It hits another spear, which, in turn, topples into another. Before anyone can stop it, a practical illustration of the domino theory is taking place on the set.

"I was waiting for that to happen," Freddie Francis beams.

The spears are repositioned. Slowly.

Every time there is a delay, the Fremen unstrap their heavy rubber collars and unplug their nose plugs. When action looks like it's going to start, they dress up again. For the past hour, they have been unplugging and unstrapping as regularly as clockwork.

Freddie Francis with second unit director Jimmy Devis.
Devis would later be the victim of a life-threatening accident.

The shot is ready for a rehearsal. Kyle steps up to the end of the sietch "stage." Everett McGill and Francesca Annis stand in the background.

There is a last-minute reshuffling in the Fremen ranks.

Kyle has a particularly difficult speech to complete. He begins it. He flubs it. He begins it again. He is going strong. A ladder falls. Chaos.

Kyle does not miss a beat. "Smell that, son?" he barks to his troops in a gruff *Apocalypse Now* voice, quoting from that film. "It's napalm. I love the smell of napalm in the morning!"

Lynch cannot hide his smile.

Technicians grapple with the offending ladder.

As workers and visitors vie for space in the background, McGill keeps in character, staring blankly ahead. Later, he explains, "If there are people moving around, people in modern costumes, you're going to notice them. There's no way you can do the scene and not notice them. You can't ignore them. If you are a spontaneous actor, like I consider myself to be, you have to use what is out there. So you use the people who are out there but in a different way. To me, they aren't visitors. They're just some other people in the sietch."

The Fremen are finally assembled properly. The ranks of visitors have been thinned out. The Fremen child stops weeping. The scene is shot. Surprisingly enough, even after the endless delays, nobody on the set seems overly agitated. Everyone walks off slightly slap-happy.

As the extras leave the area, somebody bumps into a spear.

Freddie Francis watches the entire row fall once again. A thin smile is on his face. He doesn't say a word. He doesn't have to.

Molly Wryn is ill. She is seated on the balcony of her hotel room valiantly trying to talk and breathe at the same time. It is not easy. She has been given a shot of antibiotics the night before, but a flu bug has gotten the best of her.

Today she is feeling better although she is *still* one of, as Golda Offenheim would say, the "legion of people who have felt like death during this film," the walking wounded afflicted with colds, flu bugs, stomach disorders, chronic coughs or worse.

"Aside from *this*," she says, sniffling, "it's been wonderful down here. It's my first movie and it's been magic. I'm a *Dune* child. This is a real awakening for me. I've never been so closely involved with people. I was a real introvert, shy, before this. Suddenly I'm thrown together with all these people from all over the world in this city.

Everything is new. I'm like a little kid. I'm just eating it up."

In spite of her inexperience on a film set, Wryn has been crea-tively involved with the portrayal of her character, Harah. In the story, Harah and her two children are "bequeathed" to Paul after he kills her mate, Jamis, in a fight. Later, Harah becomes a babysitter to Paul's mutant sister, Alia.

"David listens to input," she beams. "It's amazing. There was a scene when Jamis' body was going to be cremated. The way it was written, I was going to come down the stairs with my two boys and we were just going to watch it happen. I asked David how he would feel if I touched the body one last time. After all, the last time I saw Jamis, he was alive. He thought about it. He said it would be okay.

"Then we came up with the idea of me putting my water rings on his body. We also came up with the idea of Danny, one of the two kids playing my boys, placing Jamis' knife on the body. Well, before you know it, we had a really moving funeral scene there. It gave Harah a chance to come alive. And my boys? Those two boys just made me want to cry.

"This movie has really affected me. It's been so intense. I had one scene with Francesca where we're discussing how the other Fremen women dislike Alia for being a freak. Alia can hear this conversation in her mind. She comes down, faces me and uses the Voice on me. I was supposed to scream as if my head were being split open. I had to scream over and over again. It was almost like primal therapy.

"It was a difficult scene to do because, on the one hand, I've practically raised Alia. I love the child. But, then again, this little girl is really torturing me. I'd look at Alicia, who plays Alia, and she was just so intense. Those little dull eyes came at me with all that anger. She gave me chills every time. Afterwards, she'd be laughing and making jokes and acting like a normal little girl. It was creepy."

Molly stops her narrative to sneeze. "I've loved all this. People ask me if I was nervous about this being my first film. Not in front of the camera. Not for a second. It hypes me up just thinking about it."

She pauses for another sneeze and reaches for a vitamin.

It is night. Eight hundred extras are assembled in the Hall of Rites exterior set. They are standing in formation for the entire length of the football-field–size set, prepared to watch Francesca Annis, as Jessica, drink the water of life that will enhance her PSI powers. Annis and her fellow actors are standing on an elevated platform three stories above the extras. Later, through the use of matte paintings, the Hall of Rites scene will be converted into an interior shot; a moody glimpse of one of the Fremen's largest underground structures.

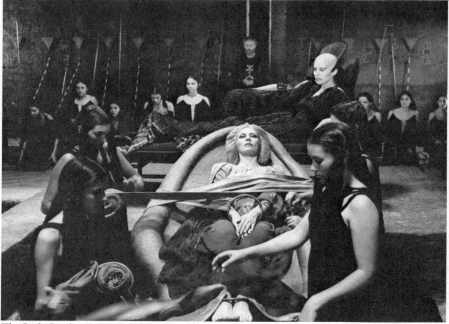

The Lady Jessica, prepared to go through the Water of Life ceremony in the Hall of Rites.

David Lynch and his crew are frantically trying to position and rehearse the extras. During these summer nights, more often than not, it rains heavily for brief periods of time. Long enough periods, however, to ruin a night shoot.

The extras run through their ceremonial behavior. "Halfway down," Freddie Francis states into a walkie-talkie, "they're not raising their knives together."

The kinks are worked out. A light drizzle begins to fall. It is not heavy enough to wash out the scene, however, and the Hall footage is kept. Nobody will know definitely whether this scene will have to be restaged and reshot until the footage is actually developed.

"It's a real gamble," says one crewmember.

Paul, Harah and Stilgar (at left) await the results
of Lady Jessica's Water of Life ceremony.

Sean Young is seated in a restaurant in the middle of Mexico
City, unwinding after a tough week. "I couldn't believe that when
we were doing the Hall of Rites scene," she laughs, "somebody
slipped liquor into the Water of Life. As I took the bottle of water
from Francesca and raised it to my lips to drink, I smelled the odor
of something incredibly alcoholic... like rubbing alcohol. I couldn't
believe it. It was really strong. Like vodka. We're up there drinking
vodka!"

She shrugs her shoulders. "At least it kept everybody's germs
away from each other."

Paul Smith flies down to Mexico a day earlier than necessary.
On the following night, he will take part in a battle scene to be
filmed at the Dead Dog Dump. He has arrived from Los Angeles
before schedule, however, just to watch tonight's shooting at the
location, a massive battle scene in which Gurney (Patrick Stewart)
leads some of the Duke's loyalists against the vile Harkonnen.

Smith is delighted to be back. "I missed everybody," he says
sheepishly. "I've never had so much fun. I tell you, honestly, that
I've never had an experience like this in twenty-two years in movies.

This film reminded me of what cinema should really be like. From Raffaella to David to the first unit crew, there's a kinship there. If you perform really well, they applaud!"

An almost childlike smile spreads across the mountainous actor's face as he recalls some of the wilder things he has taken part in during the production. "Oh, we've done such insane stunts!" he exclaims, relishing every memory. "We've *invented* a lot of really wild stuff.

"For example, after the scene where I kill Max? I'm supposed to go back into my ship and walk down a corridor to meet my uncle, the Baron. Well, this corridor looked awfully empty. I said to David, 'David. Can't we do something here? There's nothing going on in the corridor. It looks flat.'

"He thought for a minute. 'What can you do with a cow?' he asked.

" 'What?'

" 'What can you do with a cow?'

"I didn't know what to say. 'Well, I guess I could carry him,' I answered. David just grinned. 'Well, you think about it. We're going to get you a cow.'

"Where the idea of a cow came from? Don't ask me. The next day we're shooting that scene and they have a dead cow hanging from the ceiling in chains. It's been frozen. Its tongue is hanging out of its mouth. There are two little midgets looking at the cow.

"I was just staring at this thing when David came over. 'Well, Paul, what can you do with this cow?'

"I wasn't really thinking. 'Well, I can always pull out its tongue and eat it.' I was just joking, you know?

"David just beamed. '*Now* you've got it.'

" 'What?!!!'

" 'You've got it!'

"So, in the new version of the scene, I walk down the hall, pass this cow that is being worked over by two midgets, rip out its tongue and chew on it like a lollipop. I must have gone through thirty tongues in two days. Of course, what they did was take the frozen tongue out of the cow and put a cooked tongue in there instead. I got really sick of cow's tongues, let me tell you, but it was so nutty, I loved it. I love David. Where does he get images like that?"

The rotund actor sighs. His part is nearing an end. On the screen, however, Rabban has already been executed. It's never explained just *how* the Beast dies, but during the film's finale, when the Emperor and the Baron meet, Rabban's head—sans body—is seen sitting next to the Emperor.

Rabban snacks on a cow's tongue before visiting his uncle, the Baron.

"That head really frightened me when I first saw it," Smith confesses. "It's too lifelike. They used me as a model, of course. To make a mold, they put cream on your face and then pour this rubber on until it hardens. There's one straw in your mouth for you to breathe through. They plug up your nose and your ears. Talk about claustrophobia. And the whole time you're there, you feel this stuff on your face getting harder.

"A couple of weeks later I walked into makeup and there was my head with two spikes stuck through it. Whoooaaaa!

"Poor Rabban. He meets such a lousy end. I'm a little sad about that. I said to David, 'I'm very sorry that you have to kill me because I like this movie and I like everybody here.'

"David said, 'Don't worry. If there's a sequel, I'm writing the script. And if I can bring Duncan back for the second movie (Duncan does reappear in the second *Dune* novel), then I can bring you back, too!' I felt a little better after that."

Smith sits, bundled up on the sidelines awaiting the action. Before setting things up, David Lynch confesses, "I'm going to be interested to see how things go tonight. The Dead Dog Dump is sort of a power point, you know? There's something *here*. You can feel it. We haven't had a lot of luck shooting here before. Things have taken a very long time to gel. We have a lot of work to do tonight. Let's see if our luck changes."

It does. The first shot is completed by nine o'clock. There is a brief supper break while equipment is repositioned for the massive battle scene. The extras, actors and crew are fed on the side of the dump. A large, portable cafeteria has been set up, boasting countless tables and benches, a couple of circus tents, and a small army of cooks. Recruits from the Mexican army, brandishing guns, stand guard.

Crewmembers and visitors are perched in the volcano-spawned rocky cliffs like a football-game crowd clustered in bleachers. Workers scramble with the tenacity of mountain goats up and down the rockface slabs carrying wires and lights.

The battle scene will be punctuated by several dozen ear-splitting explosions rigged by Kit West. "We'll have twenty-five to thirty explosions tonight," he says. "This is a very nice site for them, really. We've dug them into convenient crevices. We've also put them in places where the ground has been nice and soft. All the explosions are numbered," he points to small tags planted in the ground above each charge.

"We'll set them off in sequence. During the rehearsals, the actors will see the tags and practice moving around the sites. Later, we'll remove the tags and the explosions will look like the result of shell fire when they go off 'at random.' All the while we'll be pumping black smoke across the set. It's specially made stuff done up in Los Angeles. It's pitch black and really looks good. Unfortunately, nobody has come up with a smoke that smells good."

West wanders down to the area where the two armies are rehearsing their skirmish. Lynch and Francis climb up to the top of the highest rockface where the camera is positioned. Producer Raffaella scurries up the side of a cliff to take her place with her crew. Characteristically, she doesn't take the safe, longer route. She digs her cowboy boots into a pathless area and skips from boulder to boulder.

The rehearsing will go on for two bitterly cold hours. The smoke will be sent streaming across the set via large fans. The fans will be repositioned constantly, to give the camera's eye a sense of the different densities available.

The battle scene will be completed...just before dawn. Lynch

Jack Nance (left), best known as Henry from David Lynch's film *Eraserhead*, **plays Nefud, a Harkonnen minion. An unidentified extra stands to the right.**

will get all the shots he bargained for. His luck at the Dead Dog Dump will have changed for the better.

The month of August is drawing to a close. Only two weeks are left of live-action photography. There is tension in the air as everyone scrambles to meet their deadlines.

Then, something totally unforeseen happens.

On a routine night shoot, second unit director Jimmy Devis has an accident. A bad one. Filming on the back lot, he is working on a scene in which a stuntman will have to fall off a man-made cliff. Dressed in Fremen garb, the stunt double is to tumble from the top of the cliff onto a recessed ledge where boxes are positioned to break the fall and send him cascading down onto his next impact point.

After a few stunt falls go badly, Devis walks up to the diving-off point himself. What happened next is anyone's guess. Devis finds himself airborne. He goes hurtling towards the ground, missing the first impact point. He plunges straight down, his arms extended to break his fall.

Word about the accident spreads like wildfire. The following morning the cast and crewmembers are stunned. For those who have worked with Devis on the shoot, the sense of shock is great. For a large number of the British contingent, however, the sense of concern is greater. Many of the camera crew have known the man well for years.

Freddie Francis is one of Davis' old cronies. "We're not certain how bad it is right now," he says, from his hotel room. "There are an awful lot of bones broken and they're not at the moment completely sure what the offshoots of that are."

Within a few days, it becomes clear that Devis has no internal injuries, despite his several broken bones. He will be in traction for a long, long time. Wheelchair bound, he vows to get back to work within a couple of weeks. While everyone realizes that Jimmy's goals are a little on the optimistic side, it's a relief to hear him so optimistic and determined.

Frantic phone calls are made to England and, within a few days, another British cameraman, Jerry Turpin (inventor of the light-flex unit) is flown in. Freddie Francis ushers a slightly jet-lagged Turpin into producer Raffaella's office.

"Raffaella," Francis says cheerfully, "this is Jerry Turpin."

De Laurentiis looks up from her paper-strewn desk. "Hello," she smiles. "What took you so long?"

18.
RAFFAELLA

If anyone has a problem, it's off to Raffaella you go.
Anne Strick, unit publicist

Raffaella is a mother to us all.
Tony Masters, production designer

Some people think I'm really tough.
I think they may be right.
Raffaella De Laurentiis, producer

Raffaella De Laurentiis can best be described as blonde steel. On June 28, 1983, she celebrated her twenty-ninth birthday. Now, she is in the midst of guiding *Dune* to the end of its first phase of shooting while simultaneously preparing the sequel to *Conan the Barbarian* (called *Conan the Destroyer*) for filming at Churubusco Studios as well. She seldom sleeps more than a few hours a night. She has been besieged by a persistent flu bug for most of the *Dune* shoot, yet she never falters, she never slows down.

Seated in the commissary, picking absentmindedly at her food, she tries to unwind, verbally, at the end of a chaotic week; a week that was punctuated by Jimmy Devis' accident. "When an accident like this happens," she begins. "It's a very sad thing. The man was badly hurt. He could have died.

"There's not much you can do about it at this point. You try to do the best you can. I'm at the hospital with him every morning before I come to my office. What else can you do?"

She sits silent for a moment. "It's like having an accident on any other job. You try to avoid situations that lead to accidents, of course. At one point in this movie, we were considering a helicopter shot in the desert, but we decided against it because of the risks involved. You take precautions all the time. You avoid risky situations. But something like Jimmy's accident is just totally unexpected. There was no risk involved. He climbed up the cliff face, slipped and fell down.

Raffaella De Laurentiis on location near Juarez.

"When something like this happens, your first concern is what happened to the man. Is he all right? Is there anything you can do? Then, and this is the sad part about it, you have to move quickly to replace him so the movie doesn't slow down."

Raffaella sits back in her chair. "I did all of that."

If Raffaella is exhausted, she has no intention of showing it. Since March, she has acted as general, den mother, psychiatrist and trouble-shooter on the production. She has been the buffer zone through which all problems are mediated. She speaks five languages—English, Italian, Spanish, French and Tahitian. She uses four of them daily to keep *Dune* running smoothly.

"Everybody here is homesick," she says. "I try my best to keep morale up. When they come and cry and complain, you listen. Once in a while, you try to solve their problems. You bend the rules a little. With a key crew of 150 people, most of them foreign to Mexico, I'm faced with a personal crisis or two a day. The secret is to sit down and listen. That's part of my job. You can't ask a person to leave their families for a year or two, work fourteen hours a day and then, when they come and say, 'My wife is leaving me,' turn your back on them. Sometimes the solution is to send them home for a while. Sometimes it's bringing their wives and families down here. I can't solve everyone's problems, but I do my best.

"I think we've been pretty successful in working together in spite of the international origins," she says. "There's no tension here. I like that. We haven't created a territorial atmosphere. I think people do a better job when they're relaxed, when they're not under social pressure. It sounds very silly to say, but we're functioning like a gigantic family here. That's how you wind up having a picture that's practically on schedule. I mean, on a twenty-three-week shoot, being four days over schedule is nothing.

"We owe a lot of the relaxed atmosphere here to David. David is cool. He handles this enormous machine with a large amount of cool. I do the same. We're not always yelling and screaming at each other the way some directors and producers do."

For Raffaella, *Dune* is the logical continuation of a career in film that started when she was a teenager. The second of four children born to Dino De Laurentiis and actress Silvana Mangano, Raffaella was educated in Italy, surrounded by her father's film world.

At the age of fifteen, she began taking summer jobs on her father's productions, working as a prop assistant and set dresser before advancing to art direction and costume design. By 1975, she was ready to get her feet wet, literally, by moving to Bora Bora for a two-year stint on the movies *Hurricane* and *Beyond the Reef.* During her twenty-four-month stay, she served as both the construction supervisor of the Hotel Marara, built to house the cast and crew of *Hurricane,* and producer of *Beyond the Reef.*

From there, she journeyed to Spain for *Conan the Barbarian,* yet another hectic shoot. By the time *Dune* was ready to roll, Raffaella was well aware of all the possible delays that could arise to hinder the production.

In spite of her meticulous planning, Raffaella admits that there have been more than a few problems on the picture. "Every day some unexpected crisis develops that you never imagined would occur. But you keep on smiling. Why not? I'm having fun. I love doing this. That probably means I'm crazy."

She smiles and shrugs in an offhanded way. "After a while, you just have to tolerate everything that comes along. Like tonight, we're shooting on location. It might rain. It's supposed to rain. If it does, what am I supposed to do with 290 costumed extras? I can't do anything about it but sit here and smile. How can I smile? What am I supposed to do, shoot myself? If it has to rain, it has to rain. That's been happening to us for the past three months. Every time we go out, it either rains or the wind shifts directions.

"I'm sitting here eating lunch, right? But I'm still worrying. I have problems to think about right now. You want to hear some of them?" She sticks out her jaw in an OK,-you-asked-for-it pose. "How are we going to get the people to ride the worms realistically? How are we going to make the worms? Will the worms look real? Will they look like the greatest thing you've ever seen on the screen? I worry about the effects living up to the imaginative standards of the book. It's difficult to match unlimited imagination."

The fear that has haunted Raffaella most during the filming of *Dune* has been that aspect of the film dealing with special optical effects. She was well aware when she began the project that the movie's effects had to be spectacular.

Now, with *Dune* about to enter its special effects phase, Raffaella is finally willing to talk about the subject and the problems connected with it.

"At the very beginning of this movie," she explains, "I felt that the biggest weakness of the film could be its effects. This is a big special effects movie and there are very few special effects wizards around; people who know everything about the subject. I wasn't confident in myself enough to handle it. So, for a year and a half I tried to farm out the special effects. I wanted to put that responsibility on someone else's shoulders.

Raffaella De Laurentiis.

"Now," she shrugs, "I'm doing them myself in Mexico... which is a challenge atop a challenge atop a challenge."

For Raffaella, who prefers direct, firsthand surveillance of all aspects of the filming, working with "out-of-family" special effects companies operating far away from her Mexico location was always considered a troublesome concept to deal with. As the months progressed, she grew even less and less enamored of the idea.

"When I realized that, in order to make certain shots work, I would have to have the effects done in Los Angeles and have it cost me $30,000 every time I turned on the camera, I began to have doubts. If the scene didn't work, you'd have to do it over. Well, you can't spend $30,000 capriciously. I thought that if we could do the shots down here by getting a great crew together, I could allow David to reshoot any scene ten times and still have it come in under $30,000. Plus, I would be using *my* crew. *My* people."

And so, in mid-June of 1983, Raffaella parted company with the stateside effects technicians she had hired. "I made the decision very quickly. I knew it was the right decision but, still, I suffered for weeks afterwards. It was difficult to put the pieces back together. On an effects movie this size which was set up for a year and a half to be run one way, to reorganize from scratch is very difficult. It was like starting a new movie."

While Raffaella grappled with the effects problem, however, she still had to keep the live-action portion of the movie running smoothly, devoting most of her time to the day-to-day problems that cropped up.

"It was a pretty bad time," she admits. "But, eventually, we came up with five people via both their work and by recommendations from people I trust. (Barry Nolan, Brian Smithies, Stanley Sayer, Charles Finance and Charles Staffell comprised the new team hired.) It's nice having five people. You can exchange a lot of ideas. When you have a production meeting to discuss one shot, you get five or six different solutions to the problem. The input is greater. You can come up with three good ideas per shot.

Raffaella's lunch is interrupted by two assistants who run over to her, detailing just a few of today's problems. "What?" she says before lapsing into Italian. One assistant leaves and Raffaella begins to laugh. "The local people are trying to invade our dump! We've put guards on duty to keep them out."

Another conversation. "We're running out of gold paint for the throne room. I need somebody to bring down paint from Los Angeles as luggage. That's going to be fun."

The second assistant leaves and Raffaella is left with a very familiar expression on her face. It is not quite a smile. It is not quite a smirk. Rather, it's sort of a hybrid grin, a physical symbol representing a mood hovering between "What, me worry?" and "Compared to me, Sisyphus had it easy."

"What can you do?" she sighs, finishing lunch. "The job is exhausting and it's aggravating and you get tired after shooting twenty weeks. It's been two years and two months nonstop at this point."

A genuine smile appears. "But I love it. You can't just be a producer for a living, at least not the way I produce. It's a way of life. You're married to the picture you're making. That's all you think about. That's all you care about."

At eight o'clock that night, Raffaella is still on the lot. She is sitting in her office, rearranging the wall-length shooting chart behind her desk. A reporter from a national news magazine is seated nearby on a couch, taking notes on Raffaella as the producer is visited by a steady stream of guests and plagued by a constant barrage of phone calls.

"Make sure the navigator's color is approved before it's painted."

"We've got the air bags out of customs? Wonderful."

"What do you mean there's been a delay on the set. Tony. There's been a screw-up somewhere."

She nods to the reporter. "The anteroom is still under construction."

Bob Ringwood enters. "Bob. Some of the stillsuits are falling apart. Can they be patched?"

A quick phone call. "I'm not going to pay a penny. You do what you want."

After a half hour of problem-solving, Raffaella is ready to take the reporter on a night shoot. "Come," she says. "Let me introduce you to the Dead Dog Dump."

She climbs into her car and, as the driver speeds out to the location, she sighs. "I suppose any other movie will look easy after this. Maybe after I'm through with everything in Mexico, I'll do a little movie. One or two characters. That would be nice."

The car enters the dump site. "It's supposed to rain tonight," Raffaella says absentmindedly, exiting the car.

As she ambles over to the site, David Lynch approaches her, beaming. He has already gotten an important shot in the can and it is not even nine o'clock. Once more, he points to the sky, there is a heavenful of stars shining down on the location. Not a rain cloud in sight.

Raffaella's spirits soar like a skyrocket. She turns to face the reporter. "Come," she says. "I'll tell you some *real* stories. Has anybody told you about the time 2,000 Mexican army extras showed up on the wrong night? No? Well, listen to this . . ."

19.
DAVID LYNCH

He is always very friendly, in a good mood every day.
You never notice anything else. That is marvelous, really.
You never feel any pressure behind his behavior.
Jurgen Prochnow, actor (Leto)

David's vision is very, very bizarre because, I think,
he's a very bizarre person. He's not normal.
He's out of somewhere... out of left field.
The reason I'm doing DUNE is to work with David Lynch.
Sting, actor (Feyd)

I don't think I'm a strange person... but what do I know?
David Lynch, director

David Lynch is wolfing down lunch at the Churubusco commissary, attempting to describe some rhyme or reason for his cinematic career which, until *Dune*, has included two black and white films: *Eraserhead* and *The Elephant Man*. "If you look at *Eraserhead*, you'll see some of *The Elephant Man*. There's also some of *Dune* in *Eraserhead*. There's a thread that links all three of them in my mind. The only big difference about *Dune* is that it's in color," he offers.

"All the movies are about strange worlds that you can't go into unless you build them and film them. That's what's so important about film to me. I just like going into strange worlds."

Tall, soft-spoken and sandy-haired, he looks vaguely preppy in a haphazard sort of way. More often than not, he wears baggy trousers and either a loose-fitting sport coat or a battered leather jacket on the set. He is not boisterous, yet when the conversation turns towards his work, he suddenly becomes very animated. Traces of his art school background emerge when he begins expounding on the mood of a scene.

If you watch him closely, you will find a sense of creative eccentricity that is as demented as it is delightful, an out-of-whack artistic slant that has been present since his days as a student.

Montana-born Lynch attended the Corcoran School of Art in Boston, the Boston Museum School and the Pennsylvania Academy of Fine Arts. While at the Academy, he began working on his first movie, *The Grandmother*, in 16mm.

On the strength of that film, he was accepted into the Center for Advanced Film Studies in Los Angeles in 1970. During his stay there, he wrote *Eraserhead*. The movie began production in 1972 and, because it was privately financed, took five years to complete. *Eraserhead* became a cult classic. *The Elephant Man* followed and, suddenly, the artistic eccentric became a commercially viable "big time" director.

The irony about his current bankable status is that Lynch is *still* an artistic eccentric. He is directing a $40 million movie, yet he still shares an office with five stuffed Woody Woodpecker dolls. Even though he is working on one of the biggest films ever, he meets his weekly deadline for the lifestyle newspaper *Los Angeles Reader*, writing a unique comic strip called *The Angriest Dog in the World*. This is a weird four-strip affair which starts off with the legend: "The dog who is so angry he cannot move. He cannot eat. He cannot sleep. He can just barely growl . . . . . bound so tightly with tension and anger, he approaches the state of rigor mortis." The strip features the same four drawings every week, with the dog emitting a small "grrrrrr" while tethered to a taut leash. Only the voice balloons of its owners emanating from inside a nearby house change. Typical dialogue: "Go ahead and divorce me you stupid, stinking idiot. I'd get a hell of a lot more out of you than I do now." "Oh yeah? Well?" Last frame: The dog: "Grrrrrr."

By no stretch of the imagination is the normally affable Lynch a filmmaker in the accepted Hollywood sense of the word. He is very much the iconoclast, albeit in a laid-back way. During one scene, cinematographer Freddie Francis notices that a prop is casting strange shadows on a wall. "Quick!" he yells. "Hide the shadows . . . David is going to want to film them!"

Lynch, still an art student at heart, smiles, shakes his head and laughs. "I *would*, too," he confides.

Despite Raffaella De Laurentiis' protests to the contrary, David Lynch is the most audacious choice to direct a movie such as *Dune* she and her father could have possibly made.

Yet, the choice has proven to be the correct one.

No one on the set of *Dune* has an unkind word to say about

David Lynch surveys the desert during <u>Dune</u>'s massive battle scenes.

Lynch and Kyle MacLachlan.

His hands bandaged after a week of work in the grueling desert sun,
David Lynch lines up one of <u>Dune</u>'s battle scenes.

Lynch. In fact, they respect him as an island of sanity in an otherwise
borderline chaotic realm.

"The set was always relaxed," says Sting. "That all came from
David. He's as cool as a cucumber. Nothing seems to phase him or
upset him. It's a marvelous quality to have on such a mammoth
production."

Jurgen Prochnow's views on Lynch are also complimentary. "You
get a feeling of friendliness, of patience. He knows a lot about people, about leading them, about bringing them to the point where
they should be the characters. He has a fantasy in his head about
the movie. The combination of his fantasy, his personality and his
understanding of people makes this something special. Not all directors are able to do it."

"I like him very much," adds Max Von Sydow. "I find him very
likable as a person and also as a director. He seems to know what
he wants. He doesn't shoot many things, which seems to indicate
that he knows exactly what he's after. He doesn't say too much to
the actors. He seems to trust his actors. That's very nice, too. It's

an awful feeling if you think that the director does not trust his actors. It's really awful."

"He's extremely kind and very, very supportive," says Francesa Annis. "That is one way of really getting very good results from actors. He always gives you, as an individual, masses of space to do what you can do. He also gives you the time. There are an amazing amount of elements that have to be tied together for this movie: the worms, the rockets, the effects. He could have been the kind of director who, bearing all that in mind, would think, 'Well, it's irrelevant how this actor says his line in the finished movie.' But he never makes you feel like that. He makes you feel that you are the most important thing in the movie. Consequently, people have been very relaxed and that's very, very nice."

"I think David as a director has been influenced by David as an art student," says Patrick Stewart. "It manifests itself in his responding very positively to images that the actors create for him and, well, the look of certain things. The relationship of an actor to an object. The physical relationships between the actors. The dynamics of the picture. The relationship of an actor to the set. It's nice to know that somebody has a view for that. It's interesting. Stage actors tend to be very aware of this because they're always thinking of themselves as part of a picture frame.

"I always have the feeling that, in his frames, nothing is there by chance. Nothing is accidental. Nothing is arbitrary. Everything is important. Everything has its proper place. It's nice to feel yourself part of something which is exquisite."

For the entire production, Lynch has held court like a benign despot, a leader who will, at the drop of a hat, eagerly dive into the role of collaborator if an actor or a crewmember has an idea that can change, twist, or improve a scene. On the set, he is often like a kid in a toy shop, scanning the surroundings for possible ideas or last-minute changes. More often than not he will respond to a stellar piece of acting with an enthusiastic "neat," "keen" or, if really moved, "peachy keen."

Even the hardened veterans on the crew respond to Lynch's infectious sense of wonder. It has gotten them through some rough times.

It is a Saturday afternoon and the crew would love to break by three o'clock. Once again, more people than are necessary are huddled onto a small sietch set. The scene calls for Paul Atreides and his cohort Stilgar to plug themselves into a large, "sound" square;

a massive black box which has large, hydraulic "legs" outfitted into each one of its four outermost sides. Paul and Stilgar are to sit cross-legged in front of the square with other Fremen, still learning the Weirding Way. They will plug in their voice modules and chant.

In the relative cool of the Churubusco lot, Lynch directs a scene taking place on the lush planet of Caladan.

The power of their voices will cause the box to spin and the legs to pump in and out as the rectangle responds to this training exercise.

The scene is not in the script. It's one of the little extras Lynch has thought of during the week to help show the development of Paul and his relationship with the Fremen.

Tempers are a little frayed on the set. It is twenty minutes until shut-down time. Either they get the shot before three or they must wait until Monday. Shooting past three, thereby going into over-time, isn't even discussed as an option.

Lynch would like nothing more than to get the shot done in one take and quit for the day.

Kit West and his men are testing the black box. It spins round and round, its legs moving in and out furiously as it does so.

"Would you like some fairground music to go with this, David?" Freddie Francis asks.

At right: Lynch and Jurgen Prochnow.

Lynch, although tense, is forced to smile.

The machine tested, the actors take their places. For Kyle MacLachlan, the shoot is doubly tedious. He has come down with a bad stomach virus and every additional minute under the lights is misery.

Lynch is as gentle as possible in his dealings with Kyle. He is under pressure. The entire room knows it. Yet, the director refuses to acknowledge that fact when dealing with his star.

Lynch rehearses a few times. The actors have to enter the sietch, walk over to the box, plug in, sit down in front of it and begin to chant. On every rehearsal at least one extra has a problem hooking up to the box and winds up sitting down too late. Finally the scene is coordinated.

Before the scene is to be shot, Lynch notices a white spot on the top of the large, black box. "Could we have someone touch that up?" he says. "Do we have any black paint here?"

After a minute or two, a studio worker walks out. He has black paint, all right, but not in a spray can. He strolls over to the box with a *can* of black paint and a brush. He plops a wad of black goop on top of the box and spreads it around with the brush.

Lynch is dumbfounded. "Now I have brushstrokes up there!" he exclaims.

Lynch's eyes dilate even further as the worker returns with a ladder and proceeds to repaint the entire top of the black box . . . with a brush.

"OK?"

Lynch stares at the box. "No! Not OK. It looks fifty times worse! One hundred times worse! Can anyone see if they can find a can of black spray paint?"

Freddie Francis is aghast. Obviously a quip is called for. "Not to worry," he says. "We've got a giant doily coming in to put on top."

At five minutes to three, the box now glistening with a coat of freshly sprayed paint, Lynch decides to shoot the scene anyway. He is silent during the filming. He is silent after it is over. It is the closest thing to anger most of the crewmembers have seen from the director.

Two days later, Lynch is in better form, battling the elements on the backlot during a night shoot as Alicia Roanne Witt as Alia wades through a man-made sandstorm, while waving a knife over the bodies of dying Harkonnen soldiers. It is a difficult scene for

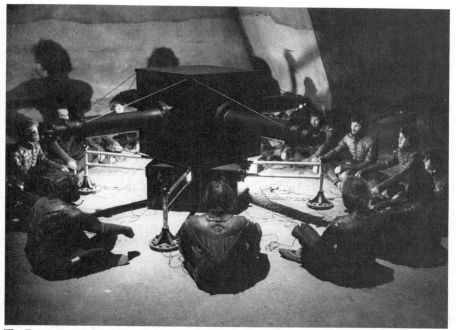

The Fremen sound gun is tested in an underground sietch.

the little girl. It is hot. It is long. And she has sand being pelted into her face by large fans. Worse yet, every time the scene is set to be shot, the wind shifts direction, sending the smoke every which way but the correct way.

Lynch is the model of patience. After each attempt, he walks to the little girl and compliments her performance. If the contrariness of the wind, the smoke and the flames is getting on his nerves, he does not betray it. In his own, quiet way, Lynch is a director of iron.

"I don't believe this guy," one visiting journalist smirks. "Most directors would be pulling their hair out by now. Or pulling other people's hair out, anyway."

The following afternoon, David Lynch prowls around his hotel suite, waiting for his driver to take him out to the studio for a night shoot. He is tired, his eyes underscored by puffy patches of slightly browned skin. His voice is raspy, numbed by too much smoke, too much sand and too many long hours. The living room does not look as much *lived* in as *worked* in, with papers and charts strewn about. The lone concession to pleasure is a stereo set. Half of the records present, however, are sample works of some of the composers being considered for the soundtrack, including, at this point, everyone from rock groups to electronic new-wave artists. A video recorder is also hooked up. Most of the movie cassettes present in the room are Dino De Laurentiis films.

Thirty-eight-year-old Lynch becomes ebullient and adolescent when talking about moviemaking. It is his great love. His passion. He relishes discussing it.

It is hard for him to sum up adequately the Oz-like quality of his stay in Mexico and, specifically, his role as captain of the *Dune* ship, but he is willing to try.

When asked about the black box incident, he only laughs and shakes his head ruefully. "That sort of crazy stuff happens all the time down here," he admits. "Someone was asking me if it was hard filming *Dune* in Mexico. I said, 'Sure, absurd things happen every day.' Then, my mind went blank. I couldn't think of any examples. But that black box bit is a good one.

"That was pretty typical of how requests get altered. It's interesting to ask for a prop, have the request translated into another language and wind up with an entirely different object being dragged in. That guy? Our painter? He's usually very good. I don't know why he decided to paint the entire top of that box while I was standing there. I was in shock.

"I mean, the box was almost shootable before he started, right? There were just a few, little white spots. As it turned out, the box looks really fine in the rushes in spite of the paint job. So, it all worked out.

"I'm *never* surprised anymore, though. For instance, one day they went out location scouting. It was Tony Masters and a few of the guys. They had two different places to visit. It was going to be quite a day. They drove high up on this mountain and the location guy took them to this ridge. He showed them the view off this ridge to the rocks below. They liked it. Fine.

"Tony says, 'Now, where are we going for the second site?' The location guy put them back in the car and they drove for two hours. When they arrived at the second location, they were about fifty feet away from where they were standing on the ridge two hours before."

Lynch leans back on a large sofa and sighs. "You just get used to it all. At a certain point, you surrender to the fates. You accept the ridiculous as part of the norm. We're all worried about what the worms are going to look like on the screen, right? I've been waiting to see some of our worm test footage for three weeks. All those dailies were impounded by customs. We sent it out by courier and the courier was nabbed on the way back into the country." Lynch squints his eyes, shifting mental gears.

"See, for me, that stuff doesn't matter. It's annoying but it doesn't matter. Making this film would feel the same for me no matter where I was because I'm surrounded by the people I would have worked with wherever. It's hard work. In my mind, the only thing that's made it harder filming this in Mexico is the fact that a lot of people have gotten sick here. The altitude and the dryness and these amoebas and the different things you pick up here have made things rough. There's hardly a day when someone isn't sick.

"But, again, after a while, you work around it. You never take note of the time you've lost. It's like, suddenly you've gotten through the day and you realize you did it without so-and-so who's been home with a hundred-and-five fever or something."

Lynch's face brightens noticeably. "To me, Mexico is really inspiring. The architecture! I still see things that I just can't believe I'm seeing. It just opens up your mind. You see things that are so fantastic! I love riding around in the car, the driver playing different music and me just staring out the window. I see different scenes. It just drives me wild. I want to make a movie down here just using Mexico City because it's a dream world."

If Mexico has been a dream world for Lynch, then the Churubusco location has been a large slice of hardcore reality. "It's a constant coping experience," he says. "I think that's what has kept the movie fresh for me. You never get a sense of relaxation. There's always something happening.

"Like last night, with Alia running around in all that smoke with the winds shifting like crazy? A long time ago, Kit West said to me, 'David, if you want smoke blowing in left to right, peachy keen. But if the prevailing winds are right to left, forget it.' There was no way our wind machines were going to overpower nature. So, right there you've got a picture in your mind that can't be filmed because the winds are wrong. If you don't change your approach, you're stupid.

"I mean, I love the David Lean approach of exhaustively searching for the picture-perfect location, but you just can't go all over the world to find the right wind conditions. You've just got to put that thinking cap on and figure out a way to make the existing conditions work. Maybe it'll even work better the new way. You've got to think fast.

"Working with Alicia, you have to be flexible. Sometimes she gets tired or sometimes she gets in a mood and lots of times you just have to stick with it and try to get that little picture in your frame no matter what. That's what last night was all about. The wind was changing. Alicia is a teeny little kid and she was up late and in a mood. Every single scene we've filmed has usually had at least one odd element that we've had to deal with.

"I think the hardest experience for me, and everybody, was filming in the Dead Dog Dump. It was really rough out there and we just got really bogged down. The movie almost came to a stop there and I'm still not sure why. It was only the third week, too. We nearly collapsed. Maybe it was the dust. Yvonne Axworthy's (continuity) script tells the story. If you look at it, you see many pages are yellow and many pages are red. They're not new scenes, xeroxed on colored paper and inserted. They are white pages that are still covered with dust. Yellow dust. Red dust. If you look at the pages we shot on that location, you can hardly see the typeface. We'd come back to the hotel and worry about being tossed out of the lobby on our ears. We looked like bums. Every day."

David Lynch and Molly Wryn.

Lynch is proud of the fact that the movie is practically on schedule, despite last-minute problems, location foul-ups, injuries and customs. "I trust in blind faith a lot," he laughs. "I don't worry too much about specifics. I know some things are going to take a long time to accomplish but I figure, eventually, we're going to get it done.

"For instance, when Bob Ringwood and I started talking about the costumes, we were dealing with all sorts of abstracts. We had some disagreements. Things were going very slowly. As soon as he had a doggone doll to dress up and work with, though, it worked out great. I'd see something and I'd say, 'This is it! Now you're talking.' I just assume people can do everything they say they can.

"Take the Baron's flying scenes. We could have stayed up worrying about those wires for endless nights but, once you get there, you see: there's the setup. There's the wires. That's the background. Freddie just goes to work and uses common sense in solving these problems.

"I can't let all the curve balls make me crazy, you know? I mean

David Lynch works with Alicia Roanne Witt, while Kenneth McMillan hangs around.

all of us on the crew are in the same boat. We've kept the set pretty light. There's plenty of joking on the set but it's not the kind of joking that screws up a scene. If it got down to that I'd be really upset. This is a really professional crew. There's a really good feeling on the set, so there's a lot of joking just before a take or if we get into a difficult situation. The kidding fits in exactly at the right places.

"Freddie constantly cracks me up. He's a real practical joker. One Friday, I was scheduled to leave Mexico at night. I had to catch a plane. Everyone knew I wanted to get this plane and we were trying to get this shot. It took a long time to get ready. Rehearsing. The lighting. We were just about ready to shoot it. A minute later, Boom! The whole set goes black. One of the guys comes running in and says, 'It's the generator. It's dead.' And Freddie says, 'Oh my God. How long is that going to take?' Then another one of the guys runs in and says that it's going to take at least two hours to get the power back on.

"I bought it. There goes my plane, right? My heart just sank. Then everyone started laughing. Freddie had rigged the whole thing up. He wouldn't have let on, either. He's really good at keeping a straight face.

"I love working with him. There's a dialogue between us, a give and take. We don't worry about anything. We just sort of go to it and have a lot of fun doing it."

The sense of camaraderie between Francis and Lynch and De Laurentiis was a definite asset when the film first moved into gear back in March 1983. "We always had faith in Raffaella knowing exactly what she was doing," says Lynch. "She had everything in control. We were relaxed enough to make jokes about the painters always being on the set when we showed up to film. Because we've always been leaping from one set to another, we've always been on the tail of the construction crew and the painters. But Raffaella is great at organization. We've been building and striking and rebuilding sets like crazy the whole time we've been down here and we've never lost a day's shooting time because of it.

"Since I have confidence in Raffaella, I don't worry about anything except the next day's work."

When informed that every member of the cast interviewed has given him straight A's both as a director and as a person, Lynch shows unbridled glee. "Great," he nods. "Great. That cast was one of the movie's biggest strong points. What a cast. What people! They have been so much fun! I just can't think of anyone else playing these parts now. It's just right.

"Kenny McMillan is a wild guy. To me, he's a cross between the Pillsbury Doughboy and Charles Manson.

"And Max Von Sydow? Everybody loves Max. I love Max. I don't know exactly what it was that got to him but he was very, very happy about working here. He was only here for two weeks or so but they were a fantastic two weeks. Watching him act is like watching him in all those Bergman films. He just dives beneath the surface of every word and every look. He produces these giant feelings. It's incredible.

"A lot of the actors really let go in this picture. I think every actor wants to let go. They want to go somewhere they haven't gone before, to go further than they trust. But you've got to feel secure. You've got to feel that you're not making an idiot of yourself. So, if I, as a director, get excited about them going into new areas, they will push further.

"Sian Phillips did some really wild things. She sort of stokes herself. We'd be talking about a scene and I'd suggest something and she'd react with 'Oh yes, yes, yes. I know exactly what you want!' Then, she'd do it.

"Paul Smith as Rabban? I just couldn't get enough of him. And Brad Dourif is another guy I just can't say enough about. He doesn't have a large role but he's just fantastic. He's one of the most intense actors around. So is Freddy Jones. So is Ken McMillan. There's a bunch of them that are way, way out there. They think up stuff for their characters and wind up really getting into them. It's fantastic to work with them.

"One thing you'll notice in this movie is that our villains are very larger-than-life. They aren't played for laughs, although they obviously enjoy their work. It's easy to get a laugh in a movie like this. There are cheap laughs that destroy the mood and destroy the picture. I don't think there are any of them in this movie. There is a sense of dark humor present, though. The Baron is slightly humorous in an intense way. Rabban. Feyd. There is humor there but I don't think you'd call *Dune* a humorous movie . . . although Alicia says that *Dune* is a comedy."

Lynch shakes his head incredulously. "I wonder if she knows something I don't."

Lynch has, during the course of the picture, constantly tinkered with scenes and dialogue in order to strengthen the movie. He has changed props at the last minute, causing shooting delays, just to add extra impact to the visual quality of a particular setting.

When he first agreed to do the project, Lynch was very much

Silvana Mangano with director David Lynch.

aware that he was a stranger in the world of *Dune*. After all, at the time he was contacted by the De Laurentiis group, he had not even read the Frank Herbert novel.

Lynch grins, remembering his time period as a *Dune* trainee. "I found out quick enough that it was a classic. Oddly enough, though, I found that there were a lot of people out there like me . . . people who hadn't heard of the book. I'm not sure who the real *Dune* freaks are, but there are a lot of them out there. There are also a lot of people who don't know anything about the novel. That frightens me. It's not like this movie is a sure thing.

"When I first started out on this, it was really difficult for me. You can't help wondering if the people who loved the book will love your script. But, if Frank Herbert is happy with the film, and he is, then I feel OK. That's super. If I love the film and really feel proud of it, then I've done my job.

"*Dune* is the kind of film that has a chance of being successful both artistically and commercially. I think that films can and should be *both* those things. It's no good doing a film that only a few intellectuals groove on while everyone else just falls asleep. *Dune* has a lot of strange elements in it that I think people will find entertaining.

"I don't think that people should approach *Dune* as a heavy-handed movie. The novel is considered a classic. I hope the film will be considered one, too. But the movie isn't set up to deliver a great, overt message. There are a lot of different elements in it. It may hit on different ideas during its course. But it's not a spoon-fed message film at all.

"It's a pretty simple, surface story. It gets complicated because of these little threads, you know, little strings just swimming beneath the surface. On the one hand, it's a strong adventure story. People escape and get into trouble. There are battles. Fear. Heroism. There are these giant worms fifteen hundred feet long and a hundred and twenty-five feet high. The sound of them alone will bring you to your knees. We have a pretty good adventure story here. As an extra added attraction," Lynch laughs, "when the characters talk they actually express thoughts! Pretty nifty, eh?"

Everyone connected with the movie has high hopes about the film's commercial and artistic viability but, at some points during production, there were concerns voiced that Lynch's approach to the subject matter would prove too dark, too brooding.

Lynch met those concerns head-on. "I never worried about that. I let other people do that," he grins. "As a director, I like something dark in the frame. If everything is all brightly lit and you can see everything, then there's no mystery. I don't think a dark movie is necessarily depressing. A movie can be bright and colorful and still depress the heck out of you.

"At the same time, I think a dark movie can be very uplifting. Like *The Elephant Man*. To me, that's an uplifting film and there are tons of dark scenes in it. I just go with the material. The material has got to reach you, to touch you. If you're true to that material, then you have a good chance of people liking your movie. If you're not true to that material and you try to second-guess your audience while you're making the movie, you could end up with a flop.

"*Dune* isn't a *dark* movie. It's well textured. It varies in tone from planet to planet, scene to scene. There are a lot of moods in it. There's a sort of faraway mood, like a distant Rembrandt painting, in some of the scenes involving wind. There's a mood that's industrial and brighter and loud and twisted. There are moods that are hot and light and foreign. There are moods that are dark and foreign. There are moods that are rich and foreign."

Lynch, in describing the space fantasy, repeatedly stresses the word *foreign*, alerting everyone that *Dune* is not your typical, all-American, Buck Rogers romp. "It has to seem foreign," he emphasizes. "It takes place on another world. Everything in this movie has to be alien. For instance, sound is going to play a huge part in this picture. To me, a picture is kind of dry until you add sounds to it. Then, it comes to life. It becomes bigger than you intended. Alan Splet (who provided the sound effects for both *The Elephant Man* and *Eraserhead)* has been working for six months on sounds. He's already got a hundred and seventy reels of sound effects and raw noises ready to go. That will be a lot of fun, just picking the sound effects and creating new effects with Alan. That's where things get real nifty. The movie will not only look different, it'll sound different, too. We're going to try to do something different with the soundtrack, as well. Having different types of music used for each different planet or civilization. We may have different artists do the music. We're not sure yet."

Lynch is dedicated to the task of making *Dune* an epic film in both an audio-visual and emotional sense. One problem he faces, however, is cutting the picture down to a functional, commercial length. Translation: the movie *can't* be three hours long, no matter how much the story begs for such a length. In America, movie exhibitors don't relish the chance of dealing with films that are so long that they can't be shown as often, during the course of a day, as a two-hour-or-under production. Worse yet, most audiences find it difficult to sit through a movie three hours long or more.

"Right now," Lynch says optimistically, "we're trying for two and a half hours. Two and a half hours is a long time for an American movie," he scratches his head. "I don't know. I sort of like the European way of filmmaking. I like films like *2001*, too. I like long scenes. I like silences. Stuff like that. It's going to be really hard for me to get the movie I really see there into two and a half hours. I still think it can be done. Right now, I know the rough cut is going to be really long. But the rough cut of every film is long. The rough cut of *The Elephant Man* was long. The rough cut of *Eraserhead* was about a *year* long. It's just something to start off from. Raw material. At this point, I don't know what parts of the script we're going to lose and what parts we're going to keep.

"There won't be any really long scenes in the film. Nothing will tax the audience. It will be cut so it rolls along. But it won't be a TV movie. I don't like fast surface films. That's popcorn. There have to be fast areas and there have to be slow areas. The slow areas *have* to be there or else the fast areas won't work. There have to be highs and lows that contrast. That's what I'm after with *Dune*."

Since Lynch is aware that trimming *Dune* down to a sprightly running time is going to be hard, why does he persistently ad-lib new scenes? During the past week, he has filmed at least two scenes that were not in the original script. He has greatly enlarged Rabban's

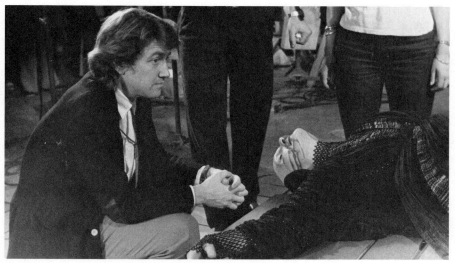

David Lynch sits thoughtfully next to Sian Phillips.

role and added bits of business for the Baron.

"Well," he laughs self-consciously. "It's like...nothing is finished until it's finished. This movie is going to *be* a certain way, come what may. The script is a starting point. It's not complete. It's the finished movie that's going to be complete. A lot of times, you'll have ideas along the way. You'll see something and you've got to just roll with it. You change this or change that. You can't be locked in when you make a movie.

"The script is like a skeleton. You can rely on it. If it works in the script, then you have a certain leeway to play with things. I don't practice what they call 'cinema verite.' I like things under control, but I still realize—maybe now more than ever—that I cannot work being locked into a script or a story. I hate storyboards now more than anything. I would hate to do what Hitchcock did and storyboard everything and stick exactly to that. All the fun of making a movie would be gone, for me.

"I mean, when you're on the set, there are so many ways to go that it's exciting all the time. Frustrating, too. Like the other day when we had that black box spinning and Freddie mentioned about the shadows being on the wall. I would have loved to shoot them but I didn't have the time. Maybe I can make that a second-unit shot. I don't know. It just adds to the mood. I love seeing things like that.

"You've got to build upon your structure to fully realize a script's potential. You find things. Discover things. Eliminate things. Sometimes I'll see something. Sometimes Dino will see something. Sometimes a member of the crew or the cast will. That's the tricky part about it. You can't let your ego get in the way. If someone's come up with a good idea and you realize that it's absolutely right, you've got to accept the fact that that idea wasn't yours.

"A film is really a group endeavor. The director is like a filter. Everything passes through me. Everybody has input and has ideas and, so, the movie has a great momentum going for it. I'm open to all suggestions but if a suggestion isn't right, I say so. Some things pass right through the filter and some things don't. It's not ego that makes you say no to some suggestions, it's a sense of what's right for the movie.

"Ego," he stresses. "Ego. That has so much to do with making a movie. Look. I can't lie and say that I'm some strange character who doesn't have an ego. I've got one but you have to strain to keep it from stopping you from letting some of these fantastic ideas come through that arise from other people. On a picture like this, there are so many creative people with insights, I'd be an idiot not to take advantage of them. Someone said that I was like a painter using his actors as tools. That's wrong. These people are not just tubes of paint. It's not like they're saying, 'OK, David. I'm here, use me.' It's much more collaborative than that. I think the finished film will show the energy that went into this process."

On this smoggy August day, with a little over a week of live shooting left, Lynch is very optimistic about *Dune*'s chances at being a success. "I have a good feeling about it," he acknowledges. "But I know that you're not out of the woods until a lot of people sit down and really love it. You can fool yourself all you want but that's what it comes down to. I've been in audiences seeing a film that wasn't working. That was pure hell for me. We've got a lot of good material done. We've got a lot more coming to be made this fall. I'm excited about it right now. I'm keeping my fingers crossed."

Lynch segues into a conversation peppered with anecdotes concerning the making of *Eraserhead* and *The Elephant Man*. Clearly, he is a filmmaker who loves experimentation and a great deal of freedom. How, then, has he managed to keep his sanity while directing a production that is a nightmare in terms of structure, logistics and budget? Has it been difficult to keep his iconoclastic streak under control for these past two years?

"I tell you," he responds with a sly grin. "People have asked me how I could do a movie like *Dune*. Believe me, this has *not* been a painful experience for me. There are plenty of nifty little things to do in this movie.

"In general, as a director, I feel like a man on a leash. We're all on leashes in some way. But I'm not stupid. I can't make personal films all the time. So, what I'm doing with *Dune*, for instance, is taking a little bit of my private world and bringing it into this movie. I think that's why I really enjoyed filming Giedi Prime so much. That's sort of the imagery that appeals to me.

"I've gotten a chance to play with Paul a lot, too. He's got a lot of things going on inside of him. There are strange moods that just come over him in this film. It's really rich."

"Here's the thing, I *like* being on a leash. A leash is nothing but a sense of restriction. Right now, I'm doing a very expensive picture. But, even if I was doing a movie on my own, a small picture, I'd still have restrictions. Restrictions are exciting. You need them. It's exciting trying to figure out how to make things work within certain boundaries. If you could do just *anything*, you might not even be able to move, you know what I mean? The freedom would be paralyzing.

"Restrictions are necessary. Restrictions are great to force you to think, to capture ideas. In that sense, this has been one of the most rewarding creative experiences I've ever had.

"I mean, you're confronted with these absolutely screwy things every single day. I usually make the best of it. I don't get mad very much . . . it takes a lot to get me there. But when I do get mad, I get really mad. I know I've gotten angry a couple of times on this movie, but I can't remember over what. Raffaella would probably know. We've argued a couple of times. But then we wind up making a joke about the whole thing. Most of us have been too busy to get angry a lot."

The phone rings. Lynch's driver is waiting outside to take him to the Dead Dog Dump for another night of cold and smoke. Lynch eases himself off the chair, grabs his leather jacket and heads for the door. The sun is setting. In a few moments, he will be curled up in the back seat of his car, listening to Mexican radio and watching the scenery pass by his window like a never-ending cyclorama.

"Mexico is magic," he suddenly offers. "It's had a magical effect on me. Just take Mexican art. I never liked it until I came down here. But now, it strikes me as being fantastic. It comes from this place. It comes from being here and breathing this air and feeling these vibes."

He climbs into his car. "There are so many ideas floating around this land and so many things that are triggers for these ideas that, if it got any more intense, it would drive you crazy. There is just so much stimulation to be gotten from this environment. Really, it's magic."

Lynch's car heads for the Great Wall of the Arrakeen palace where, tonight, Gurney Halleck will flee for his life, carrying the Duke's pet dog over the rocky terrain of Arrakis. Eight months ago, Gurney would have been tripping over a square mile of smoldering garbage. The Great Wall would not have existed. And the only uniforms in the area would have been those of sanitation workers sifting through the rotting remains of dead animals.

Chalk it up to magic.

The magic of moviemaking.

20.
MINIATURES
AND MONSTERS

I don't like to explain what I do too much.
When you see things on the screen, you should be amazed.
You shouldn't be thinking "I bet I know how that works!"
Carlo Rambaldi, special effects mechanical features modeler

We're combining a lot of new techniques with a lot
of old-fashioned ones.
Raffaella De Laurentiis, producer

I really like our Guild Navigator. He's pretty odd looking.
Pretty out there. I wouldn't have minded him being
a little odder, though. Things just
can't get odd enough for me.
David Lynch, director

As the live-action photography phase of production nears an end, everyone's attention begins to shift towards special effects work. More and more meetings are held between Raffaella De Laurentiis, David Lynch and the various heads of the different effects units.

While plans are made for the various optically enhanced scenes to be filmed during post-production, work continues on the effects sequences that are being done during principal photography.

A regular face on the set during these days is that of Carlo Rambaldi. Rambaldi's expertise lies in the area of mechanical creations. A long-time celluloid collaborator of Dino De Laurentiis', Rambaldi is the man who designed and built the blood-thirsty finned fury in *Orca, the Killer Whale*, the barbaric bison in *The White Buffalo* and the colossal *King Kong*. Rambaldi is also responsible for designing and building Steven Spielberg's popular extraterrestrial, E.T.

As *Dune's* special effects mechanical features modeler, he is re-

sponsible for the creation and execution of the titantic Third-Stage
Guild Navigator, the eerie adult/baby Alia who is born with all Bene
Gesserit knowledge, and, most importantly, the Olympian-sized,
more than slightly sinister sandworms.

Carlo Rambaldi prepares a mechanized model of the baby Alia.

On this day, late in August, Rambaldi is preparing his Navigator
for its appearance in the film. Carlo doesn't like to reveal too many
secrets, preferring to let movie audiences concentrate on the magical
qualities of his creations when they are on the screen.

During the course of a conversation, he will reveal only the bits
of information he considers less than top secret. He enjoys being
baited, however, and, in spite of his reticence to talk in detail of his
celluloid "babies," he is obviously proud of them.

Today, he stands hovering over his navigator like a concerned
parent. The 15-foot-long beast puts an appearance in at the beginning of the movie. Its scenes will be the last to actually go before
the cameras, however. The Navigator looks like a very large insect/
embryo mutation. Its head is large and bloated. Its eyes are equally
huge and heavy-lidded. Its arms are small and shriveled in comparison to its bulbous body.

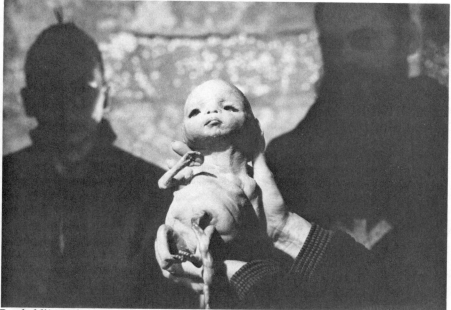

Rambaldi's mechanical model of Alia.

Rambaldi's massive third stage Guild Navigator, a mechanized beast with forty separate points of movement.

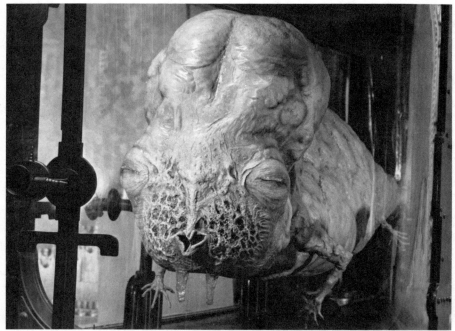

A close-up of the third stage Guild Navigator.
En route to Mexico from the States, the fifteen-foot creature was damaged
and had to be given first aid on the Churubusco lot.

In the movie, the Third-Stage Navigator is wheeled into the
Emperor's throne room in a large tank filled with gas. In reality, the
creature will be wheeled onto a set in a tank with a false rear section.
Behind the phoney wall, technicians will pump in the "spice gas"
and control the bug-eyed alien's movements via an assortment of
levers and manual controls.

"I don't use computers to work my navigator," Carlo abruptly
says, looking up at the big-orbed beast. "It's all mechanical. All
mechanics."

He sighs and shakes his head. "This arrived in Mexico all ruined.
When I got down here, I had to redo everything. The Navigator
was being shipped to the studio by truck. They changed trucks in
El Paso and no one bothered to pack it properly. By the time I arrived,
one half of its head had collapsed. It was smashed en route."

Fortunately, Carlo was able to do a nice bit of cosmetic surgery
on the creature.

"I designed the initial model for the Navigator in clay," says
Carlo. "Then, David Lynch came up to Los Angeles to see it and

we made a few changes and alterations. It took three months to construct the full-size model. Fifteen people worked on its creation. The skeletal structure is made of aluminum and assorted metal. It's all covered with rubber.

"The final model has forty separate points of movement. We have twenty-two people operating it. It is all moved by human hands. It's all mechanical."

He walks around the huge tank. "There's a single axis that holds up the Navigator in its chamber. That's the one that is never seen by the camera. It's always positioned away from the lens."

As Carlo readies the Navigator for his screen debut, he casually mentions his other work for the movie. "The weird little baby? [Alia] That wasn't too hard to do. It only took six people to operate it. It was all mechanics. Basically, it's just a mechanical baby that is a little odd. I studied what a real fetus looked like and exaggerated the features slightly to give it an alien yet recognizably human look. That wasn't hard for me.

"What *was* hard for me was making the worms." He pauses dramatically. "Those worms! They required an entirely different type of mechanical movement. I had to figure out a whole new method of construction to achieve a fluid motion.

"I built sixteen of them in all sizes. On the screen, of course, they will look like thousands of worms. They will fill the screen. But those sixteen were quite hard to build. We're preparing them for their screen test now. They are partly electronic and partly mechanical.

"They undulate, you know? They slink along. They have to be able to burrow in and out of the sand. They are very complicated because part of the worm's mechanical system extends from the

A very early model of a sandworm.

body of the worm to beneath the sand. We will have operators underneath the miniature desert working them when they move. Not only do their bodies have to move but the aperture of the mouth moves. When the worms open their mouths there are little flaps inside, like tongues. They move, too. Very complicated. It will take eighteen people to work the biggest worm."

Just what intricate devices are housed inside each of the slithering screen stars? Rambaldi flashes a puckish smile. A twinkle appears in his eyes. He realizes he is approaching a top-secret area of conversation. He shrugs. "They have a skeletal-mechanical system made out of aluminum and steel and they are coated with rubber."

But how are the worms brought to life?

He smiles again. "Very carefully."

He breaks into easy laughter. End of discussion.

Emilio Ruiz Del Rio is more than happy to discuss his work. As the effects artist in charge of *Dune*'s incredibly detailed miniatures, del Rio has been given the task of providing the science-fiction saga with an extra sense of scope.

The word "miniature" may be a bit misleading when it comes to del Rio's creations. Some of his models are nearly seventy-five feet long and thirty feet high. Most of them are filmed in conjunction with live actors as well, making these "miniatures" seem like towering objects.

"All of the models on this movie were a challenge," the wiry Spanish artist smiles. "They were difficult to construct and needed much detail. I can't single out one or two as the most difficult because they were all equally hard. But, with thirty years of experience and three hundred films behind me, I manage."

Many of Del Rio's creations are foreground miniatures that, through the use of forced perspective, are made to look like a gigantic part of a real scene. A mountain he has created, for example, that is only six feet tall, may be placed a few feet away from a camera while live actors, who are supposedly cowering in the face of this immense object, may be strategically posed thirty yards away. When the camera, properly positioned, photographs the two elements together, the final scene will show ordinary-sized people posed against a towering mass of molten rock hundreds of feet tall.

Del Rio, who has done miniature work for such movies as *Dr. Zhivago, Nicholas and Alexandria, Conan the Barbarian,* and *Solomon and Sheba* and who has worked with such directors as Franklin Shaffner, Richard Lester, George Cukor, David Lean and King Vidor, has been working his miniature magic since the late 1940s.

"I started out in the art department, working with set dressers," he explains. "When I first started doing this, I was painting the miniatures. Later, I created a new system by using cuts and pieces of aluminum that, placed close to the camera, would look large. I found that you could amplify and change sets and landscapes by adding miniature elements close to the camera. I came up with a system where you could film the live action with miniature sets and even miniature figures at normal shooting speed and have it look very realistic."

"I built a rock cliff for a scene where Paul and Jessica are hiding in a desert. They find shelter in this rock cliff. The foreground miniature was used to give extra dimension to an existing rock wall in the desert. The miniature cliff was 16 by 8 feet. We shot the scene at night using a dust effect that was later mixed with the one they were using on the set.

"The miniature Arrakeen palace I built was 29 by 13 feet. In the movie you will see real, live soldiers walking up the stairs and entering the palace. We actually constructed life-sized doors and stairs for this scene. The rest of the palace was a miniature that was 'carved' into a miniature mountainside. The model mountain-palace was placed nine feet from the camera. The soldiers and the real doors were placed far behind the miniature. There was a 'space' in the miniature castle that, when the camera was placed in its proper position, would be filled by the life-sized door and stairs and the human actors. In the finished shot, you will see the humans walk up the stairs of the 'miniature.'"

While the idea of forced perspective shots is relatively simple, its execution is anything but. In one sequence involving a fleet of Atreides ships landing at Arrakeen, for instance, a foreground model of a ship standing 28 by 19 feet had to be combined with eight other, smaller ship models as well as thousands of miniature soldiers (each .31 inch high) and live-action soldiers marching! Yet another prop was a cliff adjacent to this landing field which was 13 by 19 feet.

In the finished movie, the scene will begin with the Duke and his family calmly walking down a flight of stairs extended from their spaceship. Awaiting their arrival will be thousands of loyal Atreides soldiers lined up on a landing field already crowded with Atreides vessels. In reality, the only full-size elements in the shot were the

An Atreides ship under construction in the model shop,
with sections of a spice harvester in the foreground.

A member of the film crew stands next to a gigantic model of a Harkonnen flagship.
Next to the ship are miniatures of its crew.

Duke, his family, a small section of his spaceship and a few dozen soldiers. All the rest of the scene was created by Del Rio.

"In a scene like this," he says, "there are hundreds of details you have to think about. Whenever you use little figures and real people in a single shot in a movie, you have to take into consideration scales and the area where these models are standing in order to avoid the real people getting too close to the models.

"In this particular scene we actually built a huge, lower section of an Atreides ship, a door, a stairs, et cetera on a parking lot that was to serve as part of our landing field. The Duke and his family come out of this door, walk down the steps and salute the troops awaiting them.

"Our camera was set 312 feet away from this ship section and the actors, on a platform 36 feet high. The platform itself had a miniature scene that was spread out over an area of 54 by 36 feet. Our Atreides ship model was up there as well as the eight other miniature ships.

"Part of this miniature setup was our little landing field. On our miniature landing field were placed thousands of little soldiers, all standing in line, at attention. When the camera was angled so that the little soldiers at attention matched with the real, human soldiers at attention below us, we created an effect of sheer grandiosity. It

Using the technique of forced perspective, a miniature ship and its crew members are combined with human actors and an oversized prop to become part of a single sprawling scene on film.

takes a lot of time and a lot of patience to film a scene like this."

Yet another brain-teaser for Del Rio was the filming of the massive Harkonnen ship. "It was 48 by 26 feet," he says. "A spectacular foreground model. Part of the ship, two pilasters and a door, were real sets that we constructed at the Azteca Stadium in Mexico. We had to use the stadium area because the Harkonnen ship was supposed to be *so* big in relationship to the live actors that we had to place our camera 297 feet away to get the shot.

"The model and the camera were set on a platform thirty-six feet high. Down below us, live-actor sentinels surrounded the ship's door. Live-actor troops were in front. Our model was surrounded by little figures made at the appropriate scale. They matched the live actors perfectly. The 'live' door fit in with the miniature ship and, again, we produced a sense of colossal size."

Among Del Rio's other amazing miniatures:

Castle Caladan. "For this scene, we built a pool seventy-five feet wide. We produced waves that would crash against a rock cliff wall. High above it was the castle. It was six feet tall. We used only models, no people. We shot it all live with all the effects we needed, waves, lightning, rain. To make it all seem realistic, we shot it at seventy-two frames per second; an accelerated rate that, when shown on the screen, will be slowed down and given a natural look."

Emilio Ruiz Del Rio, at the left of the camera, supervises the filming of his marching miniatures.

A mass of Atreides spacecraft.

A Dune rock outcropping. "In this scene, 20,000 Fremen are seen entering the desert from a rock cavern. I built the rock 32 by 16 feet. In this sequence, nothing is real. We built 20,000 little Fremen figures, each 1.2 inches tall. In order to give them movement, we constructed a complicated mechanism of gears, pullies, springs and bands that was set up beneath the desert floor and operated from underneath the miniature."

A deep desert panorama. "The live-action desert scenes were shot near Juarez. We constructed a model of a desert that could be taken out to the Juarez location and matched with the real landscape. It was 16 by 13 feet. On it we constructed a similar system of movement as the one we used in the rock outcropping. We mixed live-action Fremen troops with hundreds of .008-inch figures. We filmed it all at normal speed but we used a wind-storm effects. The sand blows very hard and, in the final shot, you can't tell the real Fremen from their miniature stand-ins."

Arrakeen. "We built a model standing 90 feet by 88 feet for Arrakeen. It is a massive mountainside with the palace carved in the center. A wall surrounds the city. Outside the wall is a section of desert. We built this model for fire and explosions. Part of the material we used for this construction of the wall was very light to allow for good explosive effects."

To construct each of his miniature marvels, Del Rio and his team calmly mixed ingenuity with a great deal of sweat and whatever materials were handy. "We used the usual materials," he says offhandedly. "Resins, plaster, woods, fibers, electrical wiring. We had twelve major models. They were all under construction at the same time. Some had priority, of course, depending on when they were supposed to be filmed. It took us eleven and a half months to finish with them all.

"The models were all very, very intricate. Most of them were filmed at night so we used a lot of electrical wiring. There were lights in the interiors of the ships and castles and often we would have a series of small lights in the background to give the illusion of cities seen from a distance. We used motors to make pumps work in some models, make steam rise.

"All the ships were original designs so we had to construct *all* the pieces. In many science-fiction films you can build a ship from pieces of toy models to give them a standard, spaceship look. In our movie, everything was *different,* everything looked *unique.*"

He stifles a chuckle. "Sometimes *too* unique. The Emperor's spaceship proved amazingly difficult. It was colossal. If it was a real

Harkonnen 'thopter crash-lands in the desert.

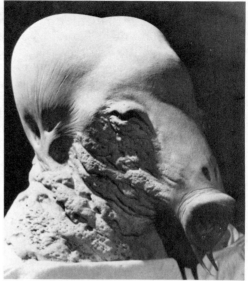

A discarded design for a second stage Guild Navigator.

The Emperor's steel tent.

ship, it would stand 650 by 400 feet!! As it was, our model was 60 by 45 feet. It was a nightmare to film. We shot it at night at twenty-four frames per second. We used oil and steam effects that were very difficult to coordinate. It wasn't possible to put the model very close to the camera because we needed to get a sense of depth in the shot.

"We set the camera and the foreground model on a platform 30 feet high and 27 feet from the real construction."

Del Rio, with over 300 movies to his credit, sees *Dune* as being one of his most "elaborate and spectacular." He doesn't have time to gloat over his accomplishments, however. As soon as he finishes his last *Dune* shot, he'll begin work on the miniatures for *Conan the Destroyer* for producer Raffaella De Laurentiis.

"There will be some challenges on that one, too," he confides. He strolls toward the backlot where part of a rock cliff he has built is being prepared for the arrival of its sandworm stars.

"Movies have changed since I started in this business," he says with a sigh. "The film industry is now making movies that are more elaborate and difficult. It's important to have effects and tricks in a movie. The more you have, the more spectacular the movie will be.

A spice harvester model chugs away on the surface of Arrakis—thanks to a metal track buried beneath the sand.

The Emperor's steel tent

A Harkonnen 'thopter, rear view

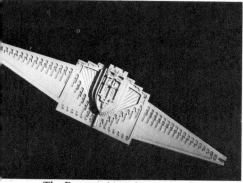

An Atreides 'thopter in flight

A Guild Heighliner

A Harkonnen 'thopter, front view

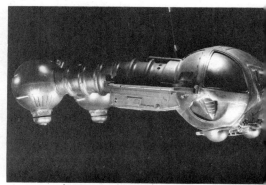

A Harkonnen 'thopter, side view

The massive Carry-All, a ship big enough to transport several spice harvesters.

An Atreides ornithopter model with landing pods extended.

"But the concept of effects has changed as well. Before, all your tricks and effects were supposed to be hidden. Movie makers wanted people to think everything was real. Today, producers publicly talk about their effects and tricks. They are proud of them. They even make documentaries that tell of the making of the film. The importance of the effects. The difficulties involved."

Del Rio, walking towards his massive cliff face, smiles slyly. He doesn't seem to mind discussing his work at all. "No," he admits. "It is good to talk about it. But," he adds emphatically, "it is better to see."

21.
THE FINAL DAYS

I hate to see this movie end. I really do.
Paul Smith, actor (Rabban)

This doesn't mark the end of DUNE.
The hard work is just beginning.
Raffaella De Laurentiis, producer

I've agreed to stay down here and work on the special
effects scenes. I will chalk that up to sunstroke.
Freddie Francis, cinematographer

The first week of September 1983 finds a mixed mood on the Churubusco lot. On the one hand, there is a sense of relief. *Dune* is ending its long live-action period of filming. There is also a sense of sadness. Cast and crewmembers who have grown fond of each other are separating and, once again, heading for their "normal" lives.

Most prevalent, however, is a feeling of tense expectation for, within a week, a gun-to-the-head post-production schedule will begin. Spaceships will have to be built and flown. Worms will have to be operated and realistically filmed. Explosions, battles, sandstorms and thermonuclear maelstroms will have to be created and staged.

In short, hundreds of optically enhanced sequences are waiting to be done.

"I don't want to think about it," moans Freddie Francis in mock exasperation. "I must be a masochist to stay."

Aldo Puccini is gazing up at the massive Third-Stage Guild Navigator. Tomorrow, the immense mechanized model will be wheeled onto the emperor's throne-room set. For now, however, the creature is sitting dormant in its tank in a darkened studio.

"The first time I saw this thing," Aldo says, "I said to Carlo,

'Carlo. Look at this thing. It is a very ugly Navigator.'

"Carlo smiled at me and said, 'Yeah. But look at the size of his head. See how big it is? He may be ugly but, by God, he's very, very smart!'"

David Lynch, realizing that there are only a few more live-action scenes to do, is getting a little nostalgic. "We've done some amazingly strange things on this movie," he says. "I love things that are absurd. Not that anything on *Dune* has struck me as *really* absurd. But seeing a group of Italians with levers operating a mechanical baby...that gets close to it. It didn't make me laugh out loud but it came pretty close. When I was filming stuff on Giedi Prime I'd get close to laughing...but that was because I loved the sets so much. I was just *so* happy."

Brian Smithies, a model builder par excellence with a host of credits ranging from such TV shows as *Project UFO* to movies like *Clash of the Titans* under his belt, arrives in Mexico to set up his model shop. He gets settled during the early days of September. His first model is required to go before the cameras in less than three weeks.

"My goodness," he mutters to himself. "This is going to be something of a job."

The scene in the Emperor's throne room involves Jose Ferrer as the Emperor being intimidated by some rather harsh dialogue delivered by the cumbersome but cunning Third-Stage Guild Navigator. Since the Navigator, according to the storyline, speaks in a different tongue than the Emperor, his "words" are "translated" into English and broadcast out of a speaker attached to his tank.

In reality, the Navigator's dialogue is prerecorded by an actor and is played back rehearsal through rehearsal. The fifteen technicians required to operate this huge Carlo Rambaldi creation rehearse diligently to coordinate their movements.

The presence of video monitors allows each controller to watch the Navigator in action as they play with their individual levers and controls.

For the most part, all goes smoothly. "We had a little problem," Carlo Rambaldi concedes. "Our Navigator ran over one of the crew. One of the British special effects team had his foot on one of the trucks we use when we were moving the Navigator back to its 'start' position. He was working the controls for the gas and didn't hear David yell 'cut.' He stayed where he was and the Navigator just ran

In the Emperor's golden throne room, the Emperor awaits
the arrival of the Guild Navigator. This was the final scene of <u>Dune</u> to be filmed.

The Emperor, Reverend Mother Helen Mohiam, Princess Irulan.

**The third stage Guild Navigator enters the throne room
with the first stage Guild Navigators.**

over his foot. The Navigator weighs around a thousand pounds, too. I heard this scream and just stopped the creature...but it was too late."

Carlo shrugs. "The man was OK. He was in the hospital for a little while. Later he used a cane."

In a sense, both the crewmember and the Emperor learned a lesson by this scene's end: When a Navigator decides to push his weight around...don't stand in his way.

During the last days of shooting a wrap party is held at a nearby arena wherein cast and crewmembers are invited to step into a bullring and "fight" baby bulls.

The mood is festive throughout the final week. Family and friends fly down to the set for one last bash.

Lynch is joined by his wife and children.

He is quite pleased by the final scenes he is filming. "The Guild Navigator is a joy to work with. He's a great actor. He's better than human actors, in fact," Lynch beams, "'cause he always says his lines right time after time after time."

On September 9, 1983, the last remaining live-action shot in *Dune*, Scene #7, is filmed in the Emperor's gold throne room.

Princess Irulan (Virginia Madsen) is dismissed by her father as the Reverend Mother (Sian Phillips) enters the chamber. The Emperor (Jose Ferrer) warns her that a Third-Stage Navigator is approaching. He asks his Truthsayer to stay nearby and try to read the mind of this strange, buglike creature.

At that point, under the carved inscription LAW IS THE ULTIMATE SCIENCE, the room's two golden doors swing open and fifty Guildsmen wheel in a forty-foot-long giant black box. The Reverend Mother is ordered out of the room.

The Emperor turns and faces the Guildsmen, still eyeing the black box, still awaiting his first glimpse of the massive Navigator.

With the small army of Guildsmen before him, and the mysterious black box sitting in the middle of the room, the Emperor attempts to win the confidence of his visitors.

"We are alone..." he says, reassuringly.

Cut.

Print it.

Dune has completed principal photography.

III.
POST-PRODUCTION

The amount of special effects work that we're trying to accomplish during this period of time is pretty amazing. If we get away with it, it's a tribute to the crazy and talented people who are working on all this.
David Lynch, director

22.
SHIP-SHAPE IN MEXICO

I'm delighted with the effects work. But, I must be honest.
In September, when we found
ourselves starting from scratch,
I was a little petrified.
Raffaella De Laurentiis, producer

What has been the biggest challenge working on DUNE?
Trying to make a successful phone call to Los Angeles.
Barry Nolan, supervisor of special photographic effects

When you actually sit down and think of the
amount of work you have to do in relationship
to the time you have to do it in,
you find yourself laughing... rather shrilly.
Brian Smithies, director of DUNE's model unit

Brian Smithies stands on a sound stage before a large miniature desert. Several technicians wearing surgical masks are doing a bit of haphazard cosmic surgery on one of the sand dunes, sprinkling wads of tinted fuller's earth onto an already formed mound.

Behind Smithies, a member of his special effects unit stands on a platform, holding a small model of a sleek Harkonnen ornithopter high above his head. The plastic model is attached to a wire. On a given signal, the ship will be released and it will zip down the wire and "crash" into the sand dune.

The technicians crawl off the diminutive desert. The cameras are turned on. The motors rev up to speed. Brian turns to the technician holding the ship. "Good luck, John," Smithies says, nodding. "Let it go."

The ornithopter glides down toward the harsh, white desert of Arrakis. It hits the dune... and ricochets off.

It looks totally unbelievable.

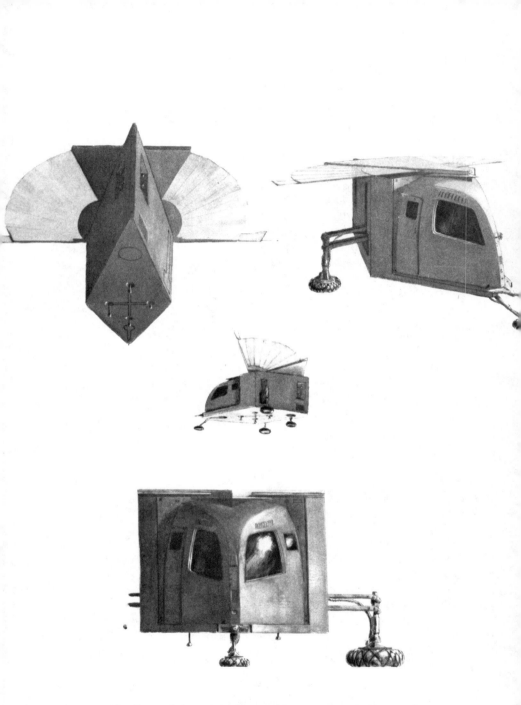

The diamond-shaped Atreides ornithopter in various flight modes.

The dark and sinister Harkonnen flagship.

Smithies heaves a sigh. He turns around, sand and fuller's earth covering his face and parts of his beard. "I'm afraid we're having a bit of a problem with our spaceship," he says, flashing a bemused smile. "It bounces."

Smithies and his men go back to work, restaging and reshooting the shot. A day later, they will finally come up with an elastic-rigging that will send the Harkonnen ship successfully smashing into the sand hill accompanied by a lethal tidal wave of grit. During the time in between, though, they will good-naturedly shrug off the pressure that is being imposed on them daily.

From the first week of September until January 31, 1984, a small group of special effects experts are being asked to do the impossible: create and film nearly 400 state-of-the-art effects sequences involving models, blue screens and mechanical monsters.

"It's not the amount of work that is the challenge," Smithies says later, "it's the relatively short period of time we have to perform it in. Still," he says philosophically, "*every* movie you work on puts that sort of pressure on you. It's an occupational hazard."

Smithies' responsibility in regard to the high-flying world of *Dune* involves building and filming the movie's imaginative fleet of spaceships.

Among the vessels he is responsible for:

• The buglike spice harvester—a sand-crawling device that travels out into the desert stretches of the planet Dune in search of melange.

• The super-sleek Guild heighliner—a mothership of incredibly large proportions.

• Both the Atreides and Harkonnen ornithopters—vehicles that can swoop low over planetary surfaces and carry from two to twelve passengers depending on the make of the ship.

• The massive Carry-All—a floating factory which picks up and drops off spice harvesters at different mining locations for a good day's work.

• The Atreides spaceships—ornate, ribbed ships that are as efficient as they are aesthetically pleasing to behold.

• Harkonnen flagships—rounded ominous vessels used by the evil Baron for nefarious deeds.

• The Emperor's ship and steel tent—solid gold vessels that are part pyramid, part deco-tech in design.

• The Giedi Prime cable car—a black messenger of evil that glides effortlessly above the steamy world of the Baron's lair.

Creating these vessels under any circumstances would be a challenge, but creating them under the conditions faced by Smithies is doubly heroic.

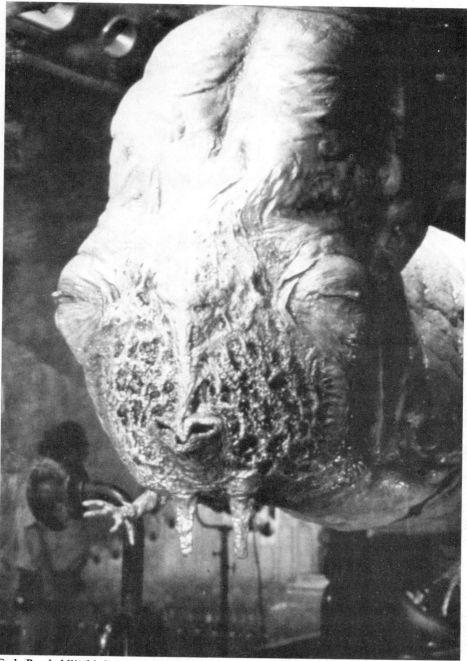

Carlo Rambaldi's third stage Guild Navigator.

**An early design
of the Carry-All.**

"I got a call in June or July and I came down to Mexico to start discussions about that time," he begins. "I agreed to do the movie but we didn't actually start getting our model shop going until the end of August.

"The time factor has always been tough. We've been building models under the gun. We had to have our first models ready to shoot by the end of September. That only left us four weeks. I've been very lucky, though. I brought a lot of my own people down here from England to supervise things and the Mexican workers we've found have been great . . . considering they've never done this thing before."

A full-sized Atreides ornithopter cockpit.

A Harkonnen ship is under construction at the Churubusco model shop.

Smithies, a bearded, affable Englishman who seems totally un-ruffled on the set, has been doing model work for years. A former artist who began designing sculptures for such films as *Cleopatra* before working on such Gerry Anderson TV shows as *Joe 90* and *Project UFO* as well as films like *Octopussy, The Dark Crystal, The Great Muppet Caper, Clash of the Titans, Superman* and *Dracula,* has found his stay on the planet Dune one fraught with irony.

"Here we are trying to design and build futuristic spaceships in a country where you can't even get hold of plastic!" he laughs.

"The main problem we've had in constructing the models lies in the fact that it's almost impossible to get parts through customs. Plastic kits and the like are just about impossible to come by in Mexico and it takes forever to try to ship them in. We've been doing some very unorthodox things. We've been designing in wood and plaster and then making fiberglass molds.

"That's not as easy as it sounds because the look of this movie is very un-hi-tech. We have some very distinct and amazing designs. Some of the plaster sculptures we've had done are really pieces of art."

In the five months of post-production, Smithies and his crew were required to build forty-two models of various shapes and sizes and film them as well.

"We've been working at a breakneck pace," says Smithies, "but I must admit I am very, very pleased with the finished models. We've just about created everything from scratch. When I first ar-rived down here we were told that there were some spaceship models left over from the previous technicians but most of them were un-usable. We've done everything ourselves in record time."

Depending on the size and shape of the vessel, Smithies would turn to a different source substance. "The Emperor's spaceship was a monster to build," he says. "It doesn't look very aerodynamically sound at all. It is heavy and ornate but it accurately reflects the taste and status of the Emperor. We made it out of wood because wood is very available down here. The actual dressing of the ship was done in wax first and, then, cast in polyester resin. It was then applied to the ship afterwards. The model was about three feet wide, in terms of wing span...if you want to call those things wings.

"We found ourselves using wood whenever we could in building these ships," he continues, "primarily because it's easy to get in large quantities."

He offers a wry grin. "Our work habits have wound up becoming as unorthodox as the designs of the ship."

An artist's rendering of the sleek Guild Heighliner,
a mothership to end all motherships.

For the super-sleek heighliner, Smithies mixed some design met-
aphors. "Basically, the ship itself is a six-foot-long plastic tube with
some decoration on it. I'm looking forward to shooting the cockpit
we've designed for it because it's very gothic. It's my very favorite
piece we've built. It's a very big interior, about twenty feet by eight
feet. It's made of wood and fiberglass, a soaring, vertical, black
cathedral-arched design. The inside of a heighliner is supposed to
be so huge that if you put a Third-Stage Navigator inside, he'd look
as tiny as a tadpole."

Smithies leaves the set and takes a walk to his model shop where
small photographs of Atreides ships are being carefully cut out and
trimmed. Later, these photos will be mounted on clear glass plates
and placed in front of a camera along with three-dimensional models
to create the illusion of hundreds of Atreides ships soaring in space.

"The models of the Atreides ships averaged about three feet in
width for the large ones and twelve inches for the smaller ones.
They were made out of fiberglass from a silicon mold," says Smithies.

He holds up a small, gold ship that vaguely resembles a jewel. "We have two types of ornithopters," he says. "This is an Atreides one. Basically it's a diamond-shaped machine with insectlike wings. Then, there's the Harkonnen ship, which looks more like a dragonfly. Of the two, I like the Harkonnen one best.

"We have three sizes of 'thopters, ranging from six to sixteen inches."

Walking quickly to another model shop, Smithies points to a large, black boiler capped by the hideous face of a laughing cherub. "This is from the refineries of Giedi Prime," he says. "I loved filming that setup. We built the entire city. It's very black. Dark. It's David's concept of Victorian industrial. It's filled with pipes and strange stuff. We made it largely out of fiberglass, using plastic pipes for the boiler area. The city itself was basically polyester resin cast in panels designed in decorative Victorian shapes. The city was modular, too, so we could pull it apart and push it back together again for different heights.

"We lucked out with the Guild ship. That was actually built before we arrived here. Emilio Ruiz Del Rio had built a large-scale miniature.

"We made several different-sized models of the spice harvester. The smallest one is just a few inches long. That's the one that you will see being swallowed by a worm on screen. The large model was beautifully sculpted in plaster by Raffaella Blank. We made a mold from that."

Smithies leaves the shop and heads back for the stage where the Harkonnen ornithopter is still poised for its dramatic dive. "We have new headaches every day," the model maker says. "It has been very difficult shooting these models because, frankly, we're short of state-of-the-art equipment. We're using motion-control cameras but it's very basic motion control. We don't have our cameras interfaced with a computer."

(In most uses of motion-control camera systems today, the movement of the camera is planned out in advance by a computer. That "flight path" program is then entered into the computer's memory. When the effects sequence begins, it is the computer that flawlessly guides the motion of the camera.)

"We're relying on technicians using step-up motors that have to be worked at the exact proper time. I think we're getting some amazing results, though. As it turns out, we couldn't have used state-of-the-art, computerized motion-control equipment down here anyhow. It never would have worked with all the blackouts and power surges and electrical problems."

Smithies steps back onto the miniature desert set, seemingly resigned to the challenge of combining high-caliber thrill sequences with low-tech filming techniques. The Harkonnen ship still dangles from a wire. "Now let's see if we can really get these Harkonnens into trouble," he mutters hopefully.

The Harkonnen ship glides down into the sand dune again. It hits the mound and slides downward a few inches. "It's still not what I want," Smithies says. On the brighter side, he notes, "But at least it didn't bounce!"

23.
WHIZ, BANG, FLASH!

*The special effects in this movie are a tribute
to creativity and a lot of insanity.*
Barry Nolan, supervisor of special photographic effects

Basically, we're working in an ad hoc situation.
Chuck Finance, special effects coordinator

Why aren't we using computerization? Ha. Ha. Ha. Ha.
*Special effects technician laboring on a miniature
desert scene for DUNE*

Special effects supervisor Barry Nolan hovers above a miniature desert constructed on a wooden platform, surveying the mini-dunes before him. "Build that area up a little bit," he says to one worker. "Mario," he calls. "Where are the storyboards for this sequence?"

Nolan is pointed in the direction of a huge bulletin board. The tall, lanky technician strides over to the board to inspect the dozen or so drawings on it that illustrate exactly what will be seen in this shot—an aerial glimpse of Arrakis' surface witnessed by the captain of a crashing spaceship.

Nolan gazes at the board. His silver-maned, bearded head nods imperceptibly. He abruptly turns, a long scarf he's wearing swinging behind him in the dust-flaked air of the studio. "Fine," he states.

With that, the soft-spoken effects man is off to another stage.

Barry Nolan is in a professional predicament. He has a lot to do in very little time. He refuses to acknowledge the fact, however. The former NASA technician (he worked on the Skylab project and made the leap into special film effects when asked to apply laws of physical science to film techniques in the mid-1960s) has a fairly bemused attitude about the carefully mapped-out craziness around him.

"These have been the worst conditions I've ever worked under,"

Kyle MacLachlan stands on a section of a moving sandworm, constructed in front of a giant bluescreen.

he chuckles. "But I think we'll be producing some of our best effects."

His shoulders slump, as if to acknowledge that this trade-off seems fair, artistically.

Nolan walks to one of the studio's editing rooms to review some test footage of worm sequences. As a member and now the head of Van der Veer Photo Effects in Los Angeles, which provided the optical effects unit for *Dune*, he has worked on over 500 films, including *The Towering Inferno, 1941, King Kong, Logan's Run* and *Flash Gordon*. Nolan has seen and done it all.

In spite of that fact, however, the *Dune* experience has proven to be *unique*.

"Unique," he says, mulling over the word. "Yes. That's a good word. Diplomatic, too."

Nolan and his crew entered the scene in July after the original special effects crew exited.

"The *Dune* people called me," he says simply, "and I came down. I've worked with the De Laurentiis organization for about ten years with Frank Van der Veer. He was one of the film effects giants and the founder of Van der Veer Effects, which he ran until his death in 1981. They're a no-nonsense group so I knew exactly what I'd be taking on.

"It wasn't too difficult to step into *Dune* at that late point because they were still shooting live action back then. We had a nice amount of time to prepare for our September start date.

"What I wasn't prepared for, basically, was the lack of technical materials down here. Overcoming that obstacle has been... interesting."

Nolan becomes engrossed in his moviola.

In the effects office one floor below the editing room, Chuck Finance, special effects coordinator and Nolan's righthand man, elaborates.

"It's my job to coordinate the work of the different effects units," says the businesslike Finance. "I make sure that they have the materials ready when they need them. I try to make sure that the different units are working in synch."

He pauses for a beat, adding with a note of humor, "That hasn't been real easy.

"Basically, we're working in an ad hoc situation down here. There was no special effects facility here when we arrived. There was no model shop. No motion control. Everything had to be assembled by Raffaella through people like Barry and Brian Smithies. A very talented group of people was gathered down here.

"The biggest challenge has been to gear ourselves up to produce the kind of effects that the script calls for. By the time we're finished, we'll have over 1,000 different effects elements that will have to be composited [combined with other bits and pieces] on the screen. Some shots will have eight or ten different elements in a single frame.

"On a purely technical level, we've had problems with our motion-control equipment in terms of what we can do and cannot do. The fact that we're working very far away from Los Angeles and don't have all the equipment we need at our fingertips is rough.

"I'm an outsider in that I'm not actually working on a stage but I imagine it must be very frustrating at times. With our motion-control camera, for instance, we have five or six different axes of motion that could be controlled perfectly if we were interfaced with a computer. But since we have no way of doing that, the person who is actually working the motion-control unit has to sit down and figure out how to work each individual movement separately. For instance, if we're panning over a spaceship zipping by, he has to figure out when the camera should speed up and slow down and

Kit West transported his workship from England in a truck,
shipping the vehicle by boat from Southampton, England, to Mexico.

run steady during the pan. It can get into a rather lengthy calculation
process. In Los Angeles, a computer would do the calculations and,
then, make sure that the camera adhered precisely to them.

"Several times we've found ourselves backlogged. Many of the
shots are difficult to work out. You see, the key to this movie is
credibility. David Lynch's vision of these planets is very unusual.
His vision is certainly not sleek and glossy, high-tech. The final
effects will be unlike most of the stuff you've been seeing in effects
pictures. It certainly won't resemble any of the *Star Wars* stuff. The
look isn't pristine or clean. It's almost baroque. It's almost old European in design. We're all sweating bullets down here trying to
get these shots done but we're doing it. I think the results will be
astounding."

Finished with his editing upstairs, Nolan strolls onto a sound
stage and pauses before a twenty-four-foot-long length of worm
"tail." Nolan pats it affectionately. "It's not looking too good today,"
he says. "But when we shot it, it looked fine. It was part of the
blue-screen shots we did with the characters riding the worms.

"The actors were rocking back and forth on these big worm
sections in the foreground of the scene. The worms are spouting

sand out of blow holes, real sand. Later, we'll composite a background on that blue screen behind them. So, you'll see the rest of the worm wriggling along the desert and a host of sand dunes zipping by. Then, optically, we'll go back and put in different layers of sand blowing by.

"In the finished shot, you won't just see a normal, one dimensional storm overlay...where the sand looks like it's been blown flat, directly in front of the camera. We'll actually have an effect of depth. You'll see sand blowing behind the foreground figures but before the background figures. Tricky stuff."

He turns his attention to the tail. "This is the back section of the worm. It's basically molded rubber built on to a wooden frame and covered with vinyl. We bolted a camera to the 'head' of the tail and then pulled the tail around this miniature desert here. The camera did most of the snakelike movement on the tail's behalf. When this is composited behind the actor riding the front part of the worm, it'll look like it's wiggling like crazy."

He leaves the worm behind and takes a tour of the Churubusco backlot. He points to a miniature desert. A three-foot-long model of a spice harvester sits forlornly on the set. "We'll photograph that chugging along in a sandstorm," says Nolan. "There's a track beneath the model that allows it to move."

He motions to a rockface cliff. "That's a cliff that collapses at the end of the movie. A wall of sand rushes out and, then, hundreds of worms wiggle down the canyon. Right now we're trying to gather up enough sand to use for the scene. We keep on running out of sand. I suppose we'll start raiding the studio's sandbag supply if worse comes to worst."

He continues his tour, pointing out half-completed sections of desert and rock. "We have about 400 optical shots planned for this movie," he says. "But we'll probably go beyond that. There are thousands of details that we have to consider on this movie. For instance, every Fremen citizen will have blue eyes because of the spice they use. Optically, we will tint every eye blue, using a process that is part photographic and part electronic. Even though I stepped in late, we had time to plan everything out on paper before we began. It was meticulously coordinated.

"We have two main effects teams. There's my unit and Brian's model unit. We each have about thirty-five people working for us. None of the shots we're doing are, in themselves, exceedingly complicated. It's just that we're going for a really naturalistic look. We don't want to produce any really jazzy effects that will stand out and take your mind off the rest of the film.

"Some of the scenes will require a lot of separate elements to be combined for dramatic effect. In one scene, for instance, you'll see a whole army of people running by the Emperor's steel tent. An atomic bomb then goes off outside the tent. Worms suddenly charge across the sand. Static electricity bursts begin going off. People will be running around firing these laser-type guns. Now, each one of those effects is a single element. The people themselves will be filmed as four separate elements. You'll see people running in the foreground. People will be running into the tent. People will be running out of the tent. People will be running away from the worms.

"The atomic bomb going off is a real treat. We've created our own A-bomb effect that's very realistic. The Mexicans don't seem to worry about the amount of explosives you use too much, so we've duplicated the flash, the mushroom cloud and the smoke movement of a real A-bomb. It looks great. Smells awful."

All the different elements for each special effects shot will be combined with each other back in Los Angeles, at Nolan's effects house via the use of an electronic optical printer. Basically, an optical printer is a King Kong–sized combination of a projector and a process camera that allows an effects man to view all the different elements of a scene as he painstakingly combines them in a given frame.

Kyle MacLachlan and Everett McGill on an oversized section of worm in front of a bluescreen—ready for a worm-riding scene.

With an electronic printer, this compositing process is accelerated. "If we were working on a conventional printer using a normal photo process it would take twice as long as it does doing things electronically. If we were working on a 100-foot-long sequence of film the traditional way, it would take us 1,000 feet of film to put all the elements together. Electronically, 100 feet of film takes 100 feet of film."

Basically, an electronic printer breaks down each and every element in a frame into scan lines, like the video lines that make up a television image. These electronic signals are then combined and mixed to form a finished shot that features all the various elements needed to complete a scene.

The detail work made possible by an electronic printer is amazing. Comparing the images with which Nolan works with the images seen on a high-priced, state-of-the-art color television tells the story. "No comparison," Nolan says. "A television has 500 lines of resolution. Our printers have 3,000 lines. The detail is unmatched. It makes color discrimination easier. Matte work easier. It takes us nine seconds to scan a frame of film to make sure that all the colors match. That's unbelievably quick. If we were working on a scene combining a group of elements using traditional photo techniques, it would take us five to seven days to complete a sequence. Electronically, we can do it in two or three hours."

Leaving the half-constructed deserts behind him, Nolan smiles confidently. "We're pretty much on top of things at present. The technical conditions down here have been causing us to scramble a little but we're bearing up. Barring any unforeseen disasters, we should be able to get everything done on time."

In mid-October, the unforseen happens. The interior to Stage 2, housing the biggest blue screen ever made for a film, catches fire. Everything housed on the huge stage—screen, equipment, props—is destroyed.

In the days and weeks following the fire, everyone involved with the film attempts to come up with a way to salvage the blue-screen shooting schedule. No one is quite sure *how* the shots will be reslated, but everyone is sure that they *will*.

"I don't panic because I don't know any better," David Lynch says one day in the wake of the conflagration. "Besides, it's always exciting to have a fire, right?"

24.
AS THE WORM TURNS

Some days, I look at our worms and say,
"Whoops, there goes our PG rating."
Barry Nolan, supervisor of special photographic effects

At times, during our worm sequences, we had three times
as much light in our studio as the CONAN crew did shooting
in full sun, outdoors.
Freddie Francis, cinematographer

I never thought little worms could cause such big problems.
Raffaella De Laurentiis, producer

The harsh winds of Arrakis whip the desert sands into a frenzy of activity. The stark, white landscape takes on the undulating quality of an ocean tossed by a fierce storm. Thick black smoke chokes the sky as, behind the dunes, fierce battles between Harkonnen and Fremen troops explode.

From out of nowhere a rumbling. A hiss. Then, a nightmarish vision. Worms. Sandworms, bigger than ocean liners, appear everywhere. They rear their heads and shake their titanic bodies angrily as, on their backs, hundreds of Fremen warriors cling for dear life. The worms open their mouths and inhale the acrid Arrakeen air. They then plunge onward...

...toward the grimiest group of filmmakers ever to be assembled on a sound stage.

Nearly five dozen people are crowded around a miniature desert all wearing masks and goggles. Large fans are blowing sand this way and that. Harsh white lights raise the temperature of the room towards the 100-degree mark. Piles of tires are burning behind the desert set, sending up plumes of thick, black smoke.

Following this scene, the doors to the stage will be opened, the smoke allowed to drift outside into the fall air and the crew will stagger out into the sunlight, exhausted and semi-asphyxiated.

Kyle MacLachlan using a maker hook to mount a sandworm
on the Churubusco back lot.

"How would I describe our worm scenes?" Barry Nolan muses.
"I wouldn't."

The climactic sandworm sequences for *Dune* have been, in a
word, nightmarish to plan, rehearse and film.

To begin with, there are the worms themselves. Carlo Rambaldi
has built sixteen worms of various sizes and with various capacities
for movement. The two biggest worms are sixteen feet long. The
next in line are three worms eight feet long, followed by ten "sausage" worms approximately two feet in length. The larger models
have fully articulated heads, featuring mouths that open and close.

All the worms are cable-and-spring-operated models which undulate along a curly Q track placed beneath their bodies. The only
worm model which deviates from this norm is an oversized worm
head and neck being used for close-up shots. The head is thirty
inches in diameter and eight feet long.

"None of the worms are computer controlled," says Barry Nolan.
"They're all run by worm handlers, a group of people who control
different sections of the model. The key to getting these worms to
work realistically is a lot of practice."

Nolan fully expected to spend a long period of time doing worm

tests with the worm handlers. He knew it would be a matter of trial
and error to achieve naturalistic motion. What he *wasn't* prepared
for was the difficult time he would have *positioning* the worms properly in front of the camera. "The first tests we did of the worms
were pretty, uh, graphic," he says.

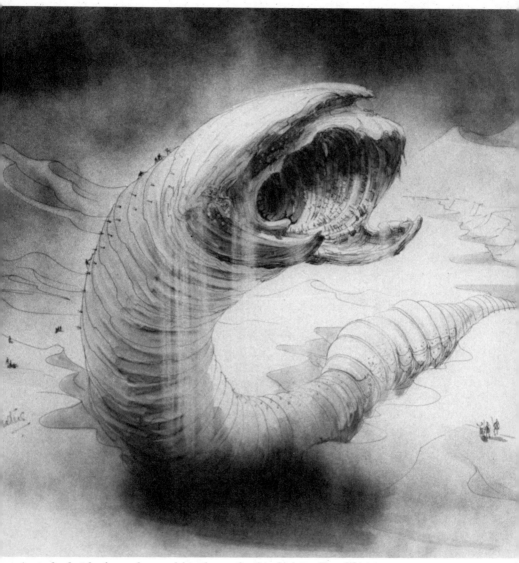

An early sketch of a sandworm drawn by production designer Tony Masters.

What Nolan is trying to say, tactfully, is that if the worms are shot from the wrong angle, they appear on the screen as not-too-subtle phallic symbols.

Raffaella De Laurentiis sums it up thus: "When we saw the first tests, we knew that the worms would work technically. We also knew that if we weren't careful, we would have the first X-rated science-fiction movie in history!"

One Dino De Laurentiis employee is a bit more glib. "After we saw the test footage of the worms, every man in the room went home with a large inferiority complex."

While Nolan tried to grapple with the worm problem, the rest of the crew puzzled over the creation of the miniature desert required to shoot the key worm scenes. A sprawling, modular expanse was created in a half-pie shape, seventy feet wide and fifty feet deep. The landscape was built in sections so that it could be pushed and pulled apart to represent various exotic geographical locations of Arrakis during different sequences.

A section of the desert was left out of the center of the miniature so that a "worm table" could be placed there; a swath of sandy terrain equipped with track that would allow the worm handlers to operate their squiggly stars from below.

Complicating the creation of his miniature landscape was the fact that real sand couldn't be used to build the dunes. "Real sand, when it collapses," says Nolan, "tends to fall in chunks. It isn't graceful at all. We needed to find a substance that, when it moved, looked as if it was flowing...like water."

Cinematographer Freddie Francis picks up the thread. "To get the correct texture of sand in miniature, we used a lot off micro-balloons mixed in with fuller's earth. Micro-balloons are hollow spheres of borosilicate glass. Each balloon has a diameter of 60 microms—2½ thousandths of an inch."

While these micro-balloons look great on camera, there is one little catch. "They're dangerous to your health if you inhale them," says Francis. "Once these spheres of glass reach your lungs, they simply remain there. They don't dissolve. So, anyone using these spheres must wear face masks and goggles. No one can wear contact lenses on the set, either."

During the filming of the worm sequences, 5,000 pounds of micro-balloons would be required. "Oddly enough," says Nolan, "we had no trouble getting the balloons through customs. Film we have problems with. Plastic we have problems with. But micro-balloons? We could have brought in tons more with no problem."

Fremen miniatures atop a moving sandworm model.

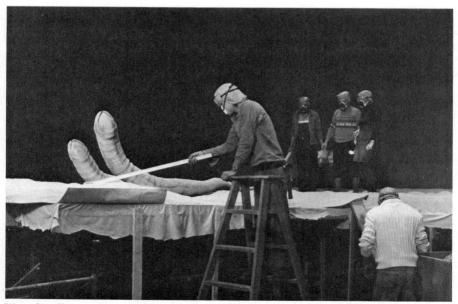

Worm handlers position model worms on the all-too-warm miniature desert set.

Once the desert was sculpted, constructed and filled with pseudo-sand, the problem of lighting the set came up. During most of the worm sequences, hundreds of pounds of sand would be blowing across the stage, smoke would be billowing, artificial clouds would be rolling. In order for a camera to be able to shoot these sequences in detail, a lot of artificial light would be required.

A lot.

"We have used 'Dino' lamps extensively on this movie for lots of reasons," says Freddie Francis between worm battles. "Dino lamps were named after Dino De Laurentiis. They were designed for him when he was doing *Flash Gordon.* That movie was using a lot of blue backing [the amount of blue-screen work used in *Flash Gordon* because of the enormous amount of space-battle footage is almost legendary], which was a huge area to illuminate with any existing form of lighting.

"So, the Lee Electric company designed these huge Dino lamps. Each lamp consists of twenty-four one-kilowatt bulbs. [The average reading lamp offers anywhere from 60 watts to 125.] After *Flash Gordon,* Dino sold his Dino lamps back to the Lee boys. He didn't think he'd need them anymore.

"We imported ten new Dinos for use in all our night shootings during principal production. But when we saw how much light we would need for our desert set, to create high light that would duplicate a real desert in the sun, we asked Raffaella to buy back those ten original Dinos from Lee. So, now we were going to have twenty Dinos to light the desert.

"In the meantime, two of our crewmembers discovered that some of the local workers on our lighting gang were very good engineers. So, we had them build another ten homemade Dinos. By the time we were ready to shoot the desert scenes, we had thirty Dinos on tap: 720 one-kilowatt bulbs all burning down on a huge *Dune* set."

But the lighting of the diminutive desert did not stop there. "Additionally," Francis continues, "we have about forty Space Lights, huge lights that hang above the set to give us reflective light, positioned to make it seem as though the light is coming from an open sky.

"We also have twelve to twenty MaxiBrutes, which are smaller versions of Dino lights. They burn between six and nine one-kilowatt bulbs. And, then, dotted all over the place, we have various strange lights that have been manufactured here by Roy Larner and his boys. Each of those consists of large pieces of tin and silver paper and 10-kilowatt bulbs. So," Francis smiles, "altogether, we have an enormous amount of light."

Francis chuckles ruefully. "Indeed. On one occasion, *Conan the Destroyer* was shooting outside on the Churubusco lot in reasonable sunlight using an f-stop of about 9. Whereas, in our desert studio, we were using an f-stop of about 22. We had about three times as much light in our studio as they did in the full sunlight, outdoors.

"We were eating up 11,000 amps of electricity on that set. Since the studio powerhouse could only supply 4,000 amps, we were forced to bring in seven portable generators which were positioned around the studio. With all those lamps burning and the sand blowing and the tires burning, the working conditions have been fairly difficult."

Adds Chuck Finance, "You have special effects men handling explosions and dust, electricians there with the lights, the camera crew and the worm handlers. Sometimes there are sixty people crowded around that set all wearing masks and goggles.

"It's really a slow, painful process. Everything has to be credible in those shots. Everything has to look proper in terms of scale. The sand has to fall off the worms in a certain way. The wind has to blow a certain way. Every single detail has to be perfect to be believable. If the audience doesn't believe these worm scenes, they'll reach for their hats and coats. More than once, we've worked so long and hard on a certain shot that we've wound up falling behind on our schedule."

"The pits," Barry Nolan grimaces. "Imagine filming this worm stuff in a room with sand swirling, black smoke blowing and explosions going off. We're wearing goggles and face masks and we can't hear each other because of the noise.

"While all this is happening, you're trying to figure out how to capture each worm at the best possible angle. In some of the scenes we also have worm riders on the worms. Each one of those figures is about two inches tall. It *can* get trying at times."

Carol Rambaldi who supervises his worm wranglers from a distance is aware of the blood, sweat and sand that is going into the filming of his gigantic sandworms. He feels it's worth it. "When people see the worms on film, they will find them more overwhelming than anything they've ever imagined."

Barry Nolan, Freddie Francis, the worm handlers and the technicians slip their goggles and masks on and prepare to reenter Stage 4. At this point on the production, they're finding the worms pretty overwhelming, too.

25.
WINDING DOWN

What have I learned from this? Some things work.
Some things don't. The ones that don't, you make work.
David Lynch, director

Every day, there is still a new problem.
Raffaella De Laurentiis, producer

I'm a lot more relaxed now. My leash is really long.
My wife says I don't have one at all anymore.
David Lynch, director

January 1984.

In less than two weeks, *Dune* will end its Mexican post-production period. The crew will take one last look at the Churubusco lot and head for home, scattering over the four corners of the Earth.

Although work at the Mexican site will cease, the post-production process will continue in Los Angeles with special effects compositing, editing, scoring and sound effects work being done until the film is deemed ready for a December 1984 release.

"We could be working on this movie until September," Barry Nolan says. "I hope we won't be, but it's possible."

In spite of the hardships, the off-putting working conditions and the occasional setbacks, *Dune* is shaping up to be the movie everyone set out to make.

"So many things have happened along the way," muses director Lynch, "but the movie itself hasn't changed. I've always felt the movie *is* what it *is*. It's still evolving."

En route to a final cut, only one major story change has been made; the subplot involving Paul's killing of Jamis and his subsequent involvement with Jamis' mate Harah and her children has been completely excised.

"That has caused me some worry," admits Raffaella. "That whole sequence was very important in the book. It's a turning point for

Francesca Annis and Dino De Laurentiis.

Paul. We had to eliminate it because it got very involved. If we kept Paul's fight with Jamis in the movie, then we had to deal with Jamis' wife and Jamis' children. It stopped the whole film.

"It wasn't a tough scene to cut out in terms of the film because we all felt it was very boring. At that point, we had to forget the book and concentrate on making the best movie possible."

Lynch echoes that sentiment. "We were forced to cut out a few scenes. But I wasn't surprised at the ones that we wound up trimming. The film, right now, is very tight. The scenes we eliminated would have slowed it down. Right now, there's no problem with the movie's pacing. If we hadn't done that cutting, there would have been.

"In the book, the Jamis confrontation is important because Paul gives water for the dead [he cries after killing the Fremen warrior]. For that one bit in the movie, though, the audience would have fallen asleep before they even witnessed that. It was a tremendous sideline to a story that was just barreling along.

"We just didn't have the luxury of going off like that. It jeopardized the whole film. There are things like that in the book that just can't be in the film. The *feeling* of giving water to the dead, I think, is still in the movie. I'm not positive of that at this point. We're still fine-tuning."

Brian Smithies is working on a miniature ship shot. Supervising the lighting is Jimmy Devis. He is walking around Studio 4, but four months after his near-fatal fall, without the aid of crutch or cane.

"He's remarkable, isn't he?" Smithies says. "He's a miracle man."

Devis dismisses the fall with a shrug. "I'm perfectly all right," he says, "except that I don't have all the movement in this arm."

He holds up a slightly stiff left wrist. "But, they tell me that I'll recover fully after a bit of physical therapy."

Devis excuses himself and returns to the more important matter at hand, lighting a spaceship crash for maximum reality.

Unit publicist Anne Strick is working double duty. Now in a newer, larger office, she is juggling both *Dune* and *Conan the Destroyer*. While Arnold Schwarzenegger stands before her desk, scrutinizing possible publicity photos for his next sword and sorcery epic, a minor emergency has arisen.

Kyle MacLachlan has arrived at Churubusco to do some overdubbing, to rerecord a few lines of dialogue.

The *Dune* office felt that it would be an ideal time for Kyle to pose for a beautiful, color portrait shot to promote the movie. Kyle arrives on the lot and the collective blood pressure of the *Dune* production office soars. The actor, who had a thick crop of hair all during the *Dune* shoot, has had his hair cut short for a play he is appearing in.

Very, very short.

Strick gets together with the movie's hairdresser. The hair stylist comes up with a solution. Over a three-hour period of time, the hairdresser takes individual strands of real prop hair and weaves it between strands of Kyle's short mop. She then takes a curling iron and laboriously fluffs all the hair up.

By the time Kyle walks in front of the cameras for his portrait shot, he looks like good old Paul Atreides, bushy-haired space messiah.

Barry Nolan is prowling around a ten-foot platform on the backlot. Atop the platform is a small desert scene. Below the platform is an eight-foot-long neck and head of a sandworm.

"This is where we're going to film the worm swallowing the spice harvester," he explains.

"We'll place the small harvester model over here," he says, pointing to a section of the desert which (barely) conceals a large, circular hole.

"There will be people underneath the platform operating the worm. When they release a weight, that worm head shoots up, its mouth open, in one second flat. We'll film the sequence at fifteen times the normal speed so, when it's shown in the movie, it will be slowed down and will look very big and very creepy."

Nolan scrambles down the platform and walks over to a large miniature of a rock chasm. The chasm stretches back some fifteen feet. Lining its sand flooring are a batch of worms. "We still have to film our worm charge," he explains. "We tried it once and we didn't like it."

He points to the three eight-foot worms in the lead. "We have all our little Fremen warriors on their backs. The worms up front will have more of a sense of movement than the sausage worms (the two-foot models) placed behind them. The small worms in the background are supposedly the same size as the charging worms up front. They're supposed to look smaller because of the perspective of the shot. Way in the back of the chasm," he points to a group of slender black objects perched on the sand, "we're using pieces of rubber tubing as worm stand-ins. On the screen, they'll be so small that you'll barely see them in the distance."

He watches three worm handlers reposition one of the large worms. "We'll have about twelve people working the worms. In most scenes the worm handlers can stand right next to the camera and watch the way their models are responding to their commands. For this scene we may have some video monitors set up so that the handles can watch what they're doing from the side of these rocks."

He smiles as the sun beats down on the sandworm models. "We've really come a long way filming these worms," he says. "The handlers are a lot better at working the controls and we've come up with all the right angles to shoot the models. Why, sometimes, we don't even notice that the worms look like...what they look like anymore."

Raffaella De Laurentiis sits in the Churubusco cafeteria with a few friends. It is late in the morning. The *Conan* crew has not broken for lunch yet and most of the *Dune* crew is still hard at work on the sound stages. The producer takes a few minutes to relax before running off for a meeting.

She is still concerned with the *Dune* shooting schedule. "We finish here on January 31st," she says. "There are still at least five important shots that I have to get. If I get those five, I can go home and sleep well in February. Anything over that is gravy. We still have to stage the crash of the ornithopter, the explosion and the sand flood in the desert, the worms coming across the desert. . . what else?"

"The explosion of the steel tent?" a friend offers.

"Oh yes. We've done it once and it wasn't very good. If we can, we'll redo it here. I don't want to try to mess around with it optically."

She offers a sly smile. "As you can see, I'm still going crazy over these effects. I'm delighted with the effects work that is being done. I don't think I could have made a better decision. I picked the right people. I have all my own equipment. All my own models. I answer to no one for the effects.

"But," she adds, "I am still concerned. Do I still encounter effects problems? How about every day? Two times? Three times? This morning we saw dailies of yesterday's work. There wasn't one shot in there we can use. We'll just have to redo them until we get them right.

"I mean, yesterday's shots were usable. They are good enough to appear on the screen. *But* they are not good enough to appear in *Dune*. I haven't taken any shortcuts so far. I am not going to start now."

Raffaella nurses a cup of coffee. "I think the effects part of this movie was harder than the live-action shooting. There was always something unexpected happening. During October, for instance, everything on Stage 8 burned down. Our blue screen. All the special equipment. All the stuff that cost us $50,000 to build. Gone. Big disaster. We just sat there, stunned. 'We're going to lose all the blue shots for the picture.'

"We didn't know what to do. We sat down and figured out that it would cost us half a million dollars to rebuild everything. We didn't have the time because another movie was getting ready to use Churubusco and the studio had promised them Stage 8. I went berserk."

She shrugs her shoulders. "Sometimes I go crazy. It's not a pretty sight.

"Anyhow. We didn't know what we were going to do. Someone, at that point, said, 'Let's build a blue screen outside.'

"'Huh'?

"Well, it turns out that this was done years ago for movies. Our old blue screen was 35 feet high and 105 feet long. Our blue screen outside was 200 feet long but only 8 or 9 feet high. We did all our blue-screen work outside using ancient techniques. We shot all the scenes in three days. We had been scheduled to use the screen on Stage 8 for three weeks. It came out wonderfully and we wound up saving time.

"Not that there weren't problems. For instance, we had to figure out how much paint we needed to cover this screen we built. The day before we were going to shoot we realized that we needed eight more gallons of blue paint. Of course, this country has problems getting paint. So, I decided to bring in eight gallons of paint from El Paso, Texas. Naturally, I was stopped at the border."

Raffaella rolls her eyes heavenward. "The last five months have been a nightmare for us in terms of customs. Things have gotten *worse*, if that is possible.

"It was important to get plastic down here for our models and miniatures. I was going to be up in Los Angeles and Brian Smithies said that he needed these little pieces of green plastic for a scene. They look like straws. It was one of those 'If we don't have them, we can't shoot this scene correctly!' routines.

"Fine. When I was in Los Angeles, I bought a handful and tossed them in my handbag. I arrived in Mexico. They kept me in customs for three and a half hours! I said, 'Look. These pieces of plastic might be worth $10. I'll pay you $25, OK?' They almost put me in jail! It turns out that every plastic product brought into this country needs some sort of dispensation from the government!"

She shakes her head ruefully. "Such craziness. Sometimes I think I thrive on it. The wildest day I ever had as a producer was, one day, when we went to reshoot a *Dune* shot in the desert. We reshot it while we were shooting a scene from *Conan the Destroyer* at the same location.

"It was insanity! On one side of this hill was Conan, riding on horseback with Wilt Chamberlain next to the skeleton of a big mammoth. On the other side of the hill, we had these Fremen warriors running over these sand dunes. You just had to laugh at the sight."

Raffaella heaves a sigh. "This movie has involved so many last-minute decisions. The tinting of the Fremen's eyes blue, for instance, will now be done through rotoscoping. Each eye will be colored on the film. For a while, we were thinking of using dyes. I used the dye on myself before I tested it on the actors. It was a disaster. I would come home with blue eyes, red eyes, brown eyes. I'd be crying blue tears all afternoon.

Dino De Laurentiis, Raffaella De Laurentiis, David Lynch, Freddie Francis.

Frank Herbert and Dino De Laurentiis.

"Then, someone came up with the idea of large contact lenses made out of clear plastic that covered only the whites of the eyes. You couldn't turn your eyes. It would have been a disaster for the actors to try to act wearing those things. Poor Molly Wryn. She actually tried a pair of them up in Los Angeles. It hurt like hell! So, we decided to film all the live action first and, then, worry about the blue eyes later."

Anne Strick enters the cafeteria. A minor emergency. A European magazine has run color photographs of the behind-the-scenes variety. No one has seen the magazine as yet but the "top secret" photos supposedly show a lot of special effects work being done.

"Do they show the worms?" Raffaella asks.

"We don't know yet," Strick replies.

The entire table wonders how the photos were leaked. "Have you noticed how many people who operate the worms go around with cameras hanging around their necks?" Raffaella queries.

"The worm operators are mostly people who worked as extras in the movie," Raffaella sighs. "Local people who speak either English or Italian well. They stayed on to help but..."

She is clearly worried. "We have to be careful about what photographs of the worms are released. If they are shot from the wrong angles they look like, uh..."

Finally, she blurts a fairly succinct colloquialism. The table is reduced to laughter. The crisis dissipates for the moment. Later, a series of phone calls will be made. No one will find out how the photos made their way to Europe.

David Lynch sits in his office. Behind him, a hand-drawn "poster" for a future collaboration with Dino De Laurentiis, *Ronnie Rocket*, is tacked on his wall. Unlike *Dune*, *Ronnie Rocket* will be a lighthearted excursion into science fiction, detailing the life and times of a rock 'n' roll star who is literally out of this world.

On Lynch's window sill, his bevy of Woody Woodpeckers sit, surrounding a cheesecake photo. Outside his door, several members of the *Conan* cast and crew bellow at each other like true barbarians.

Lynch takes no notice. He is on his walkie-talkie with Jimmy Devis, discussing the lighting of a scene and the positioning of a Harkonnen spaceship.

When he is not on the lot in his office, Lynch is in his hotel room, working on the scripts for two sequels to *Dune* based on later novels by Frank Herbert. Lynch hopes to shoot them both, back-to-back, during 1985–1986.

Following the conversation, Lynch leans forward in his chair. "Things are shaping up," he smiles. "We have close to a fine cut done—minus the effects, of course. Every day, we're shooting the effects with three crews. Little by little we're getting all these holes plugged in. We have a really good idea about how long the movie is going to be and what it will look like. We still haven't done any sound effects or music. That will make a huge difference.

"Everything is falling into place," he acknowledges. "But it's still touch and go. I really feel confident that everything is going to work but this is the kind of movie that you won't be sure of until the very end.

"It's like the worms. When we first started filming them, they were working but they just weren't very dramatic. All the models that Rambaldi builds depend on the operators for their effectiveness. The operators need a lot of time to rehearse. They need to get with it. At this point, the people working the worms can do a lot of things with them that they couldn't when they first started. It's a learning process. They can move them a lot faster and smoother now. There's a sense of personality involved."

Lynch says in mock-serious tone. "They *know* their worms now!"

As for the helter-skelter miniature schedule, Lynch admits that,

more often than not, it's a source of concern. But, he views it all with characteristic aplomb. "Boy," he says in genuine amazement, "were those models done in a hurry! It's been hard on everybody involved. Maybe we'll put it all off. If we do, it'll be because of the fantastic people involved. We never really have much of a second chance to do most of this stuff. Almost every single sequence is thought up, built, set up, shot and, then, torn down because the next shot is waiting to be done. We have a really crazy schedule we have to keep. There have been a lot of disappointments and some reshootings but, despite that, we're really doing some neat things.

"We even wound up coming out of that fire looking good. I was really happy that we did all the blue-screen stuff on the backlot. I think it turned out much better. We had a much bigger sense of the desert out there. The blue screen was very low to the ground, which turned out to be an improvement. We discovered concepts and angles that we never thought of in our old storyboards.

"After the fire, we realized that all we really needed was a blue screen that would rise just above the actors' heads as they were coming over the sand dunes. Originally, we had had this gigantic blue screen built at 3M. The biggest blue screen ever built for a film. We didn't need it. Since our old blue screen was on a stage, it meant that we would have needed billions of lights to have lit it for a single day. We had this enormously complicated rig set up behind this little bitty piece of desert. Going outside, we had all the desert we needed and all the light we needed.

"It turned out really peachy."

Raffaella De Laurentiis is rushing off to the studio screening room to look at another batch of dailies. "Right now," she offers, "it looks as though the movie will run about two hours and twenty-three minutes. The rough cut ran about four hours but we had everything in it filmed from four different angles. I think the final movie will have a nice balance between adventure and drama."

Faced with the prospect of returning to Los Angeles and spending the next six to eight months working on the final version of *Dune*, the producer simply shrugs her shoulders and smiles.

"How could I mind something like that? I've been wanting to do this movie for—what—ten years? It has been my dream to film *Dune* since the first time I read it. In December, after all this work and craziness, my dream will be realized."

She enters the screening room. The lights are dimmed. The screen flickers to life. Spaceships slice through dense sandstorms, flying low over sprawling desert terrain.

A faint but approving smile appears on Raffaella's lips.

A dream is evolving into a reality.

A dream that started nearly two decades ago.

In December of 1984, nineteen years after its first appearance as a novel, *Dune* will be a motion picture at last.

ABOUT THE AUTHOR

Los Angeles-based writer Ed Naha is best known as the West Coast movie columnist for *The New York Post* as well as the author of such film-oriented books as *Brilliance on a Budget—The Films of Roger Corman, Horrors—From Screen To Scream* and *The Science Fictionary*.

His articles on the world of entertainment have appeared in such diverse publications as *Playboy, Oui, Science Digest, Starlog, The Twilight Zone* and *Heavy Metal*.

His novels include *The Paradise Plot, The Suicide Plague* and *First, You Fight* (as D. B. Drumm). He is currently working on a mystery novel to be published in 1985.